FAILING
DESIRE

Karmen MacKendrick

Failing
Desire

STATE UNIVERSITY OF NEW YORK PRESS

COVER IMAGE: *Aquamanile in the Form of Aristotle and Phyllis.*
Southern Netherlands, late 14th or early 15th century. Bronze, 32.5 cm x 17.9 cm.
Robert Lehman Collection, 1975 (1975.1.1416).
Courtesy of The Metropolitan Museum of Art.

Published by
STATE UNIVERSITY OF NEW YORK PRESS, ALBANY

© 2018 State University of New York

For information, contact State University of New York Press, Albany, NY
www.sunypress.edu

Production, Laurie D. Searl
Marketing, Kate R. Seburyamo

Library of Congress Cataloging-in-Publication Data

Names: MacKendrick, Karmen, [date] author.
Title: Failing desire / Karmen MacKendrick.
Description: Albany, NY : State University of New York Press, [2018] |
Includes bibliographical references and index.
Identifiers: LCCN 2017018231 (print) | LCCN 2017041860 (ebook) |
ISBN 9781438468921 (e-book) |
ISBN 9781438468914 (hardcover : alk. paper) |
ISBN 9781438468907 (pbk.)
Subjects: LCSH: Failure (Psychology) | Shame. | Humiliation.
Classification: LCC BF575.F14 (ebook) |
LCC BF575.F14 M33 2018 (print) |
DDC 128—dc23
LC record available at https://lccn.loc.gov/2017018231

10 9 8 7 6 5 4 3 2 1

What exceeds the system is the impossibility of its failure, and likewise the impossibility of its success. Ultimately nothing can be said of it, and there is a way of keeping still (the lacunary silence of writing), that halts the system, leaving it idle, delivered to the seriousness of irony.

—Maurice Blanchot, *The Writing of the Disaster*

Contents

Acknowledgments

While the chapters in this book have not been previously published in their current forms, they do draw concepts, conceptual moves, paragraphs and passages from many of my presentations and essays over the years. These should be acknowledged, along with my deep gratitude to those who invited me to say or to write them, and those, too many to name, who listened.

Material related to obedience was presented at *The Body: Ethos and Ethics*, the meeting of Foucault Society Conference in 2006, at the invitation of Terri Gordon; and at the seminar *Desire, Love and Sexuality in Medieval Thought*, at Lewis University in 2010. The Augustinian material there was refined for a seminar presentation with Virginia Burrus and Mark Jordan at Berkeley's Graduate Theological Union, at the invitation of Daniel Boyarin. We eventually developed the seminar material into *Seducing Augustine: Bodies, Desires, Confessions* (Fordham, 2010).

Impossible Confessions, the basis of chapter 2, was refined over the course of two presentations: *The Sacred and the Debased in the Work of Georges Bataille*, at Occidental College in 2008, at the invitation of Malek Moazzam-Doulat; and *The Space of Community in the Work of Georges Bataille*, at the Society for Phenomenology and Existential Philosophy in 2010. A version of that presentation was published in the anthology *Material Spirit*, edited by Carl Good and Manuel Assensi (Fordham, 2013).

An invitation from the graduate students in religion at Syracuse University to present an opening keynote at their conference "The Monstrous, the Marginalized, and Transgressive Forms of Humanity," in 2013, first prompted me to think about the kinds of visuality that are central to chapter 3.

Finally, material that is related more broadly to the book rather than to any particular chapter appears in *Pornotopias: Image, Apocalypse, Desire*, edited by Louis

Armand, Jane Lewty, and Andrew Mitchell (Litteraria Pragensia, 2010); *Analecta Hermeneutica* vol. 4, 2012, guest edited by Michelle Rebidoux; and *Querying Consent*, edited by Jordana Greenblatt and Keja Valens (Rutgers UP, forthcoming). I am also indebted to Ed Casey, who invited me to discuss Jacob Rogozinski's work at the symposium in his honor, *Envelopes of Flesh*, at Stony Brook University in 2014.

This is the sort of book for which people may not be especially eager to receive thanks or participation credit, but I am at least indebted to those friends and colleagues who provided me with references and useful suggestions for sources, including Jennifer Glancy, Virginia Burrus, Cary Howie, and Kathleen Costello-Sullivan. I believe that it was from Catherine Keller that I first heard Keats's idea of negative capability. Orly Nave recommended to me the Velleman essay on original sin that I've used here, though the essay itself is more intriguing than my use might suggest.

I am particularly grateful to the Research and Development Committee at Le Moyne College, which supported my work through a summer grant in 2016. I continued to work on the manuscript during part of my time as a fellow at the Cornell Society for the Humanities, surely one of the best work environments in the world.

The manuscript reports from Kent Brintnall and William Robert were invaluable resources for improving this text, and I am lastingly grateful to both readers for their intelligence and insight. SUNY's Andrew Kenyon is the very model of an academic editor, managing to combine encouragement, efficiency, and an impressive measure of patience; it has been a great pleasure to work with him. I have been delighted as well by the privilege of working again with production editor Laurie Searl, who produced my first book when we were both young.

Finally, as the one who endures the disorderly distractedness of me-writing and the grouchy anxiety of me-not-writing with equal aplomb, Alan Griffin has once more earned my deepest thanks.

ONE

Unworking

THE FAILURE OF WRITING

THE SHAME OF THE TEXT

What is this madness that must be excluded (tragically) in order to constitute our culture, the modern West? It is nothing else, Foucault replies at once, than "the absence of oeuvre."
—Mark Jordan, *Convulsing Bodies*

This book is about secrets and failures, so it is unsurprising that it resisted its own writing. As Eve Sedgwick has pointed out, we are deeply susceptible to the shame of others, and it is shame—at the depths of humiliation and subordination—that I take up here; shame, the various kinds of failure occasioning it and occasioned by it, and the ability to find in that failure a strange, secretive, and curiously resistant pleasure. To speak or write about what is shameful, many authors agree, is to risk doubly shaming oneself, adding the subject matter to the shameful imposition that characterizes all speech, acknowledging one's own complicity in the act of embarrassing oneself.[1] We cannot even be sure of speaking truly: "To risk making truth," writes Virginia Burrus, "is . . . also to risk perjury."[2] Our words are too many and never quite right, and we are not even sure whether what we are telling is truth-making or embarrassed elision. It is as if, deeply uncertain that we are interesting, quite sure that we talk too much, we nonetheless had to say. "The writer," says Maurice Blanchot, "finds himself in this more and more comical condition—of having nothing to write, of having no means of writing it, and of being forced by an extreme necessity to keep writing it."[3] What necessity compels such repeated failure?

I begin with the suspicion that humiliation and failure are entangled. The necessity that seeks each one is driven by will, and knowledge, and the will to know.

The necessity that they recur is driven by the impossibility of that will's perfect satisfaction. In the first chapter following, I explore the question of obedience, making use of the lives of some exemplary ascetics as well as Michel Foucault's work on pastoral power. Perfect obedience not only demands an extraordinarily strong will, but also presents an unsurpassable paradox—from which much of its interest derives. That in the will and the flesh which eludes even the most deter- mined obedience will elude knowing as well. The second chapter, on auricular confession, makes use of some of the same Foucauldean theory, but also of work from Georges Bataille's theories of speech and sacrifice, to explore the strange infolding by which the construction and undermining of the speaking subject oc- casion each other. The effort to know the depths of the confessing subject turns those depths inside out, leaving us to suspect that they were in fact flexible sur- faces—and that something remains, unsaid, however thoroughly we try to unfold them. The will to know and our ability to say what we know run into a mystery, a secret. The secret, we begin to see, will not allow us to hold on to a sense of self with a clear inside and out. Just as we necessarily fail to obey perfectly, so too we are unable to confess everything.

The third chapter changes senses, turning from sound to sight. We hear our- selves speak; we do not see ourselves seeing—but as part of our urge to know, we may well want to. We especially want to know what is "inside," but this will elude us just as a stable interiority does. The gaze on skin is not enough to know the flesh; various probing means attempt to know more by opening up the skin, but here too we may document a range of failures—not least in the desire to turn the gaze back and understand the seeing self. Again, we run up against an unknowable, against what remains beyond knowing; we run up against a remainder that seems to evade even the most thoroughgoing knowledge.

Obedience, confession, and exhibition cover a considerable range of humili- ating pleasures, but by no means all. Chapter 4 therefore considers a range of roles by which we may deliberately abandon autonomous dignity as the measure of be- ing human, in favor of roles ranging from fool to furniture. The secrets of the will, the self, the flesh, and rational humanity all entice us, as secrets will. But they are able to do so in some measure because they also elude us. Each of these practices and performances tells us that there is a mystery, a resistant remainder to remind us of our failure.

In what follows, I have not distinguished between shame and humiliation. The distinction is sometimes made, but I have not found in the particular cases I explore that it holds up strongly (this is not to imply that it might not hold up elsewhere, especially where no pleasure is involved). In this respect I am inclined to agree with Martha Nussbaum, whose philosophical work on shame has been widely influential: "[H]umiliation is the public face of shame. . . . [I]n most cases to inflict shame is to humiliate."[4] I want to know, however, what happens when the one humiliated has fully sought out shame.

A HISTORY OF FAILURES

The tendency of a person to allow himself to be degraded, robbed, deceived, and exploited might be the diffidence of a God among men.
                            —Friedrich Nietzsche, *Beyond Good and Evil*

Though they were little spoken for a long time, by now I hardly take up these
themes of pleasure and shame on my own. There are whole movements already.
Judith Halberstam's *The Queer Art of Failure* alerted us all to a range of playful possibilities, and I draw extensively on it here.[5] Earlier, David Halperin and Valerie
Traub introduced the anthology *Gay Shame* with an essay called "Beyond Gay
Pride." Gay shame, they declare, is for those who "feel out of place in gay pride's
official ceremonies: people with the 'wrong' bodies, sadomasochists, sex work-
ers, drag queens, butch dykes, people of color, boy-lovers, bisexuals, immigrants,
the poor, the disabled," whose marginality or overt sexuality "can be a cause of
shame."[6] The gay shame movement, as Jennifer Moon writes in the same volume, "provides a radical queer alternative to consumerist pride parades and as
such helps constitute a queer counterpublic. . . . A specifically queer counterpublic
would, following Michael Warner and Lauren Berlant, reject a politics of assimilation and instead foster an independent, sexually rebellious ethos of antinormativ-
ity."[7] This entails not shame about being proud, and not exactly pride in being
ashamed, but a sort of defiant joy in shame and the shameful, in failing to be
proud in the proper ways, about the right things.

Counterpublics engage in what Foucault calls "counter-conduct"—a term
characterizing the behavior of those who resist modern governmentality, and so
modify the strategies of discipline and normalization imposed upon them.[8] Lynn
Huffer argues for eros as such a contestation, one that fights the reduction of life
to scientifically quantifiable bios. Biopower works by imposing norms; eros resists
them, emerging "as a new name for an unreasonable, corporeal ethics of living in
the biopolitical present," an unsystematic, nonnormative, and occasionally surprising ethics.[9] Can the pleasures of failure be erotic and ethical, too—ethical, and
resistant, startling, and surprising? Can they be these things, and still fail? Can we
be humiliated by these failures, and still take delight? My affirmative answer to
these questions unfolds over the following chapters.

It is particularly difficult to lose neither shame nor joy in the other, not to be
so proud of embracing shame that the shame vanishes, nor so humiliated in reject-
ing pride that we lose all joy. Shame celebrates the exclusion and marginality that
pride fights, and we already suspect that there is something perversely sexy about
it. But it cannot be unequivocally celebratory: that's pride again. It is too easy to
recenter stubborn, edgy shame, and, in celebrating without hesitation, turn it into
its own sense of pride—losing in the process the defiance and excess, the perversity and pain that brought the joy in the first place. "Shame" movements easily and

understandably become demands for a wider circle of pride. Considerable stub-
bornness is required to keep failing; to, as Halberstam has it, make "peace with the
possibility that alternatives dwell in the murky waters of a counterintuitive, often
impossibly dark and negative realm of critique and refusal."[10] For all the defiant
effort that it takes, pride is a little bit easier. But failure, it turns out, is interesting.
And shame attends only where we are interested.[11]

Even before the recent interest in shame, there were traditions that valued it,
and valued its attendant pleasures of subordination, confession, exhibition, and deliberate disempowerment. The Greek Cynics (like the much more accepted philosopher Socrates) saw themselves as living out truth—in their case, by a devotion
to that truth above and against all convention, and an insistence upon following
only it. Their way of life struck most, however, as decidedly discordant with reason. Cynics were ascetic,[12] but more famously, they were also eccentric: the Cynic
Diogenes of Sinope was said to live in a tub, wear only a cloak, and embrace
bronze statues in the winter. In warmer months, he was even less well behaved,
having no hesitation about urinating or masturbating in public.[13] He is also said to
have gone through the streets carrying a lantern in bright daylight, with the claim
that he was seeking an honest man, and ordinary illumination had not sufficed
to show him any. In the nineteenth century, Friedrich Nietzsche adapts this story,
writing of a madman who carries a lantern in the morning, seeking the god we
have killed. Like the Cynics, the madman is the object of jeers; for Nietzsche, he
is wiser than those who laugh.[14]

Others seek to shame the Cynics, but in his *Lives and Opinions of Eminent
Philosophers*, Diogenes Laertius calls the Cynics "shameless": they are not only willing, but apparently eager, to endure rejection and laughter.[15] In this, they offer an
odd precursor to later quests for humiliation: the Cynics delight in the humiliating responses they generate, but there is no indication that they seek thereby to
humble themselves, as later Christian monks will. Nor is there an indication that
they indeed experience shame. Their cynicism is directed toward those foolish
enough to disdain their behavior.

Still, they remain of interest to those intrigued by both social norms and bodily disciplines. Michel Foucault describes a Cynic who "has suffered, has endured,
has deprived himself so that truth could, in some way, take body in his own life, in
his own existence, take body in his body." Citing this passage, Mark Jordan points
out that Foucault is paraphrasing the Christian Gregory of Nyssa, who in turn "is
describing a Christian Cynic (and who relies on the incarnational tropes of Christianity)."[16] The Truth, for the Cynic or the Christian or the Christian Cynic, is
divine and fleshy, not factual; the will is subordinated to it by refusing the demands
of willful flesh so that the divine (will and all) can take that flesh as its own. Flesh is
only disowned so that it can be re-owned, and better. For ancient Cynics, the standard of truth is reason. But in Christianity, that standard may come to include not
only humility, but actively sought humiliation, on the model of a crucified god.[17]

In another failure of reason, Christian Cynicism is taken up by the holy fool, one who appears absurd by common standards. Holy folly originates in monastic asceticism, with its rejection of the trappings of pride and worldly success.[18] These fools deliberately court public contempt, sometimes by encouraging misperceptions of themselves as criminal[19] or insane, though in some cases the latter perception is arguably accurate. ("If the sacred walks along the borderline between the social and madness, what can you do?" asks Catherine Clément. "If one of its functions is to cross over, how can you stop it?")[20] All push the monastic quest for humility into a quest for humiliation, for which the appearances of criminality and madness are excellent sources.[21] So too is scandal—the cynical saint Symeon tied a dead dog to his belt, overturned vendors' carts, feigned seizures, harassed churchgoers, and associated with outcasts, actors, and prostitutes. Onlookers were horrified, despite the fact that he evidently retained his chastity—though chastity might strike few of us as his primary issue.[22]

"Cynicism," Jordan goes on to say, "presents a series of breaking points at which philosophy must confront its own inconsistencies. It is a carnival but also a race to the limit."[23] Holy fools subvert not only convention, but submission: their carnivalesque "freedom" from all social constraint pushes the limits of obedience to a considerably more difficult imperative. Cynicism is resistant to the norms that constrain others, but it is under the strict constraint of obedience to the more abstract demands of an ethical truth—with its edge of the unknowable. The holy fool obeys not even a moral imperative, but the impossible demand of holiness.[24] This demand for something more, for greater difficulty, is common to those who seek the pleasures of failure, who may find it impossible to fail by ordinary standards.

That stricter obedience characterizes the lives of many other Christian saints and martyrs, too; here again, humiliation is often deliberately sought, and eagerly written afterward. This gives hagiography a prurient appeal that has been noticed, and condemned, for a long time. As David Frankfurter points out, hagiographic narratives often appeal not just to eros, but specifically to a perverse eroticism, a "sado-erotic voyeurism." The positioning of pornographic violence in hagiographic context "allows the enjoyment of erotic display at the same time as the disavowal of that enjoyment. . . . It also allows masochistic identification with victims' eroticized brutalization and dissolution."[25] The increasing scholarly interest in these bodies does not meet with Frankfurter's approval. Citing Tertullian, he asks, "Why should it be lawful to see what it is shameful to do?" Frankfurter extends "the question to martyrology itself, in which bodies—often erotically charged bodies—are imaginatively put through sexual display and graphic torture for a frankly prurient gaze."[26] Precisely here, however, our interest lies: in what is shameful, and in what is at best in uneasy relation to what is lawful. Rather than disavowing either the eros or the perversion, rather than turning our intellects properly away, perhaps we too can learn from these triumphant failures—instead of repudiating the pleasure and sublimating it into a rage against the martyrs themselves, as Frankfurter argues was the primary effect of such texts.[27]

More avowedly sadomasochistic eroticism has seized on humiliation as well, from the texts of its titular figures onward. Several of the libertines in the Marquis de Sade's *120 Days of Sodom* rhapsodize on its delights. The banker Durcet, in a precise reversal of Tertullian, declares, "Nothing more logical than to adore degradation and to reap delight from scorn. He who ardently loves the things which dishonor, finds pleasure in being dishonored and must necessarily stiffen when told that he is." Joining in, the Président de Curval reminds the group of the tale of "the brave Marquis de S★★★," who ejaculates joyfully when he finds himself "at last; covered with opprobrium and infamy . . . !"[28]

Like many after and, undoubtedly, before them, Sade's characters wonder about the cause of the "undisputed facts" of shameful pleasures. Curval explains that the soul is changed "once a man has degraded himself, debased himself through excesses;" then "from the state in which one is when one has ceased to blush, to that other state wherein one adores everything that causes others to blush, there is no more, nor less, than a single step." The ways of such shameless people cannot be mended, since they will only enjoy any punishments inflicted, an "enigma above all else" that we must suspect pleased Sade greatly.[29] That this is the sadistic perspective is already evident, however; the masochist or submissive who has ceased to blush will find humiliation at best uninteresting, and this will be uninteresting to the sadist in turn. What these characters' delight suggests is that the sadist who retains interest in shame must work to avoid its characteristic contagion, delighting in it without feeling ashamed in turn.

Leopold von Sacher-Masoch is likewise invested in humiliation, though his take on it evinces less delight in the paradox. Though *Venus in Furs* contains a range of small humiliations (my own favorite is Wanda's insistence that Severin travel in a third class rail car),[30] the greatest come when Wanda enjoys the attentions of another lover in Severin's presence, and encourages this second lover to whip him: "I almost went mad with shame and despair. What was most humiliating was that at first I felt a certain wild, supersensual stimulation under Apollo's whip and the cruel laughter of my Venus, no matter how horrible my position was."[31] Here the arousal through humiliation is even more humiliating than the initial shame. Perhaps worse still, Severin may be ignored: "I served her at dinner, she ate by herself, but had not a look, not a syllable for me, not even a slap in the face. I actually desire a slap from her hand. Tears fill my eyes, and I feel that she has humiliated me so deeply, that she doesn't even find it worth while to torture or maltreat me any further."[32] Failed visibility and visibility as humiliated tangle themselves together: if Severin did not suspect that Wanda enjoyed ignoring him, he would find much less of both pain and pleasure.

Sade and Masoch are less distant from the martyrs' stories than we might suspect. Masoch compares himself to a Samson brought low by the beauty of Delilah.

One of the four libertines of the *120 Days* is a bishop, and in general Sade loves to populate his texts with clergy.[33] No doubt the entanglements of the sacred and profanity are more readily acknowledged from the side of the latter. I think, though, that we do well to recall a point raised by anthropologist Michael Taussig: "[D]esecration is more than the inverse of the sacred or of sacrifice. Something more complicated than inversion is going on."[34] In desecration, as he hints, perhaps we find a sacred reenchantment of a world that has become too mundane.

RUNNING INTO LIMITS

He did not at all want to consent to suffering, but he was detained . . .
by Limit . . .

—*A Valentinian Exposition*

Desires that pull against pain or displeasure are often about testing the limits of our capacities, whether or not those limits are understood as physical (almost always, they will be experienced physically in no small part: even the resistance to speaking is strongly felt in the throat, the jaw, the tightly pressed lips). They are pleasures that try to break from the limitations of words in opening the spaces between them, from the limitations of flesh in embodying sensation, from the limitations of desire belonging to a subject. Burrus asks whether shame might be inherent to finite creatures.[35] As finite, we are constantly frustrated and humiliated by limitation as we run up against it—and stubbornly pulled to what we know is not knowable at all. The play of limitation and excess appears throughout humiliating pleasures.

Anne Carson points out the "inevitable boundary that creates Eros: the boundary of flesh and self between you and me. And it is only, suddenly, at the moment when I would dissolve that boundary, I realize I never can."[36] Both desire and the desiring self arise in failure, and failure arises at the limit.[37] "Words have edges," Carson points out. "So do you."[38] The edge that forms identity is sharp enough to open desire: "Infants begin to see by noticing the edges of things. How do they know an edge is an edge? By passionately wanting it not to be." Desire, made at an edge, is made to fail—and is made, we realize, in stubborn opposition to knowledge (we know an edge by desiring a dissolution).[39] The very limits that make us may also unmake us, as William Robert points out: "[P]assion binds its subject—one subject to passion—to a limit, but enduring at that limit entails a subjective dis-integration or de-formation, thanks to which this subject is no longer himself or herself and, therefore, no longer fully self-knowing or self-determining."[40] Limit, after all, is not just finitude but definition.

Excess is outside (or, rather, it is not within) the limits of knowing; it is a mystery, a secret. I have used both of these terms, rather than one or the other, to allow me to draw upon a wider history: literary and queer theory tend to use the term secret; theology, though not without exception, mystery. "The excess of the secret is marked by a disproportion for which no progress of knowledge could ever compensate," Pascal Massie writes of Blanchot. "The secret cannot be mea-sured; for a measure encompasses what it measures, while it is proper to the secret that it exceeds any knowing."[41]

This may sound odd, since there are all sorts of secrets that we can know. Taussig writes of "public secrets," things everyone knows, but everyone knows very well not to say, in realms ranging from deeply traditional religious rites to contemporary politics. There are what I think of as everyday secrets, bits of in-formation, usually about people, that are shared only among a small group. The demand that they not be shared beyond that group may have penalties ranging from quiet disappointment to, if the information is, say, governmentally classified, imprisonment. There are data that we know must be there, as in a natural science, but that we haven't yet found. But there is also a sense of secret as mystery.

Mysteries, in the history of mystery religions, are traditionally secrets not to be told to those who are not initiated. In the *Symposium*, Plato deepens the meaning of mystery. After laying out the lesser mysteries of love, Diotima (who is, we must remember, an invention of Socrates) teasingly remarks, "Even you, Socrates, could probably come to be initiated into these rites of love. But as for the purpose of these rites when they are done correctly—that is the final and highest mystery, and I don't know if you are capable of it."[42] Whatever this highest mystery might be, then, it won't be accessible to reason, at which Socrates is masterful—it is a mystery that taunts him with the humiliating likelihood of failure. "Diotima" leads him, and us, through the ascent from lust for a single beautiful body to *philosophia,* the love of wisdom itself. Yet Socrates is a brilliant ironist. In his Diotimatic drag he surprises us by going beyond the love of wisdom to a higher or better object still, one that in the perfect simplicity of its beauty eludes exact description.[43] From that which is guarded from telling by the constraints of rite and rule, the mystery becomes that which is guarded from telling by impossibility itself. Even Socrates's presentation of it harbors an impossibility: he creates the very speech in which he acknowledges his inability to understand what he is saying. Eros must lead us to failure, and in failure's intermingling with pleasure and desire mysteries stir.

Even speaking becomes excessive—out of the bounds of the subject who speaks. Bataille writes, "Not that one must or could speak . . . , but it speaks . . ."[44] The authority of speaking is self-expiating; it is never mine, as Socrates's use of a surrogate already shows. The "it speaks" likewise characterizes what Blanchot calls "the neuter," which precedes speech yet murmurs within all speaking. Massie writes of the neuter as something like a mirror image of the secret; we might un-derstand the latter as pure interiority, and the former, harboring nothing, as pure exteriority. He adds, "The neuter, as secret of the secret ('which is no secret') is beyond meaning, pointing both to the limitlessness of language and to the limit that gives rise to meaning."[45] The "it says," unsaid by anyone, surrounds the unsay-able, unknowable secret. This means that the kernel of the possibility of saying, the neutral murmur said by no one, is itself not sayable. There is no secret if secrecy means inside with no outside; there is no meaning without what exceeds it.

The difficulty of saying is pronounced in failure and humiliation. We cannot easily claim what shames us—nor, in many cases, the closely overlapping set of what we find exciting. Such expression encounters the difficulty of pornography, which is also an effort to reveal excitement, to portray arousal in hopes that it will prove as contagious as shame. The language of obscenity is as difficult, as resistant, as that of confession. Bataille writes in *L'Abbé C*, "It takes energy for [the priest] Chianine to raise his skirt but even more to speak of it properly."[46] Reader, writer, and fictive subject all resist even as they push on. Language betrays us: it will not do what we want it to do, and yet it tells, in its stutters and gaps, the secrets that we spoke in order to keep.

The reluctant shame to admit or to reveal is a pornographic commonplace, in tension with the pride in displaying the desirable body. Related to this reluctance is inadvertence, the claim that what is revealed would have been resisted had those represented known about it. It is not unusual for works of pornographic fiction to include avowals of their reality, as if to reassure the reader that this too is something we were not quite supposed to hear, something overheard or reluctantly told, with a blush still in it—or manifesting an astonishing shamelessness, rather than simply a vivid imagination. Likewise, the viewer is assured that an impressive percentage of online and other visual pornography is amateur and thus, presumably, a little shocking, a little embarrassing, in its display of those not jaded or hardened by the profession—those who cannot simply leave a sense of the personal behind and act altogether professionally, so that their arousal and expression must somehow be "real." Of nearly equal popularity are claims of successful voyeurism, implying that those displayed would be shocked and embarrassed by the use thus made of their images. Each attests to the desire to catch something revealed rather than some-thing created to make money from revelation—innocents who know no better than to show themselves, or the even more innocent with no idea that they are on display. It is true that a great deal of what is available is at least amateurish, but equally so that the claim of inadvertence is often, to put it gently, exaggerated. It is perhaps even less likely to be true, on grounds of imagistic composition as well as legal liability, that all of the caught-by-surprise voyeurism really does show its subjects unawares. What the popularity of these genres suggests is that we want to feel as if there is something still a little naughty here, a little bit forbidden; some-thing someone ought not to have been doing, some gap in the deliberate display of the self. The resistance is in and to the revelation; what is revealed is its failure. When that failure is successfully sought by those revealed, however, something stranger still must be at work.

Halberstam begins *The Queer Art of Failure* "by addressing the dark heart of the negativity that failure conjures." She turns to "the happy and productive failures explored in animation," but then back again "to darker territories of failure associated with futility, sterility, emptiness, loss, negative affect in general, and modes of unbecoming," which "allow for the fact that failure is also unbeing, and that these modes of unbeing and unbecoming propose a different relation to knowledge."[47] One reason we cannot say secrets is that we cannot, in any of our customary senses, know them; in secrecy we must be in a very different relation to knowledge. Among the most important of the excessive desires at play is just this desire to know; among the most important of our failures is that of knowing. We are not always humiliated by ignorance (one hopes), but we may seek the failure of knowledge through a quest for humiliation.

WHOSE FAILURE?

T'es qui toi, t'es qui moi?
T'es pas qui, t'es pas quoi! T'es qui toi, t'es qui moi?
Mais toi, t'es qui? T'es quoi?

—Rachid Taha, "Tekitoi"

Mirroring this unknowable, unsayable failure is a correlation between power and knowledge, and even a mutual constitution: we know in order to have power; we have power in order to find out. A comprehensible, graspable world is a more readily governable world. As Jon Simons summarizes, "[P]ower can only be exercised over something that 'techniques of knowledge and procedures of discourse' were capable of investing in.'" Political power requires that we make people and populations into objects of knowledge.[48] If we turn ourselves to what avoids being known, we may fail, but we may also resist.

But who are this we? A counterpublic that courts failure and troubles identity makes itself and its members difficult to identify. Yet stubbornly, like Jordan, "I want the possibility of an embodied authorship that can contest power by writing across assigned identities, their privileges and inhibitions."[49] The unsettling pleasures of humiliation do, certainly, take identity as among the elements unsettled: like other painful pleasures, they can induce a shattering of the sense of self, from which a return to the selfsame is impossible. So I interpreted several such pleasures, many years ago, and I do still think that there is value to disturbing the sense of a too-steady, securely established ego—the value of an identity that disturbs identification.[50]

But this is not altogether unproblematic. Stephen Bush, considering the possibility of a Bataillean ethics, phrases the concern nicely: "[W]hereas a good dose of self-negation could be just what is needed for individuals at the top of the social hierarchy, whose agency needs to be restrained, it could be precisely the wrong thing for those already marginalized or repressed."[51] Kent Brintnall points out a recurrent and related queer concern: if we delight in undoing the sturdy, nicely bounded, self-directed ego, we risk offering delight only to those who are culturally positioned for such strength in the first place. If these twisty pleasures belong only to those whose privilege—in class, race, gender identity, able-bod-iedness, and more—has already smoothed out many of the daily challenges that others face, then these pleasures don't resist anything; they just reinforce those normative conceptions, offering one more thing to which only the privileged have access. To value them seems to ignore those for whom incoherence is a less chosen reality. It seems, even, to turn against the needs of some particularly vulnerable groups.[52] Writing of the urge for shame in early Christianity, Burrus remarks that her students respect

> the yearning for transcendence, transformation, and freedom . . . evident
> in those . . . texts. But they resist . . . transcendence bought at the expense
> of the shaming of the body (above all the sexual body), transcendence
> that produces the flesh in and through shame, inscribing it as a matter
> of shame—the shame of matter itself. Many of them do not fail to note
> that women, sexual and racial minorities, and the poor or uneducated
> seem to carry more than their fair share of such shame.[53]

Burrus herself both takes note of the concern and fails to resist the yearning, a delicate doubling.

And this doubling, however delicate, is essential to understanding these plea-sures. Brintnall points out that what is at play may be something less obvious than we think: not the existence of sturdy egos, but the cultural value placed on them. "Western conceptions of autonomy and dignity generate strong affection for the coherent self," he points out, and so long as those are affections are strong and those selves are normative, are what we are all *supposed to* want, there is value in undoing and resisting them, value in valuing otherwise.[54] This seems to me accu-rate and important, as an argument both for a political edge to shattering pleasure and against the queerer-than-thou urge that occasionally runs through politics as much as through theory. Following Foucault's claim that the analysis of power is an analysis of the ways in which individuals are made into subjects (who may be subjected), we might also suspect that failures in identity and even selfhood are again modes of resistance; they need not presume a clearly identified subject in order to make it problematic. I have come to suspect that we might do better to begin not with the a priori subject who chooses, but with the directions of desire, including paradoxical directions (pain, submission), and impossibilities (succeeding at failure). Failure, as Ellis Hanson points out, "renders identity politics an inex-haustible resource for shame."[55]

And failure does more. Like madness, it cannot quite be expelled from reason, remaining as "the unsettling force that puts the subject into question."[56] Huffer points out that Foucault's *History of Madness* is "the story of a split that produced the queer."[57] The split between reason and unreason is both constitutive and resisted. The exclusion of unreason, she adds, is also "about the internalization of bourgeois morality which produces, eventually, the 'fable' of an inner psyche, soul, or conscience."[58] What is perceived in this fable is an interior, the place where we look for the secret truth of the subject displayed on the skin. In inside and out, as each complicates and refolds, something remains of the other. With the effort to expel it, the tragic dimension of being human is pushed aside as well, and all pain becomes a problem to be solved by science.[59] The unreasonable, however, continues to haunt the rational subject. It remains.

Phenomenologist Jacob Rogozinski theorizes this unknowable other-in-self as the *remainder*—a slippery concept, an attempt to conceptualize precisely what eludes, cannot be caught up, or will not stay in place. He writes, "The remainder is the untouchable of my touch as well as the invisible of my vision and the inaudible of my hearing."[60] It cannot be encountered. Our means of knowing, "inside" or "out," are frustrated. The distinction itself is threatened. Rogozinski reads the remainder as a constitutive, necessary impossibility at the heart of the self. The I touches upon and is touched by a strangeness, a break—but this strangeness, this throwing into question, is constitutive of it rather than transcendent to it, as the will begins in a fracture, as the self begins where an edge is cut into the world, or as late antiquity argued that God is found within those who are not God, as their own centers. In the beginning, there is multiplicity. The heart of the I is broken. Rather than being tidily harbored, the remainder would necessarily rupture, or disrupt, the neatness of the self's boundaries. The edges of the self are jagged and uncertain.

Rogozinski suggests that the embodied self demands both an enveloping flesh and an opening to the world; the envelope is perforated. But we have to hold on to the sense that in the beginning is the break; there is no primary integrity. Rogozinski's understanding of openness includes the possibility of incorporation, taking more into the self, even enlarging it. But it includes an unbearable vulnerability too—the impossibility of excluding with sufficient force. We may literalize the remainder as small separated and abjected bits of ourselves, objects that can excite both desire and disgust; we may project it in hate or in love, in an effort to exclude.

Julia Kristeva, for whom remainder is likewise theoretically significant, writes in *Powers of Horror*, "Remainders ... pollute on account of incompleteness." This concept of incompleteness is essential, she adds, to nontotalizing thought.[61] Pollution links the remainder to the abject—the impure that is nonetheless crucial to any possibility of purity, the pushed-aside that haunts the center.[62] We reincorporate the remainder constantly and incompletely. At heart, our hearts are restless.

These three entangled constructs will emerge repeatedly in the discussions that follow: the interior, the secret or mystery, and the remainder. The interior is never wholly nor securely enclosed; the secret that it seems to harbor is never quite there, but neither is it somewhere else to be found. Something remains and resists, and without that remainder, the enclosed self, which the remainder seems to break, would not be at all.

The identity of the self is in play, not at base. It is fairly common to defend unusual choices in pleasures by appealing to freedom of choice: even if a choice might displease us, we are obligated to respect the autonomy of the chooser. Paradoxical desires and pleasurable failures undermine this option. Does this undermine their value?

"The value of some aspects of historical gay identity . . . have been diminished or dismissed with successive waves of liberation," Halberstam warns. "Central among these is the association between homosexual love and loss—a link that, historically, has given queers insight into love's failures and impossibilities (as well as, of course, wild hopes for its future). Claiming such an association rather than disavowing it, I see the art of losing as a particularly queer art."[63] The queer embrace of failure is both aesthetic and political.[64] Halberstam suggests "that there is something powerful in being wrong, in losing, in failing, and that all our failures combined might just be enough, if we practice them well, to bring down the winner."[65] Bringing down the winner, do we win instead? We do not: the queer art is far subtler.

WORDS FAIL

For now it would be heavier than the sand of the sea: therefore my words are swallowed up.

—Job 6:3

"Free me from the too-long speech," writes Blanchot, fifty pages into *Le pas au delà* (*The Step/Not Beyond*).[66] Blanchot's style here is fragmentary and aphoristic, each little speech brief in the extreme. Success! But he repeats the line on page 137, and now we wonder—if he was becoming concerned eighty-seven pages ago, what must be happening now? The line is typical of Blanchot: concise to the point of opacity, yet just translucent enough to be almost endlessly provocative; self-reflexive (the imperative is exemplarily brief), epigrammatic, enigmatic—and almost prayerful. In his repetition, Blanchot awakens in us an uneasy awareness that no speech, no text, is quite short enough to be safe. It would be safest not to speak, not to write. Perhaps he has failed, after all; perhaps despite their brevity those aphoristic bits have accumulated until he worries at their excess. Perhaps that particular request is one that *must* fail; maybe every speaking is too much, somehow, already—and not enough, either, too, again. In excess, and too limited.

In theory as in practice, religious history has important connections to the unsayable pleasures of paradoxical shame. The negative or apophatic theological tradition, denying the ability of language to grasp anything about "God," declares instead that we can only use words to say what-God-is-not, or, in many versions, that-God-is-not. Western negative theology traces back at least to the Platonic "One" that Socrates's creation Diotima sets forth in the *Symposium* as the object of the highest love—not a body nor a body part, she says; not "one idea or one kind of knowledge . . . not anywhere in another thing"[67] Negation might take the form of simply defining very narrow limits to theological language—insisting, for instance, that such speech must be analogical, or approximate. As a rule, though, such language courts failure. Apophasis, literally "saying away," is focused upon the necessary failures of speech, but its attitude to those failures is not one of discouragement. Words are used *so that* they fail; so that, in reading them, we are struck by the hints of what exceeds the grasp of saying, peeping through the gaps where words cannot perfectly mean. Such indirect expression serves as a reminder of humility, since it emphasizes that human concepts and words are inadequate to divinity, no matter how powerful the intellect that produces them.[68] We sometimes find warnings against using words at all, given our temptation to prattle on once we begin to speak: "So be silent, and do not chatter about God; for when you do chatter about him, you are telling lies and sinning," Meister Eckhart sternly warns in the fourteenth century, channeling Augustine from the fifth.[69]

But theirs is the less common perspective—and in fact, neither Eckhart nor Augustine is short on words. The paradigmatic negative theologian in Christianity is probably the fifth-century author known as Pseudo-Dionysius, who joyfully piles up the names of God, delighting in the revelations created by each new failure to designate the divine. Those images may harbor more than one mode of negation. They may negate simply by saying not-this. But they may also be "negative" in the sense in which we speak today of a negative attitude; that is, they may say that God is worthless, or other bad things. In fact, declares Dionysius, the shock of saying unattractive things about God is great enough to make those associations even more revealing than positive ones: they show up our inadequacy all the better.[70] If we say that God is a worm, then we are not so tempted to try to work out the logical accuracy of an analogy as if we say that God is a flower.[71] Unsaying inheres within saying, as a failure essential to the possibility. For Pseudo-Dionysius, nonsensical seeming images that appear to be humiliating to the divine allow "interpreters of the secret wisdom" to "keep [it] undefiled."[72] This is nothing so simple as the presentation of special facts that the best people keep for themselves; rather, it is the interpretation of what nonetheless is and remains mysterious. Language that sounds nearly contemptuous is appropriate to its own inadequacy.

This interest in the failure of words is taken up by literary theorists and extended beyond descriptions of divinity. For Blanchot, writing is bound to fail, and that is just what it should try to do. "Express only that which cannot be expressed. Leave it unexpressed," he instructs in *L'Attente, l'Oubli*.[73] The "work-lessness" of writing, Ann Smock points out in introducing Blanchot's *The Space of Literature*, does not call upon a writer's strength, as if she could gird her mental loins and confront failure successfully with her sword-surpassing pen. Instead, it "calls upon ... weakness, the incapacity ... to achieve anything at all."[74] It's not just that writing is very hard to do successfully, but rather, that what it does—no matter how successfully—is to fail.

This literary tradition is perhaps best known through Samuel Beckett, who famously mutters in *Worstward Ho*, "Ever tried. Ever failed. No matter. Try again. Fail again. Fail better."[75] As Leo Bersani and Ulysse Dutoit point out, this is a text that seeks its own failure, gradually divesting characters of identifying attributes, sentences of completion and structure. It aims worstward, never failing enough. In fact, "The text would appear to be concerned with little more than obstructing its own progress."[76] A proper failure of writing would be "to fall permanently into silence," but in this, Beckett fails to fail.[77] His writing never quite manages the "unlessenable least" that would be "best worse."[78] One of the central paradoxes of humiliating failure emerges: to succeed is to fail at failing.

It's hard to accept failure, even better failure, and Beckett's epigrammatic line has been bizarrely taken up as a mantra of success—keep trying! A better failure is a success! (Or, at least, it shows us the way to the success! Try more! Fail heroical-ly!) It is hard to overestimate how appalled Beckett would likely be—or perversely delighted, perhaps—by seeing how completely his own remarks have failed. They fail, in part, because they are cut short. *Worstward Ho* in fact continues, "Better again. Or better worse. Fail worse again. Still worse again. Till sick for good."[79] As insufficiently uplifting, this more thoroughgoing expression of failure fails to make it into the popular culture of self-improvement, of always seeking and look-ing after one's own interests. Apparently, even Beckett can be reappropriated for entrepreneurial enthusiasm, but his texts offer us still more strongly a resistance to that constant boosterism.

Closer than corporate mottos to Beckett, Blanchot, and apophasis alike is the queer embrace of failure with which we began, an embrace that does not refuse its dark ineffectiveness, its weakness—the depths of its powerless shame. The very term *queer* begins its political and theoretical life apophatically, as an attempt to name a defiance of categorization. Queer failure is necessarily embar-rassed, necessarily tangled up with rejection—and older than we might think. An image of shame lies behind the famous phrasing of Alfred, Lord Douglas, who wrote, in 1891, of a dream in which there appears a beautiful sad youth calling himself "Love." A much happier and more outgoing youth, however, declares this name false: "He lieth, for his name is Shame ..." The happy, shameless love adds proudly, "I fill / The hearts of boy and girl with mutual flame," and the sad replies, "Have thy will, I am the love that dare not speak its name."[80] This shameful Love, refused its name, is nonetheless the love that Douglas prefers. In another poem, he declares, "Of all sweet passions Shame is the loveliest."[81] It is a bit embarrassing to see such a surplus of sentimental sighing. But it is just a bit of an embarrassment, too, to feel this fondness for shame drawing us in, ashamed and embarrassed and desirous ourselves.

Language, like shame, is contagious. Language, said Laurie Anderson in the 1980s, is a virus—a notion she may have taken from William Burroughs, who suggested novelistically that language began as an extraterrestrial virus that lodged in the throats of prehumans, mutating from biology to information.[82] This is disappointingly unlikely, but language remains information and biology both, and as both, it travels across us, (sub)vocal vibration and conceptual sharing. Failures of words belong necessarily to bodies as well. Jordan quotes Foucault: "Really, writing tries to make the whole substance—not only of existence but of the body— pour itself out, through the mysterious channels of pen and letters, in the minute traces that one deposits on paper." As Jordan drily points out, "The effort cannot succeed."[83] This might be some part of the reason that it matters.

Bodies even more than words are frequently, inadvertently ridiculous, and it is embarrassing as well as delightful for language to depend upon our physical capacities. Failures of words and failures of flesh, as I shall try to show, are quite caught up in each other. The relation between word and flesh can be itself one of failure; as Jordan reminds us, bodies resist the legibility of writing.[84] Bodies are not quite legible and not quite speakable; like the divine of the negative theologians, they cannot quite be read, nor quite known. They cannot quite truthfully be said, in the face of constant contestation; they are all the more difficult to say because the theological, the literary, and the queer are entangled together—and are an embarrassment sometimes to one another.

Speaking is an exposure, though apprehension regarding it is unevenly distributed. Some people seem, even, to be eager to speak. Perhaps they feel exposed insufficiently: "In the beginning," says Jacques Derrida, "I would like to entrust myself to words that, were it possible, would be naked."[85] Derrida might be among those for whom the imperative to truth is especially strong, those who must speak or be faced with their own sense of dishonesty. Perhaps others are sure, somehow, of their right to occupy the aural space. These experiences of speaking confront little of the resistance that Blanchot voices. Few of us in or out of academia today can quite manage Blanchot's wonderful pictorial reticence, but we may well ask along with him when it comes to language: Free me from the too-long speech. Allow me, even, to remain in the innocence of silence, not to speak: to remain whole within it, and safe, as if wholly inside myself, keeping secrets. Yet the pleasures of failure show us repeatedly that neither inside nor self is undisrupted. Shame attaches to the need to speak, to impose—to the desire inherent in language, to the fear of the body convulsing there on the page rather than proceeding to the conclusion at a stately pace. It attaches to words' inadequacy, to our inability to make them say exactly what we want them to, to our inability to present our bodies just as we think they ought to be. The pure, blissful freedom from the too-long speech, from too-much saying, would be silence, were it not for the perverse urge to say the silence too, to lay out the body on the page.

We want the safety of silence because we accept the imperatives of words. All language use responds, says Michel de Certeau, to "an infinite volition," an "inner yes." In fact, he declares, "to say is to want."[86] The infinity of this volition is most marked in what he calls "mystic discourse," language in which desire is especially bare, and words especially likely to fail in reference. This affirmation is not so distant as it seems from Beckett's crystalline pessimism, Blanchot's self-effacing imperative, or Halberstam's queer and resistant art. Between body and body, word and word, word and flesh, desire moves, and desire—like the Cynic or fool, saint or martyr, sadist or masochist—is indifferent to reasoned measures of success.

One reason that desire is so obvious in mystic discourse and apophatic speech is that such language must try to say what it acknowledges must be unsayable. Mysticism and perversion alike are suspended in this pair of tensions, to reveal and conceal, to say too much and to respect silence by trying to keep it.[87] Every speech is too long, and insufficient.

BARE TEXT

> One ought only to write when one leaves a piece of one's flesh in the ink-pot each time one dips one's pen.
> —Leo Tolstoy, with Aleksandr Goldenweizer, in *Talks with Tolstoy*

Too long and too little, speech sins by saying at all and by its failure to say what it seeks. We are returned to my opening concern, to the shamefulness of writing shame. Stretched between excess and inadequacy, hyperclarity that reveals too much and illegibility that cannot tell what it wants, words try to place upon the page the body's excessive desires. We find ourselves, as soon as we try to say any of this, at an impasse. It is not by chance that Blanchot writes so often of mystery and secret, of silence that can neither stay unsaid nor be well spoken. We cannot expose the secret; it eludes the grasp of our words. Our urge to exposure, as much as our failure, can shame us.

The more words we pile up, the less we are able to hide behind them, as if, using them and using them up, the writer gradually and paradoxically laid herself bare. What's more, we are uncomfortably aware that the dramatic display might reveal a bareness that no one is very interested in seeing. As Derrida writes, "As soon as I leave a trace, I have to ask for forgiveness, because I imply, I assume, that it is interesting. . . . And then of course, there is guilt and I'm ashamed."[88] We are exposed, ashamed, and unable to deny our responsibility for this intrusion on the world. Against the constraint of brevity, one pushes on: one has spoken too much, already. There is little to do but fail more ("fail without fail," says Blanchot).[89]

Michel Leiris (like Blanchot, a close friend of Bataille) "cites a sentence that Picasso said to him: 'Reading poems in public—it is as if I was being asked to strip in front of everyone.'"[90] For Leiris, as presumably for Picasso, an exhibitionistic streak is not quite enough to keep this possibility from being horrifying. Against the urgent desire for silence and shelter, though, we sometimes find the perverted pull and pleasure of the risk. People do, after all, read poems in public. People do strip. In perverse and ascetic pleasures, we find an effort to bare, but one that fails again.

Milo Sweedler writes of Colette Peignot, who wrote under the pen name Laure: "Leiris and Laure seemingly agree that communication and nakedness are intimately related, but whereas one wants to keep his clothes on, the other would strip herself bare before the world."[91] What complicates this binary, and makes it far more interesting, is that Laure's sense of shame is no less developed, and no less entangled with words, than is Leiris's—only differently complicated by desire. In fact, Leiris's autobiographical writings suggest that they are perhaps not even all that different; the lady only doth protest a bit less.[92] Leiris, Laure, Bataille, Blanchot, Derrida—even Picasso, as a poet—are all writers; their very bodily, tangled-up erotic shame is also the shame of speaking. "[L]anguage is always involuntarily ridiculous," Bataille remarks, in his novel *L'Abbé C*; "that aspect is deliberately obscured: which is the reason for all the subterfuge, the circumlocution, the 'tricks' serving to disguise the horror that disarms one's pen." In this text, Robert, the titular Abbé, stutters to speak what is shameful, because it eludes words and because we would rather it were still more elusive, that it kept itself out of our speaking altogether. "[A]n unspeakable shame was perceptible apart from the sentences that were lying; it was perceptible directly: in the feeling I had of a suffocating silence. For that silence was so precisely what Robert wanted to say."[93] To speak of it is no less awkward than to silence it. Either one fails.

Complete truthfulness is impossible. The unsayable does violence to words, echoing in them as a reminder of surplus and tragedy. Certeau writes, "Thus, in a thousand and one different ways ... the sayable continues to be wounded by the unsayable. A voice comes through the text, a loss transgresses the ascetic order of production, an intense joy or suffering cries out, the sign of a death is traced upon the display windows of our acquisitions."[94] The unsayable secret is kept in mystic discourse, apophatic theology, obscenity, and the language that struggles to theorize them all. "What if philosophic writing—or philosophic writing so far as it is resistance—is more like a convulsed cry than voluntary speech?" Jordan asks.[95] And cries are limit-sounds, voice at the very edge of sense: "Foucault's longing to record these sounds—he crouches again and again to hear them—is always checked by his conviction that they occur at the limit of language. They resound in the place he sometimes associates with the poetic but also with the holy."[96] What if we try to take philosophy to the limit where it must be poetic, holy, obscene, and wholly corporeal, to the truth sounding only in the frustrated, wordless humiliated cry of failure?[97] The sense of the cry must register imperfectly, in the incompleteness of truth. In it, a mystery remains unsaid, but it may yet register, and the arrogance of trying to tell it may leave us ashamed. Shamelessly, we cannot help but try.

TWO

Unwilling

THE FAILURE OF AUTONOMY

AFTER SUCH KNOWLEDGE, WHAT FORGIVENESS?

Of Man's First Disobedience, and the Fruit
Of that Forbidden Tree, whose mortal taste
Brought Death into the World, and all our woe,
With loss of *Eden*, till one greater Man
Restore us, and regain the blissful Seat,
Sing Heav'nly Muse . . .

—John Milton, *Paradise Lost*

Whatever we may think of it now, obedience has an illustrious history both religious and secular, a history of association with goodness, properly accompanied by happiness and dignity. For the Abrahamic faiths, disobedience occurring in an original paradise is the first disturbance in the blissful relation of human to divine. In the Quran, the trouble is brief—the passage forbidding the humans in paradise to consume one tree's fruit, their temptation and transgression in eating it, and their repentance and forgiveness consume a total of three verses.[1] Though humans may no longer dwell in the garden after they've disobeyed divine directives, they know that they will be able to return to it in a heavenly afterlife. God's mercy, which makes this return possible, is stressed. But it has one limit—it does not extend to "the defiantly disobedient" (2:26).

The Hebrew Bible makes considerably greater drama of the matter. The forbidden tree in the garden of paradise is more specifically designated in the book of Genesis as the tree of knowledge of good and evil. Though the connotation seems narrowly moral, good-and-evil is probably a merism, a figure of speech intended to show, by juxtaposing opposites, that a wide or even comprehensive sweep is encompassed (such as we might mean in saying "search high and low"). This is the tree of knowledge. The humans are not wholly ignorant before they eat from the tree (the man, for instance, knows the names of animals), but this fruit will provide new and wider insights ("your eyes will be opened," says the helpful serpent, urging them to eat [3:5]). Perhaps they are offered more knowledge, perhaps new ways of knowing. Certainly, having eaten, they can make new observations.

And they see that it is not good. In verse six of the third chapter, they eat the fruit; by the end of verse seven, having realized that they are naked, they have "made themselves loin coverings," and in verse eight, they hide from God, who suspects that they are up to something and is looking for them (like children, they arouse suspicion by being quiet). This covering and hiding suggest shame, previously unknown to them. Suddenly vulnerable and aware of their own vulnerability, needing to cover themselves, human beings become susceptible to being shamed, to humiliation. This ancient God is less forgiving than the later God of the Quran. Each human, and the serpent, receives a specific condemnation, and all are exiled from paradise. Mortality is imposed upon them.[2]

Perhaps the most influential interpretation of this chapter is proposed by Augustine of Hippo, following certain Pauline texts.[3] Paul writes that "through one man sin entered into the world, and death through sin, and so death spread to all men, because all sinned" (Rom. 5:12). Augustine develops this into a notion of an original human sin passed on to all subsequent humanity as the tendency to sin, the impossibility of wholly getting it right. This might well seem a peculiar mode of punishment, and it depends upon the way that Augustine views punishment generally. In his understanding, punishment is implicit: that is, the punishment is in the transgression, rather than being something imposed afterward. Sin is punished by being what it is: a distancing from the divinity that is the source of all joy. The punishment for the sin of disobedience is more specifically to be what it is; that is, the punishment is further disobedience.[4] Augustine sees primal disobedience as a turn away from God, a split between divine and human will, an increasing distance. In consequence, the human will is split not only from divine will, but from itself and from the human body. Humans disobey God and their own better impulses, and their flesh disobeys their wills. The rift is then inherited by all subsequent human beings.

The division between will and flesh is especially important for an understanding of shame and humiliation. Knowledge becomes shame, so far as we can tell from the story, instantly. Humiliated by their own nakedness, the couple hides it away; humiliated by their own disobedience, they hide their bodies from their God altogether (though not altogether successfully). Augustine argues that it makes sense that they would cover their loins, since genitalia are the least obedient of the visible parts of the body, often acting quite against the rational will in fairly obvious ways.[5] Though the first sin is not sexual (it is more nearly gastronomic—but it is disobedience at base), sinfulness and sex rapidly become connected, and not infrequently conflated.

What is inherited, Augustine argues, is concupiscence. This term, too, has taken on a sexual sense, but for Augustine it implies simply the tendency to sin, to make wrong choices. While he does not think that this tendency is one that any human can overcome, he does think that the sinless god-person of Christ creates the possibility of a sin-free, wholly blissful reembodiment for all humans (like most early orthodox Christians, Augustine holds very firmly to a carnal resurrection).[6] In that glorious state, he adds, our divided wills are wholly mended, and we can be free from sin and frustration—and from shame. The beauty of entire bodies, wholly exposed, is cause only to sing out at the sheer gloriousness of creation.[7] It is not clear, really, that we shall will at all in this condition, as there is no need: in perfection, the best option is always already assumed, already taken. Eve and Adam had, and gave up, the power not to sin; risen humanity lacks the power to sin at all.[8] Will's perfect harmony would mean its absence, because that harmony would include a oneness with divine perfection, where the best choice is a given. That is, *there is no perfecting the will*: it becomes perfect only in ceasing to exist.

Human will is made as something broken. We have will when we are separated—when we are imperfect, individuated, and error prone. Similarly, we can only know our selves when we are separated—in distinction from the other things of the world, marked by our edges and our distance. But these splits keep us at once from perfect goodness and from full knowledge either of God or of ourselves, Augustine argues.[9] Humans find themselves unable to obey God, at least with any completeness and consistency; unable to harmonize flesh and will, most obviously unable to suppress involuntary genital arousal and movement; and unable even to be at ease within, such that we find ourselves with multiple and contradictory desires, often unable to decide among them.[10] And having known knowledge, we find it incomplete: no longer immersed in a divine world, we cannot see past the edges, cannot fully know any thing. Insofar as we are us and in our lives and in our world, the split is irreparable. We know ourselves as we become ourselves, by our separation. And our knowledge is our shame. To be a self is to be ashamed of that self, of the exposure that separation creates, of the imperfect wandering will, of knowing at all, and of knowing that one never knows enough.

AUTONOMOUS DIGNITY

"Why all the fuss?" asks one critic.
"She wanted liberty. Well didn't she have it?"
—Anne Carson, "The Glass Essay"

Culturally formative though these myths are, we can find quite secular valuations of obedience as well—though they mightn't appear that way at first. In *The*

Grounding of the Metaphysics of Morals, a small book of enormous importance, Immanuel Kant links dignity to the autonomous will, and both to the very possibility of ethics.[11] For Kant, the rules of ethics are universal and absolute, but they are also empty formulae into which the specifics of a situation must be entered. That is, they do not prescribe or proscribe particular actions ("Be kind to animals"; "Do not commit adultery"), but rather tell us how to figure out what to do—first, by asking whether we would be okay with everyone following the same rules that we set for ourselves. This universality, though, is pegged to individual freedom. A truly ethical rule cannot be given from the outside; rather, a person is ethical only when she, acting freely, determines on her own to act according to the laws of reason. We cannot be ethical unless we can be rational. (The same is true for Augustine, for whom the joys of paradise are wholly reasonable joys.) Kant writes, "[A]ll maxims are to be repudiated that are inconsistent with the will's own giving of universal law. Hence the will is not merely subject to the law but subject to it in such a way that it must be viewed also as giving the law to itself."[12] He reiterates, more succinctly, "An action that is consistent with the autonomy of the will is permitted; one that does not agree with it is forbidden."[13] An act is ethically permitted or forbidden, of course, only by the autonomous will itself.

From autonomy, which is this capacity to give *oneself* the laws that one obeys, it follows for Kant that rational creatures have a unique kind of worth.[14] Reason allows us freedom; because of it, we are not bound by instinct, nor by purely physical causes and effects. We can make rules rather than following only the laws of biology. We may justify obedience to rules by declaring it in defense of freedom, thus attaching obedience to freedom's pride rather than to the humility of subordination.

Because we must respect freedom, free beings have dignity. Dignity is perfectly distinct from exchange value: no will can rightly command another (that is, will for another); in parallel, no reasonable being can replace or be exchanged for another. The will directing itself is directing itself well. The will divided by heteronomy is split, like Augustine's will after the Fall, taking its direction from lazy sensuality, inclination, or other people. Obedience to another becomes a threat to the rule of rationality.

Autonomy is self-legislation, but it is not necessarily the contradiction of someone else's legislation. In fact, Kant argues, a community of truly autonomous, rational people would be perfectly harmonious, as all of them would follow the same law without that law ever being imposed from without.[15] Each would reason her way to the same conclusions. And so, once again, disobedience is disharmony. A very particular obedience is at the base of dignity: obedience only to the law, as Augustinian obedience is only to God; in each, the will would be perfected.

Reason is not—emphatically and decidedly not—God in the Kantian system. But Kant's reason and Augustine's God do share morally relevant traits. Each is the source of universal rules, which, if we understand them properly, are infallible.

(Kant is far more optimistic at each step—that we might know, understand, and follow.) Each is the source of a particular kind of knowing, which may exceed mere understanding of the workings of the sensible world. Each works against our lower instincts, and our laziness. We must obey the law; our moral duty is, Kant agrees, a form of subjection.[16] And for each, the failure of the will is a loss of dignity.

The relation to dignity may be the most difficult aspect of humiliation, ethically and aesthetically both. Kant is not alone in basing dignity solely on this obedience to one's own will, where will is assumed to follow rationality. Political theorist Jeremy Waldron writes, "[O]ur dignity is thought to be based on conscious aspects of our being such as reason, understanding, autonomy, free will and so on. And often too human dignity is associated with an element of normative self-regard."[17] Martha Nussbaum also argues that "human dignity and the closely related idea of the social bases of self-respect and nonhumiliation" must be our ethical touchstone.[18] She grounds dignity, not quite in autonomy, but in capability, meaning that each being is free to develop as it can, and each finds its dignity in that development.[19] The developing being must not be inhibited by others in developing these capacities, which for humans include reason, Kant's ground of autonomous being. Respect for free development means that we allow others choice in developing their capabilities, with one conspicuous exception: the choice to decline dignity is firmly off limits.[20] So, in some manner, autonomy as foundational to ability (however wide or limited) grounds self-respect, as well as the respect of others for oneself. While humility and dignity are compatible, humiliation and dignity appear to be firmly opposed. Obedience to another, especially in extremes of submission, undermines autonomy, and to obey humiliating instruction seems clearly undignified.

Though the concept of dignity has a long history as a sense of human value, it has not always been so straightforward as Kant suggests. The English term *dignity* emerges in the early thirteenth century. It is rooted in the Latin *dignus,* signifying both worthiness and propriety; ultimately, like *decent,* it is traceable to the root **dek-,* which means equally to accept and to be suitable.[21] For centuries the concept was reserved for kings, or at least for nobility. It only very gradually came to be attributed to all persons—just as the possibility of general autonomy came only slowly to be attributed to the masses.[22] Dignified, we are never indecent, but accept what is suited to us, to us in our proper worth. Even when, under the Christian inversion, humility comes to be valued positively, and arrogance or undue pride to be more strongly condemned, "*Superbia* and *humiliatio* are vices and virtues of the aristocracy, lay and ecclesiastic, not of the peasantry," as Patrick Geary points out.[23] Catherine Clément suggests an intriguing connection when she writes of the medieval European orders that Georges Duby analyzes, "the nobility, the clergy, and the 'clerks'. . . . As for the servants, they did not belong. The servants are the 'rest,' the 'remnants,' of humanity."[24] Another remainder. That which is beyond the order of dignity is all that sustains dignity's possibility. And those beyond dignity are those who take orders from others.

A more egalitarian sense of dignity emerges again with the rise of humanism; for instance, Pico della Mirandola's fifteenth-century *Oration on the Dignity of Man* foreshadows Kant's link between dignity and freedom.[25] Recent decades have seen a resurgence of interest in dignity, with political philosophers such as Waldron, Michael Rosen, and Ronald Dworkin,[26] and ethicists including Martha Nussbaum urging that we re-center the concept, now universalized with a dual status of innate characteristic and human right.[27] For all of them, dignity is linked to self-legislation, personal responsibility—and human worth.[28] Yet complications still emerge—dignity seems to be both something innate to us, and thus inalienable; and something that could be taken from us, though it ought never to be.[29] It is also seen as both a quality that one has and a right that one may exercise. The tensions in this multiplicity emerge clearly in the obedient subject, who must at once be and not be self-determined and must voluntarily give up voluntarism for the impossible pleasure of a paradoxical failure and the humiliation of an incomplete submission.

FROM ONE, MANY

> Abstractly taken, why is "one" more excellent than "forty-three," or than "two million and ten"?
>
> —William James, "The One and the Many"

It must seem that I have gone on at some length against my own claims, or at best both against and for. Obedience to God, particularly in Christianity, is wholeness and joy; obedience to the law, in Kant's influential ethics, is autonomous dignity and thus the very ground of human value. But these connections apply only to the singular obedience to a perfect source: it is in turning obedience elsewhere, indeed anywhere else, that we connect it instead to our shame, because we cannot obey the perfect will (belonging to God or to reason) and any other will at the same time. Why abandon a pure and good obedience for the humiliating subordination of the will to mere, and sometimes multiple, humans? The commands of reason to the imposition of others, or, for that matter, to a God who demands the abandonment of one's own best interests, who insists that one act against one's desires? It is here that the delights of imperfection, and the nagging pull of the desire to know, both begin to matter. And if knowledge must lead us to shame, then the desire to know may take its own pleasure in humiliation, in knowing its own shamefulness. Obedience is not "about" knowledge, but we can already see that it is well entangled with knowing and with the strange double shame of knowing and of not knowing enough.

The connection of obedience (to another person) to humiliation is significant, but it is not direct, and we should review a few caveats before taking it up.

There are people who accept instruction because it is useful or comfortable for them to do so. Most of us probably do so, in fact, at one time or another, and most of us appreciate the instructors' expertise. There are those who take pride in their own obedience, particularly if it is the result of long training and effortful discipline—we need only envision a military force on parade to see this. There are social and political reasons to value obedience, ranging from the totalitarian and conservative to the coexisting and communal. Obeying another person may accompany a more singular obedience; in monastic practice, obedience to a superior is generally understood to be in the service of obedience to God; military obedience to an officer is understood as obedience to a patriotic imperative.

The complexity of the connection between obedience and humiliation emerges clearly in monasticism, where obedience even now is valued as leading to humility, but where both at the level of humiliation were once less foreign and alarming. Some of our earliest monastic rules begin with simple humility. Basil of Caesarea, writing in the fourth century, already urges, "First of all then, and this truly is first, [the monk] must give such evidence of humility in the love of Christ, that even in his silence the example of his deeds will serve to teach others." As such evidence, monks should occupy themselves "in menial tasks" in order to "cure the malady of arrogance."[30] "The first degree of humility," writes Benedict of Nursia in his sixth century *Rule for Monasteries* (widely regarded as a basis for most later rules), "is obedience without delay."[31] Several further degrees of humility in Benedict's *Rule* develop this connection: "The second degree of humility is that a person love not his own will nor take pleasure in satisfying his desires"; "The third . . . is that a person for love of God submit himself to his Superior in all obedience"; "The fourth . . . is that he hold fast to patience with a silent mind when in this obedience he meets with difficulties."[32] Since Benedict wrote, we have come to value this self-abnegating humility considerably less, and the freedom that is opposed to obedience considerably more, and perhaps this is one among a great many reasons for the decline of monastic life. There are evident egotistical and cultural reasons for this revaluation; perhaps more importantly, there are ethical reasons as well—exactly the reasons that Kant has given us. Yet, as Sara Maitland warns, "It is easier . . . to reduce the concept of the holy from the mysterious to the ethical, and make it refer solely to moral goodness, than to address the inevitable destabilization of psychological well-being involved in the decentralized location of the liminal. But the liminal is a key value here."[33] In our desire to understand the religious life in ethical terms, and in our love of secure and stable selves, we have moved too far from the edge. The demands of humility are not solely moral; those of humiliation mutually sought are scarcely moral at all.

This difference involves a shift in the understanding of freedom. Augustine writes to his God: "[W]here through so many years was my freedom of will? From what deep and hidden recess was it called out in a moment? Thereby I submitted my neck to your easy yoke and my shoulders to your light burden"[34] Freedom of the will is called forth only by its submission. Prior at least to the will-lessness of postresurrection flesh, there is no passivity in this submission, but the active desiring of God's desires,[35] which ideally accord with one's own, but which are not desired on that account but because they are God's.[36] The ever-authoritative *Catholic Encyclopedia* reminds us that obedience is less about the particular instructions and more about the imperative to follow.[37] Obedience must willfully give over the will while retaining the will to give it. For the Christian tradition, the giving-over is necessarily imperfect (the only perfect submission being Christ's, particularly in his acceptance of death)—human disobedience is ineluctable and insurmountable. We must be humble enough to think ourselves below Christ, who displayed ultimate humility.

This creates both a practical impossibility and a paradox: the will must be simultaneously retained and given up. To be an individual, a subject who might obey (a subject, even, who wills or wishes to obey, a subject constructed under the will to obedience) is to be finite and separate, with a will distinct from that which one endeavors to obey (as the Genesis myth suggests, we are made in separation). The obedient will, ideally, subordinates itself to the will of another—in the monastic mode, to the will of God or of the Abbot; in the perverse mode, to the will of the dominant—*because* that will is God's or the Abbot's or the dominant partner's, and not because of what the will instructs. Thomas Aquinas writes that "obedience to a superior is due in accordance with the divinely established order of things."[38] One who displays perfect obedience, carrying out every expressed impulse of the commanding will, is either engaged in a perfectly interiorized struggle with his own will against itself, successfully keeping it away from any impulse contradictory to the superior's, yet imperfect, *because* of the very element against which he struggles, in this obedience—or else he is will-less, all desire and struggle stilled in the empty purity of his heart. The latter seems to be the perfect triumph of the superior, a final win. Yet in this case too, despite the appearance of pure perfection, the one who obeys is not obedient after all, because his is not even a subordinated will. His will simply isn't there, or is already so perfectly in accord with that of the superior that there is no need for obedience, with its salutary humbling effect. Obedience is self-undermining because it is impossible both in practice and in principle: it requires the subordination of a will that must subordinate itself imperfectly if it is indeed subordinating itself at all. (Nor does this stop at the level of the human superior; it also renders incoherent the doctrine of divine omnipotence. Power exists only when power pushes back.) The human will heals from its foundational fracture by breaking itself; it breaks out of its limits by a maximum of restraint. Even if we are optimistic about the perfectibility of the will, one who is perfect need not, and cannot, obey: there are no flaws to subordinate. Such perfection could only obey a worse will, making itself imperfect again.

The perfectly obedient will could only will itself into oblivion, thus annihilating its own perfection. What keeps obedience interesting is its necessary imperfection, the struggle not only against insubordination but also against not struggling—the ineluctability of failure. Even a happenstance accord will not work; there must be something to subordinate. As we can readily imagine, what is less than ideal in monastic humility—the accord of wanting what the superior wants anyway—is unbearably dull in perverse eroticism. The will is redeemed only by absence. But this absence must be desired; it must be willed. The medieval Beguine Hadewijch exemplifies this desire even better than those monks we have already encountered; as Giles Milhaven writes, she "affirms several times that she has the very desire that takes over her and puts her out of her control only because she wills so freely, so strongly to so desire."[39] And we are returned to the paradox again.

INSIDE OUT

> Then you will teach him again to dance inside out as in the delirium of
> our accordion dances and that inside out will be his true side out.
> —Antonin Artaud, "To Have Done with the Judgment of God"

Further problems arise from our lack of knowledge—not only about the superior, perhaps in figuring out just what she wants or intends, but about ourselves as well. Both mind and flesh retain a suspicious opacity, so that neither our motivation nor our success is as certain as Kant clearly hopes—though, to be sure, rule-generating reason is likely to be less opaque than another person. Augustine, as we've noted, is less optimistic, already aware of the tendency of mind to hide from itself and of flesh to evade the will. If the inward gaze cannot be sure of clarity, even inside and outside cannot be distinguished as neatly as the terms suggest. And this adds to the problem of opacity; we cannot simply hope to get past a barrier when the layers and levels decline to remain in order. Obedience is meant to evade just this problem, by making the subordination of the will into something visible. "For in what way shall he put his humility to the proof," asked Basil, "if there is no one before whom he must be humble?"[40] Obedience makes the subordination of the will into something exterior, something knowable—or, at least, it tries.

The difficulty begins in the flesh, not because it is bad, but because it is elusive. Contrary to his popular reputation, Augustine is not hostile to the body, which he sees as part of the lost Edenic harmony.[41] He is not even opposed to corporeal pleasure; he only worries, as Peter Brown points out, that such pleasures tend to override more rational movements of the will.[42] In this, bodily pleasure reminds us of the original schism of sin.[43] Sexual pleasure can even be altogether involuntary: like many of his contemporaries, Augustine was concerned with nocturnal emission and the behavior of the dreaming body, which he regarded as evidence of a concupiscence beyond the reach of the conscious mind and the rigor of self-control. These somnolent behaviors become especially important as objects of restraint: if we could know even our dreaming bodies, if we could get them under control, then surely we would be well on our way to full transparency? To a corporeal will that obeys, even in sleep?

Here traditions differ. The depth of Augustine's mistrustful stance is not universal, despite his success in making original sin into Western Christian dogma. Others, including John Cassian, whose work is fundamental to Eastern monasticism, believe the monastic body to be truly susceptible to retraining.[44] He admits that the perfection and purity of the sinless soul are very seldom attained. But perfectibility is *possible,* and this marks an immeasurable difference from the Augustinian view. Here too, however, an "interior" perfection can only be brought about by the submission of the will to the outside, to the will of the superior. And as we have already seen, this perfection undoes its own possibility.

Cassian tells a striking story at the opening to his Nineteenth Conference, one worth citing at some length, as it brings this peculiarity into a fully fleshed visibility:

> [W]hen one of the brethren had been rather slow in fetching and bringing in a dish, the ... Abbot Paul, who was busily hurrying about among the troops of brethren who were serving, saw it and struck him such a blow before them all on his open palm that the sound of the hand which was struck actually reached the ears of those whose backs were turned and who were sitting some way off. But the youth of remarkable patience received it with such calmness of mind that not only did he let no word fall from his mouth or give the slightest sign of murmuring by the silent movements of his lips, but actually did not change colour in the slightest degree or (lose) the modest and peaceful look about his mouth ... if this paternal correction had not disturbed his patience, neither did the presence of so great a number bring the slightest sign of colour to his cheeks.[45]

The novice's obedience appears to be perfect. Moreover, it appears to be perfectly freed from shame; the abbot's success is not in shaming the young monk, because what is admirable about the latter is his utter *lack* of shame—yet we would use the term incorrectly if we called him shameless. Shame, signified in angry word, tightened lips, or embarrassed blush, would imply some lingering and injurable pride, and this pride would imply an impurity of the heart. The novice has no fear of exposure, because there is nothing to expose. His once-willful body is a blank page, not unwritten, but perfectly erased. And to offer nothing on the surface, it must have no palimpsest of resistance hidden beneath.

In an early and important study of the affect of shame, Léon Wurmser writes, "There is above all an area of inwardness and interior value that should not be violated by any agent from outside or even by other parts of one's personality. If this area of integrity and self-respect is infringed upon, shame and often violent rage ensue." He compares this "power sphere" to the territorial space of other animals, but adds that in humans there is "an inner limit covering this intimate area that one does not want to show."[46] Anything that breaches or even seriously threatens this barrier can arouse shame.[47] Will and knowledge converge again: control by the will is especially important when what it controls is something that one does not wish to have known, or uncovered. If there were nothing that we wanted to keep to ourselves, then there would presumably be no boundary to breach. A very old argument holds that we need no privacy where we fear no shame: "Prudentius [in the fifth century CE] emphasizes that, after victory over the Vices, the Virtues avoid all recesses and hiding places: their tents stand open, their flaps drawn back, lest anyone take advantage of secrecy to relax their vigilance (*Psych.* 741–45). Exposure is not feared. The inside is as the outside."[48]

If we have no shame and no cause for shame when there is nothing we wish to conceal, then perhaps when we get rid of the illusion of interiority, shame vanishes too. We create this illusion for ourselves by trying to hide certain truths and desires; we put up little barriers of silence or hiddenness around them. If purely disciplined obedience is wholly visible, as it is in the novice's case, then the barriers can come down, because there is no interior space that they protect. Yet the will of the superior must cross the boundary of the self that the monk makes by obeying it; without this duality, there is no obedience. The religious person, as Maitland reminds us, must have an autonomous self to give away. If the novice is perfectly obedient, it is because his will is gone, and so he is not perfectly obedient, but simply, in some fairly fundamental way, absent. The paradox of perfection returns again when we try to understand the will as interior.

If we are to know our own wills perfectly, then those wills must be made visible: not interior, not guarded by shame. What's more, if we are to be obedient, then the visible action must be a perfect match for the superior will. But we cannot perfectly know our superiors, either, even when they are not incomprehensible gods. In fact, Thomas Aquinas tells us that obedience is *not* a theological virtue, "for its direct object is not God," but a moral one, according to which one is to follow "the precept of any superior, whether expressed or inferred, namely, a simple word of the superior, indicating his will."[49] It's a serious moral virtue, and disobedience can be a mortal sin (though Thomas allows some pragmatic exceptions, such as circumstances in which there are just too many rules for anyone to follow). That the monk is to obey the superior is basic to all monasticism. This moral virtue is fundamental, and, says Thomas, pleasing to God. So it seems that obedience itself is so salutary that it is the fact of obedience, rather than the particulars of the orders followed, that accords with God's will.[50]

An implicit tension already emerges: from the earliest monastic rules, we are told firmly that the superior must not issue instructions contrary to the will of God. Thomas characteristically finesses the issue: disobedience is always a sin, but it is worse to disobey God than to disobey a human being. Even when a superior issues orders, those orders contrary to divine will ought not to be followed.[51] This means, however, that obedience meets with an added complication: How does one know or find that divine will? Here Augustine is helpful, if also rather abstract. Despite his role in the ecclesiastical hierarchy, he nonetheless insists that God is found by turning within; the way we know both God and our obedient or disobedient selves is a kind of contemplative introspection. Introspection creates a version of self-awareness by which one realizes that God is at the heart even of one's fallen self, and is the place of rest to which one will always desire to return.[52] The self at its center is not selfsame; it finds itself when it finds God, but it does not quite find God as itself (Eastern Christianity is more open to this latter possibility). Nor is this God some separate entity parasitically lodged in the human being. Somehow it is other within the self, yet constitutive of it. This version of the self divided at heart is more optimistic than the view given by the analysis of original sin, but no less intractable. The will must turn outside to the superior, inside to God, inside out to a harmony that the subject nonetheless knows is unfindable.

Knowledge entangles with desire in the original sin, as the desire to know more impels disobedience, and disobedience leads to dismaying knowledge, including the knowledge of knowing's limitations. But conversely, even the most stubborn and best intentioned obedience fails because of failures to know. We do not fully know our own wills, nor the superior's will. We do not fully know or control the bodies in which obedience makes willing visible. For monks, there are the added problems of knowing neither God's will nor the harmony or disharmony of God's will with that of the superior. Even if God's will is found within oneself, one can never be certain of knowing it; we lie to ourselves all the time. The problems of harmony with divine will and moral certainty do not tend to emerge within perverse erotic subordination, but the problems of interiorizing another will, of knowing and properly interpreting that will, and of retaining an obeying self—even if only for the pleasure of the willful dominant—all recur, all displayed in the stubbornly illegible and resistant flesh.

The remainder, the other-within, even if divine, threatens the boundary that the desire against shame so strongly endeavors to preserve, a boundary that clarifies the borders of the self. The demand that all secrets be told and shown, all mysteries demystified (that is, obliterated), is also an attempt to rid ourselves of the invisible in the visible, the silent in speech—the mysteriously, annoyingly unknowable in the possibility of knowledge. The demand is never met; we can no more constitute a perfectly displayed obedient self, its tent flaps virtuously open, than we can create a wholly inner self, tucked away from all evidence.

Obedience is both a renunciation of one's own will and a greed for more difficult demands. It may become an exaltation not despite, but *in,* shame—at the lack of strength in one's own will, at the failure to hide the inside, at the nature of the orders themselves. It fails as autonomy, and it fails to obey completely. Shame takes pleasure from the break always in the middle of self-construction, from the giveaway of the rigorous ego. Obedience, so often in the service of conserving the given, resisting novelty, or even giving up on the power of thought, can resist not only by disobedience (as it often must), but by pushing itself to an extreme. This is true for the early monks; it is true for the perverts too. The will wins in submission when it demands its "own" loss, and more: when it turns another cheek, feigns a more severe unreason, invites derisive laughter. But it can "win" only if there is some division in it, some over-which—some failure. "To resist temptation," writes Burrus, ". . . is to triumph *against* oneself, and thus it is crucially not a triumph *of* the self. The encounter with temptation produces a splitting within the subject that continues, in theory *ad infinitum,* ever approaching (but never quite reaching) a state of utter dissolution. To triumph is also, then, to submit extravagantly . . . to one's own humiliation."[53] We are dissonant with ourselves, and not in a simple dualism of will and flesh. The duality of inside and out may feel like security, threatened by its imperfection, by the sense of an interior exposed. But it may feel like entrapment, too; like the boredom and frustration of a limited subject; the ability to refold and display the obedient will may seem inadequate. Bottomless and soaring, humiliation of the will reaches the highs and lows of the sacred—and turns inside out again and again.

EMULATING FAILURE

Now he came that we might become glorious through the humiliated one that dwells in the places of humiliation.
—Anonymous Valentinian author, *The Interpretation of Knowledge*

That *sacred* has a double sense of high and low is particularly crucial to Christianity, which is much concerned with the ways that the low sacred seems to emerge in the person of Christ. The tension between high and low, exalted glory and abject humiliation, generates another of the paradoxes and pleasures of obedience, though primarily within the Christian context. The very humanity of Jesus is regarded as an abasement for a deity (and thus is much contested in early Christianity). Rogozinski writes speculatively, "God's 'emptying-out,' which the theologians have named his *kenosis,* his descent in flesh and his death on the Cross, are the condition of this invocation allowing him to call him by his Name. It is indeed the . . . story . . . of a living flesh that is disfigured and transfigured, that dies and is resuscitated—and it is the story of *our* flesh, our life, the intrigue of the ego and the remainder."[54] The concept of kenosis comes from Christian scripture, where a passage in Paul's letter to the Philippians tells us that Christ "emptied Himself, taking the form of a bond-servant, and being made in the likeness of men" (Phil. 2:5-7).

The "emptying" is not of divinity entirely, but of some of the privileges that go with it, especially those of sovereignty and invulnerability.[55] It is widely associated with humility and with obedience both, as the next verse of the letter demonstrates: "He humbled Himself by becoming obedient to the point of death, even death on a cross" (Phil. 2:8). Only a few lines later, Paul makes it particularly clear that this obedience is meant as a model: "So then, my beloved, just as you have always obeyed . . . work out your salvation with fear and trembling; for it is God who is at work in you, both to will and to work for His good pleasure" (Phil. 2:12-13). God empties out of godself as Christ, but empties into the addressee, within whom God wills and works toward God's own pleasure. (Once more, within and without become untrackable.) Christian Passion narratives further emphasize the obedience inherent in accepting mortality; all of the synoptic gospels feature some variation on the line "not my will, but yours, be done," as Christ accepts his impending crucifixion.[56] The gospel of John does not include the story of Christ's antemortem agony and acceptance, where these lines occur, but features several remarks regarding Christ's work as "the will of the one who sent me."[57] This act of obedience can only be displayed in the flesh, at its most vulnerable in its mortality, its most obedient in agreeing to death. Rogozinski argues that "it is our relation to the remainder that most often gives us access to the divine: the immanent experience of its disfiguration and transfiguration subtends the madness of faith."[58] It is important, I think, that this transfiguration is a disfiguration too, emphasizing the obedience and humility that the crucifixion requires.

Unsurprisingly, a story this strange gives rise to further oddities. Self-abjection, as Kristeva notes, becomes "the ultimate proof of humility before God."[59] It is true that there are passages in the Hebrew Bible, particularly in the Levitical prohibitions, that focus on abjection—that is, on what is pushed out or exteriorized as impure, like indecency from the heart of the monk.[60] But "a subjective interiorization of abjection," Kristeva writes, "will be the accomplishment of the New Testament."[61] What is to be pushed out or abjected folds into the depths of the subject. Humiliation is often an aspect of abjection, the act of pushing outside of the acceptable and bounded body, whether somatic or social. Slow, inglorious execution as a criminal announces the abjection of an agitator and blasphemer; Christianity proclaims this criminal God.

Most of the time, monastic submission is explicitly modeled on Christ's, presenting again the desirability of the forbidden limit. Slightly lesser exemplars are sometimes permitted; John Chrysostom, for instance, approvingly cites Paul, who took "pleasure in infirmities, in insults, in persecutions."[62] But invocations of Christ's submission are far more common: "Submitting myself completely to the Abbot," writes Cassian, "seems in some degree to emulate Him of whom it is said: 'He humbled Himself, and became obedient unto death'"[63] Benedict writes of monks as those who "desire to have an Abbot over them. Assuredly such as these are living up to that maxim of the Lord in which He says, 'I have come not to do My own will, but the will of Him who sent Me.'"[64] In a more contemporary reading, Hans Urs von Balthasar elaborates upon the example: "The prayer-agony on the Mount of Olives has as its unique object a saying 'Yes' to the will of the Father," a yes that is part of a "wider programme of living ... which received its final illustration in the gesture of the Footwashing, that pure piece of slave's service (John 13.13ff)."[65] The emulation of slaves is not what one expects of a God, and so it makes a remarkable theological move, one that might retain even now a tiny bit of its ability to surprise. Lest we be tempted to assume that the crucifixion is merely a following-out of fate and prophecy, and therefore as effortless as it is inevitable, von Balthasar adds, "Even Christ's self-giving remains obedience (Philippians 2, John 5), and the harshest obedience, bitter obedience, at that."[66] For the monk, Christ's is the exemplary life, and as most people cannot attract disciples or generate miracles, obedience is widely chosen at the point of imitation. But tension arises from the fact that Christ as the ultimately humiliated, obedient person, who subordinates any personal will, remains God in the very tradition that exalts his humiliation. To aspire to such lows, then, is also a self-exaltation, a high measure of arrogance. The monk cannot rest until he has humbled himself to the level of ... God? Such a consummation, however devoutly to be wished, is just as devoutly the temptation to enormous pride.

Bataille captures the poles of this perverse pleasure: "[A]t the very instant of the disgrace ... the most bitter saint knows himself to be chosen."[67] To be like God, when God becomes Trinitarian and so is the degraded sacrifice as well as the all-powerful to whom sacrifices are made, is necessarily a paradoxical undertaking. In its exaltation, the surrender of the will nonetheless risks pride. To humble oneself before humility is to risk being arrogant about one's absence of arrogance; to emulate a paradigmatically humble God is necessarily to place oneself into the paradox of identifying oneself with divinity by declaring oneself the most debased sort of human. Yet it is precisely Christ's abjection that will inspire his followers; not the triumphant resurrection and ascent, but the deepening enfleshment, a lived pain and humiliation, death as one in a row of criminals, not even unique.

Granted, there is a strong and understandable tendency for contemporary Christianity to focus upon the triumphal vision of the resurrected body, upon death defeated—sublimation of all that is evil and ugly, such that even our remains are perfected. One of the sites of resistance to this triumphalism, however, has been mysticism, as Bataille points out: "The mystic's love even demands that God put Himself at risk, that He cry out His despair on the cross. The crime of saints is essentially an erotic crime. It is linked to these transports, to these torturous fevers that brought burning love into the solitude of convents."[68] Not all modes of mysticism attend to the body, but those that do so within Christianity have often dwelt upon vulnerable woundedness. Rather than dualizing body and spirit, or sublimating carnality to transcendence, such mysticism is intent upon the wounded spaces that paradoxically undo separations. While religious ortho-doxy carefully veils both eroticism and criminality, their presence in "transport and fevers" emerges both in erotic mysticism and, with or without the specifically Christian content, more overtly in the perverse pleasures that delight in eroticism and a sense of transgression—of which we shall shortly see more. One who obeys faces the double risk and the double demand of being unable to obey and of fol-lowing commands too easily; transport demands the rupture that the constitution of self by abjected remainder makes possible. But where this demand is met, the willful self seeking it has failed.

Kristeva argues that Christ's role is to demonstrate pure sublimation, to show what it is to be without flaw. This role emphasizes the clean purity of the resur-rected, rather than the crucified, flesh:

> Christ alone . . . is a body without sin. What others must do, because of their fault, is to achieve that sublimation, confess the part of themselves that rebels against divine judgment, a part that is innerly impure. Because the unrivaled existence of Christ is nevertheless the vanishing point of all fantasies and thus a universal object of faith, everyone is allowed to aspire to Christic sublimation and by the same token know that his sins can be remitted. "Your sins will be forgiven," Jesus keeps telling them, thus accomplishing, in the future this time, a final raising into spirituality of a nevertheless inexorable carnal remainder. Sin then remains the only token of difference from the sublimity of Christ.[69]

This reading of the incarnation as a perfect overcoming of abjection in the flesh, a triumph of sublimation and sublimity (even as the carnal remains) seems to accord far too readily with Christian triumphalism, but Kristeva is subtler than that. The possibility of such transformation fits with her insight that in Christian-ity sin and evil on the one hand, love and beauty on the other, have a curiously convertible quality:

> [T]he Christian conception of sin also includes a recognition of an evil whose power is in direct ratio to the holiness that identifies it as such, and into which it can convert. Such a conversion into jouissance and beauty goes far beyond the retributive, legalistic tonality of sin as debt or iniquity. . . . [T]he beautiful penetrates into Christianity to the extent of becoming not merely one of its component parts, but also probably what leads it beyond religion.[70]

We must resist the temptation to read this passage as if beauty (particularly in the mild sense of prettiness) and monotheism win out over multiplicity and erotic complication. Emphasizing the excessive character of beauty, Kristeva notes that here excess is also a wanting: "The idea of 'want' tied to sin as debt and iniquity is therefore coupled with that of an overflowing, a profusion, even an unquench-able desire, which are pejoratively branded with words like 'lust' or 'greed.'"[71] Like Anne Carson's mobile verb *eros,* this is a wanting that bursts.[72]

Excess and insufficiency come together in desire, and the experience is both bewildering and, as Burrus notes, sometimes shameful. "As Silvan Tomkins re-marks, we frequently feel shame when our physical wants are not satisfied. I would add that we also frequently feel shame when they *are:* what is perhaps crucial to shame is the very exposure of our fleshly wanting, of the immensity of human need."[73] Perverse pleasures may well involve such exposure, drawing attention to the body's desirous responses in the obedience of humiliating instruction. The as-cetic demands of monastic life likewise force attention to the body's demands and desires, taking pleasure and struggling against pride in the satisfaction of remain-ing unsatisfied. Obedient behavior renders visible an obedient will, but the visible flesh, unless it is as utterly blank as that of Cassian's unshamed novice, also shows the disobedient remainder. The remainder's stubborn link to abjection humiliates.

Kristeva acknowledges the dependence of the spiritualized upon the perverse body. The "body that is pneumatic since it is spiritual, completely submersed into (divine) speech in order to become beauty and love" can only exist as the sub-limation of "the 'body' as eager drive confronted with the law's harshness." She attributes this insight to Christianity, which has "gathered in a single move perver-sion and beauty as the lining and cloth of the same economy."[74] The relation goes beyond dependence to entanglement, even to the impossibility of disidentifying these two strains: into a perverse beauty, in which mystery remains and remainder murmurs, and in which mystery's submersion into a speech recognizable by hu-man ears and minds, or a sight that leads to knowing, must remain incomplete after all.

The incarnational complication—the abject divine body—is at this inter-section. To desecrate and to consecrate cannot be put on either side of a tidy boundary. They cannot be perfectly identified, but neither can they be exactly distinguished.

WHAT GIVES?

> All things to which I give myself
> grow rich and spend me.
> —Rainer Maria Rilke, *Sonnets to Orpheus*

Other readings of this sacrifice of a god embodied draw us back to our story of disobedience in paradise: the divine sacrifice (the death of God) is the only way to reopen those closed bounds between gods and humans. Primal disobedience is widely read as *pride* (taking one's own willful desires as equal to God's), which in the Middle Ages will become standardized as chief among the mortal sins. The sacrifice of the will, undoing sinful pride, is meant to echo the sacrifice of the god. Obedience, as Bataille puts it, sacrifices autonomy, which he regards at least as suspiciously as Augustine does. Foucault, too, sees the monastic "spirit of obedience as a permanent sacrifice of [the monk's] own will."[75] For both, obedience is tangled up with the demand that we be autonomous, and we are returned at last to our Kantian considerations. The result, however, is at some distance from Kant's love of orderly reason.

This is because, as Bataille argues, the desire to rule the self cannot stop with the self. This is how autonomy becomes entangled with pride. Self-will extends into the desire to impose ourselves upon the rest of world; it must, because otherwise the world might interfere with the rules we establish.[76] Such extension is a less benign version of Kant's claim for the universality of the moral law. Kant says we should be sure that our own rules are the laws that we think everyone should follow. For him, however, this is not to suggest that we should *impose* those laws upon others. Kant is able to hold to both points because he assumes benevolent and universal reason, an assumption that Bataille, like many thinkers after the world wars, cannot quite grant. If reason is not perfectly good, then autonomy is not perfectly benign; it harbors the very dictatorial tendency that it must resist.

Quite apart from the resistance of others, our desire to make the world over in the mold of ourselves meets up with our own desire *not* to be everything, says Bataille, with his typical love for contraries. "[T]he necessity, where the autonomy of human being finds itself, of imposing one's value upon the universe—introduces from the outset a disordering in all life. What characterizes human life from the outset . . . is not only the will to sufficiency, but the timid, cunning attraction on the side of insufficiency."[77] After all, we cannot be us and be all: we are, to say it again, made ourselves by our limits and edges. We are perpetually lured not only by the pleasures of irresponsibility (neither making nor imposing the law), but even, perversely, by incompletion and insufficiency: not only toward not-everything, but into not-enough, into humiliating inadequacy. Failure also entices.

It's a shameful variety of enticement. That "cunning, timid" attraction is an embarrassment, not an open admission. "We don't dare affirm in its fullness our desire to exist without limits," Bataille declares—we don't wish to be obviously arrogant. "But we are even more uneasy at feeling a moment of cruel joy in ourselves as soon as the evidence of our misery emerges."[78] The desire for incompletion, for feeling at once the narrow constraint of our own limits and the open space of our own possibility, doesn't merely oppose our desire for limitless dominance over all that is: it inheres within that desire, always implicated in it as the self-tormenting pleasure of our necessary failure, of impossibility. We are afraid not only of our desire to exist without limits, but of our desire for our own desire's frustration, our desire against satisfaction—our inability to obey perfectly, our willful frustration with inadequate demands. What may sound very strange is nonetheless familiar to us as the desire for desire: completion ends desire, which has nothing left to seek.

The sacrifice of will in obedience becomes a sacrifice of self. Even our every-day sense of "self-sacrifice" implies not fulfilling one's own wishes, not following at least one direction of one's will. The Christian self is a paradox of this self-sacrifice founded in obedience. On Foucault's reading, the modern secular self is molded, in no small part, by the pastoral power of observation and obedience, which translates readily enough into later centuries' perpetual observation and tightening gover-nance of the flesh, in the disciplined individual or the governed population.

The dual extreme of self-control and self-sacrifice is the pulled-apart meeting point of obedience that resists itself, and finds itself not enough. Sean Connolly identifies this movement in the life of Colette Peignot: "[L]ife enters into a kind of eternal contract wherein it vows to 'give itself up' to an impossible end in order to (re)acquire itself as that which *has* given itself up. The movement of life, the 'response' of life ... therefore describes a form of sacrifice wherein life itself is both expropriated and (re)appropriated in a movement that is always 'on the way,' always 'returning' to itself—and (also) to that which is other."[79] That this move-ment is always en route keeps it from being simply an investment for a reward; neither divestment nor return is ever wholly achieved. We are neither immortal nor dead. Might we, in suspension and recurrence, in striving between impossible extremes, be most alive? Like Bataille, Peignot sought intensities of experience that made the very category of experiencing problematic—as problematic as a pursuit that can only succeed in its own failure.

With Laure's strange suspension between death and immortality, we circle back to the beginning in the stories of Paradise, to the question of autonomy as a requirement for dignity, to the joys of indignity, to the garden where tempta-tion grows on trees. "Masochism," writes Halberstam, "represents a deep disrup-tion of time itself." More specifically, the masochist reconciles "the supposedly irreconcilable tension between pleasure and death. . . . She refuses to cohere . . ."[80] Masochism "invite[s] us to unthink sex as that alluring narrative of connection and liberation and think it anew as the site of failure and unbecoming conduct."[81] The lure is not death as a cessation of all sensation, but a disregard for limits that becomes careless of the bonds holding together the coherent subject, a disruption that psychoanalysis identifies with the death drive. Not only sex, but a much wider eros, can become shameful, disruptive, incoherent—humiliatingly unbecoming.

Obedience to humiliating instruction takes a powerful will. The will fails in its own intensity. Perhaps only failure is sufficient for a will so strong that it be-comes bored with its challenges and seeks an escape from itself, for the desire so devout that it becomes careless of convention, for the most demanding obedience. Catherine of Siena, an exceedingly stubborn saint, faced her mother's punishment when she refused to marry. But she "does not reject the punishment her mother is preparing to inflict on her: she appropriates it and transcends it. It is not the mother who punishes, but the daughter who corrects the mother and punishes herself."[82] Only a demand so difficult that it undoes the self can satisfy the self that demands the breakage, but there is an irresolvable tension in the self's desire to experience that break, to know the fragile but essential remainder that the self would abject. If disobedient, such a will, bent on its own strength and failure, is insistent upon punishment—punishment keeps it within the rules of obedience. We remind ourselves of our failure in the autonomy to which we pretend. And for the ascetic, the mystic, the pervert, there is a queer pleasure in this failure.

Foucault helps us here with a vital qualification to the sense he has developed that pastoral power has as its aim the creation of the obedient subject: "[T]his expression does not have as its end the establishing of a sovereign mastery of oneself by oneself; what is expected, on the contrary, is humility and mortification, detachment with respect to oneself"—thus far, still, sounding like perfect obedience, until Foucault adds, "and the establishing of a relationship with oneself which tends towards the destruction of the form of the self."[83] This destruction leaves a disfigured, transfigured remainder, whether of masochist or monk. Self-destruction reminds us that there is not a will that is the proper, possessed power of a neatly rational self. Entangled desires may pull against one another. As Bataille writes, "There is an irreducible discord between the subject seeking ecstasy and ecstasy itself. However, the subject knows ecstasy and senses it: not as a voluntary direction coming from himself, as the sensation of an effect coming from the outside."[84] Coming from the outside, which is not quite other than in. This is the need for an other—to obey, to hear, to see. Another before whom to be ashamed, another who will humiliate with impossible demands. Bataille's curious sense of seeking as opposed to willing clues us in to the complexity of the pleasures that we seek. We seek and we will, we do not seek and cannot will, at once perfection and obliteration.

"Will" is never truly singular, and "subject" never stable; rather, multidirectional desires stretch and fracture the envelope of a self split at its center. Yet it seems clear enough that we can, and do, label a particular collection of will and sensation and memory, roughly bounded by the skin-barrier of a body, as a self, a self in the face of an other, or others. It is the multiplicity of wills "within" a subject at a given time, "within" a self, that allows the possibility of the effective will from "without"—"The forces that work to destroy us find in us such happy—and sometimes such violent—complicities that we cannot simply turn ourselves away from them as interest would lead us to do."[85] That will-from-without must resonate with, catch onto, some will from among the multiple desires gathered into a self. I can, perhaps, however briefly, escape myself by escaping my will—desiring against my own desire.

This is how Simone Weil (whom Bataille and Peignot knew well) understands supplication. "Attitude of supplication," she writes: "I must necessarily turn to something other than myself since it is a question of being delivered from myself."[86] Hers is a religiously devout supplication. Nietzsche's is not, and yet he writes of the ascetic, "The secret love of that which grows in him directs him to situations where one relieves him of thinking of *himself*."[87] Deep obedience is not the lazy relief of letting someone else make decisions (not always, at any rate). It is, rather, the delight of exceeding the knowledge of self that is gained in disobeying; the delight in shame that exceeds the shame of knowing the disobedient flesh. It is, in some curious sense, a pleasure in freedom—as it was for Augustine—but with a more acute attention to the pleasure's perversity.

Freedom is not least from oneself, as Burrus points out: "In imitation of Christ, holy men and women of late antiquity engaged in elaborate rituals of self-humiliation through which they might hope to escape the unbearable weight of selfhood."[88] The desire to escape oneself is not the desire to end oneself. Weil's own relation with the desire for death does not seem to have been a very distant one, but she insists that she needs her living materiality. "I need God to take me by force, because, if death, doing away with the shield of the flesh, were to put me face to face with him, I should run away."[89] Yet she also writes, "The obedience must, however, be obedience to necessity and not to force."[90] It is hard to know what to make of a contradiction quite so direct, but I suspect that divine force is for her necessity itself; human force, on the other hand, is an imposition. Need gives to force a feeling of necessity, for anyone who demands it. This is not a materiality that gives way to spirit, but a spirit that is mortal matter. After the self, what remains?

ONCE IN A WHILE, I WANT MORE

> I don't know
> Why you've got to be so undemanding . . .
> —Sisters of Mercy, "More"

The influential rule of Benedict shows us how the paradoxes of obedience slide toward those of humiliation along the path of humility. Benedict continues past humility's first four degrees, each clearly a mode of obedience, and moves closer to the limit where humility cannot evade humiliation: "[W]hen struck on one cheek, they offer the other; when deprived of their tunic, they surrender also their cloak; when forced to go a mile, they go two; with the Apostle Paul they bear with false brethren (2 Cor. 11:26) and bless those who curse them (1 Cor. 4:12)." A monk must "be content with the poorest and worst of everything, and . . . in every occupation assigned him he [must] consider himself a bad and worthless workman;" "he [must] consider himself lower and of less account than anyone else, and this not only in verbal protestation but also with the most heartfelt inner conviction."[91]

Not every demand for humility is a quest for failure and shame. Contemporary theorists argue that humility may serve as protection *against* humiliation, as

one who starts with an uninflated opinion of self can scarcely be deflated by others. William Ian Miller remarks on the gradual split between humility and humiliation in monasticism, noting that until about the eighteenth century, both terms
were used in Christian moral discourse, and both highly valued. Now, though
humility retains some value there, humiliation does not.[92] The degree of humility
demanded by monasticism, like that of Cynicism, shades into humiliation, even by
the self. I have long thought that Nietzsche was right about at least some aspects
of the ascetic will: it is strong and easily bored.[93] No doubt most of those in monastic communities endured humiliation reluctantly and for the sake of humility—
but there are others, like the holy fools, who seem to have sought it for its own
sake, whether or not they thus labeled it. They have sought humiliation as a sign of
the depths of their humility and more—in their pleasure in insults, in persecutions.

Augustine shares Benedict's emphasis on submission as an imitation of Christ,
but he nowhere parallels the superior to God the Father, as Benedict does. Rather,
he regards the role of superior as an enormous difficulty, full of temptations to
pride. He urges monks to be gentle about demanding too much of their abbots,
who face the dual temptations of pride both in their power and in the display
of their humility. He warns the monks that though the superiors "shall hold the
first place among you by the dignity of their office . . . in God's sight let them lie
beneath your feet in fear. . . . It is by willing obedience, therefore, that you show
mercy not only toward yourselves, but also toward superiors, whose higher rank
among you exposes them all the more to greater peril."[94] God alone is not im-
periled by our obedience, not tempted to pride, because God alone cannot think
himself better or more powerful than he is. In keeping with Augustine, though
more contemptuously, Bataille calls the bishop Christianity's "most submissive
slave."[95]

Occasionally, particularly strong-willed monastics or ascetics, such as Catherine of Siena, have taken the line that they are obeying God's will rather than that
of a human superior, whether ecclesiastical or otherwise. In most of these cases,
strikingly, the superior has not been demanding *enough*. Catherine firmly informs
her family, "I must obey God not men."[96] Catherine of Racconigi finesses her
obedience nicely: "Father, I am a daughter of obedience, and I am obliged to obey
until death in all things governed by the rule to which I am pledged; but those
things to which the rule does not obligate me, *for now I do not want to obey*. And
since the rule does not require me to [return to Racconigi] and especially since
it would be against the express will of God . . . excuse me, but I am not coming
back."[97] Teresa of Avila has a gift for obeying and even declaring the rightness
of so doing while, just once in a while, subtly suggesting otherwise, as when the
finger snaps commanded by her superiors, as an effort to dispel hallucinations, just
makes her feel disrespectful during her visions of Christ.[98] Elizabeth of Hungary,
famous for meticulously and devoutly following the sadistic orders of her confessor Konrad von Marburg, chose those orders against the demands of her family

that she eat normally, remarry, or even remain with her children.[99] The obedience that saints and monks and masochists seek is never the easier option. Janet Hardy, co-author of *The New Bottoming Book* (and, for that matter, *The New Topping Book*) writes of a discussion with a submissive. "She told me, 'No, I really have no power, I really have no limits. Whatever my master wants is OK with me.' I proposed, 'Suppose your master woke up tomorrow morning and told you, "I'm tired of the S/M stuff. From now on, we're only going to have gentle, consensual, egalitarian vanilla sex." There was a long pause. Finally, sheepishly, she answered, 'You win. I'd be out of there in a minute.'"[100]

Obedience is not demanding only of the one who undertakes it. In *Oranges Are Not the Only Fruit*, Jeanette Winterson writes, "I don't even know if God exists, but I do know that if God is your emotional role model, very few human relationships will match up to it." Though the narrator misses "the God who was my friend," she adds, "I want someone who will destroy and be destroyed by me."[101] This is indeed a challenge for any human. Augustine takes on God more directly: "Grant what you command," he insists repeatedly, "and command what you will."[102] The demand to be commanded is a demand against too much ease. The will disciplined to obedience may nonetheless be unable to obey the command of satisfaction. Those who want to obey often want more than another can demand—the superior is endangered in monasticism; the erotic dominant, if less endangered, may at least be tired.

There is paradox again, and not mere weariness, for those commanding as well. When they are not God, those destructive demands call for an almost unbearable balance of violence and care, of selfish desire and selfless attention, of a nearly awed respect for the will one sets out, just for a moment, to destroy—so that the one, and will, and self are no more knowable than those under destruction. Certainly some people take pleasure simply in destroying things or in giving orders, but theirs is a less interesting pleasure. Destruction without the recognition of that ascetic strength acknowledged by Nietzsche, a strength he admires even as he deplores its tendency to turn upon itself,[103] is too uncomplicated, too hostile, to allow the interweaving of persistent pleasure.

MAKE ME

That I may rise and stand, o'erthrow me, and bend
Your force to break, blow, burn, and make me new.
                    —John Donne, *Holy Sonnets*, Sonnet 14

And so one struggles to create and believe a supreme fiction, to use Wallace Stevens's marvelous phrase; the impossible fiction of the perfect dominant will.[104] There is no power where there is no relation, and there is no relation where all wills are one. And if maximum obedience is nonresistance to the master's power because it is that power, then the power not-resisted must be not-powerful either—a paradox that exists as much for the obeyed as for the obedient. Perfect obedience, to say it again, would not be obedience at all. Whether we contract ourselves inward to the site of our splitting or reach out toward a superior who will push us to our knees, our obedience carries within it the necessity of its own resistance, undoing not only the obedient subject but the one who must be obeyed. And thus, by resistance, obedience sustains itself too, never dissolving into its own perfection. The "truth" of the self is that the self eludes, inverts, and fractures, and this very elusion maintains the resistance that exists at the heart of every power, no matter how well it makes its subjects. In resistance and pleasure, submissive shame seeks itself in a spiral of pain and delight, failing to succeed in failure. If obedience shows in behavior, it must also bear a trace of resistance—a blush, a hesitation, a tension in the muscles—or it may simply be happenstance accord.

Paradoxical impossibility sustains desire, and the resulting failure before it reinforces shame. The nearly inadmissible pleasures of shame demand not only obedience but resistance to obeying. They demand not only humiliation, but a pride transformed and enhanced by its depths. Against the demands of subjectivity, against the boredom of selfhood, against all the requirements of identity and its politics and its laborious demands, the subject seeks for itself the abject, or the extroject; seeks to be out of itself—or so deeply within itself that it encounters its remaining other. Against the self that it is made, it makes a contrary demand that gives an illusion of more of the same: *make me.* Insubordination is no pleasure without the subordinating demand. Allow me to finish here with a rather long excerpt from a performance piece by playwright Neil Bartlett, in which the performer's speech is juxtaposed with religious imagery, in which the submissive demand for *more* becomes downright imperious.

> Make me forget my own name
>
> Make me not care, *come on, make me!*
>
> Make me do it again, and slower.
>
> *Turn the light on.*
>
> Make me do it for money. Make me do it in public places. Make me
>   do it in my parents' house.
>
> Make me do it with your son.
>
> Tell people all about me—and then forgive me.
>
> Flood me; dissolve me; wash me away;
>
> Scatter me in drops, spill me, pour me out;
>
> Make me despair.
>
>   . . .

Make me despair—and then forgive me. For I acknowledge my faults;
     make me a clean heart, *break me* . . .

And then forgive me.[105]

A forgiveness that reaches all the way back, before knowing, demands an obedience that scrubs the heart clean, an innocence no individual can have, a prelapsarian or postressurection harmony in which obedience can make no sense. If perfect obedience is indeed impossible, not just practically but in principle, then the effort to attain it must fail. It might, failing, undermine the very self who would obey, the very authority that would demand obedience. It might signal the inherence of resistance, in a Fall much happier than Augustine suspected.

THREE

Unmaking

THE FAILURE TO SAY

A BRIEF HISTORY OF CONFESSION

If you have to lay yourself bare, then you cannot play with words, trifle
with slow-marching sentences. Should no one unclothe what I have
said, I shall have written in vain. . . . This book has its secret, I may not
disclose it. Now more words.
                                        —Georges Bataille, *Madame Edwarda*

Obedience, as Foucault and the various monastic orders agree, is fundamental to
Christian virtue—and indeed, if we follow Foucault, to the very self, first in and
then well beyond monasticism. It is foundational to humility, and can be followed
with shameful delight into humiliation. But we cannot know how much the desire to obey is itself a desire independent of the superior's will. We have just seen
that some remnant of desire remains disobedient if there is willing at all—if, that
is, there is obedience at all. How do we know what remains? There lingers a well-
founded worry that there may be some hidden niche of the soul and the flesh in
which will remains unknown. This will not do.

It is perhaps concern for these possibilities that underlies the inseparability
of obedience and confession in monasticism, and the intriguing if less central role
that confession plays for perverse eroticism. Power, after all, is always entangled
with knowing, and not least with knowing subjects. The knowledge necessary
to pastoral power (originally the power of the priest or abbot), with its roots
in the obedience of monks, depends heavily on speech and on what we can
know by means of it. The purity Cassian envisioned requires that the self become
"something to be renounced and deciphered," as Foucault writes, and deciphering

demands that the self be made into words.[1] And as David Brakke has pointed out, "Foucault's work may dovetail with Charles Taylor's claim that Augustine . . . bequeathed to the modern self a 'radical reflexivity' predicated on the notion of the self as being an *inner* space."[2] Attempting to get beyond a report of actions, monastic confession also attempts to get before or behind those actions, ideas, or desires; before the will itself—thereby requiring and constructing the self as actor, thinker, and agent of desire. The monastic demand to report continually on one's thoughts, involuntary actions, and inner states actually, slowly creates that inner space, bringing it into being through words given to the superior.[3] The power play, the creation of interiority, and the fleshiness of confession will all concern us here, as we try to tease out the forms of humiliation that belong especially to it.

Pastoral power may begin in the monastery, but it is not ultimately restricted to monastic or even religious settings. The abbot's labors mark an early effort to keep track of the movements and inner workings of a community's members. In the Middle Ages, the obligation to confess is extended to the laity. After the Enlightenment, the human sciences take up the effort to "renounce and decipher" the self, to both know it and (re)construct it. So at least some of the effects of monasticism hold on, long after its cultural power seems to have faded nearly to nothing. Both pastoral power and modern state power individualize and monitor, "in the name of well-being" for all those they govern—that is, on the assumption that their effects improve the lives and selves of those who undergo them.[4]

Means of monitoring multiply. In modern governmentality, the power to know individuals and small, contained communities is integrated with more totalizing concerns; that is, with the need to know whole, larger populations. Along with this comes a change in what counts as well-being. In the monastery, the health of the spirit—its devotion to God—is all; every other mode of doing well is in its service. In the modern state, however, autonomy is paramount, seemingly against subjection. We must above all be free, and obedience begins to lose its shining reputation. Of course, when autonomy becomes a cultural imperative, freedom loses its flexibility. Jon Simons points out that the "acquisition of capabilities" that initially seemed so fundamental to autonomy and dignity (the more we can do, the freer we are), "has been accompanied by the development of political technologies, disciplines, and normalization processes."[5] In fact, Simons continues; "Modern pastoral government invests in the capacities of the individual, developing qualities of rationality, autonomy, and decision-making."[6] These are, of course, just the quality that eros resists, not least by failure. The capable contemporary subject offers a sharp contrast to the ancient self, for whom the absence of any truth-of-self implies the freedom to become otherwise.[7] So the autonomy and capability that modern governmentality is invested in creating through, among other measures, deciphering the truth-of-selves, would ideally (impossibly) recreate the freedom that preceded the invention of such truth. Between the two, monastic confessional speaking creates a more honestly subordinated self, finding a nonautonomous freedom in its obedience.

We continue both to extract and to worry over individual confessions, certainly in talk show revelations or reality television, or in the lesser publicity of psychoanalysis, but also in sacramental contexts, in erotic play, or in penumbral practices such as the eliciting of "information" by "enhanced" interrogative techniques—the latter distinguished by their refusal of mutual desire. Even in their antiquity, monastic confessions can tell us of the ways in which we are made by knowing, and the ways in which our flesh is entangled in words.

Though confession fully develops in monastic communities, Kristeva places its origins in the desert. She quotes the Egyptian hermit Anthony, who preached, "Let everyone of us take note of and write down his acts and feelings, as if he were to apprise other people of them. . . . Just as we shall never fornicate in the presence of witnesses, if we write down our thoughts as if to make them known to others, we shall abstain from obscene thoughts for fear of being found out."[8] To put into words is to put before witnesses, and, Kristeva argues, to "[usher] in judgment, shame, and fear."[9] In the seventh century, more frequent confessions came to be permitted for the laity, and by the thirteenth century, all Christians were required to confess in full at least once a year.[10] The imperative of annual confession eventually became standard, though it met with some initial resistance from both laity and priests.[11] This turn to widespread verbal confession works with the Christian construction of interiority. Penances previously could have been very long indeed, lasting years, and involving public display, so that there could be little question as to whether or not they were accomplished. But if long penances were imposed annually for the sins confessed each year, a complicated and unwieldy overlap would have occurred. Public display thus diminished in importance and, consequently, the significance of "inner" repentance increased, and the way to know this repentant "inside" is through words.[12] As Kristeva points out, "[A]cts of atonement, of contrition, of paying one's debt to a pitiless, judging God, are eclipsed by the sole act of speech."[13] She argues that as confession takes on strength, power is no longer the sole prerogative of God; "Power henceforth belongs to discourse itself, or rather to the act of judgment expressed in speech."[14] It is not the abbot who takes over the double divine power of knowledge and forgiveness, but speaking. Speaking itself, necessarily, is changed: "[T]he practice of confession . . . does nothing else but weigh down discourse with sin. By having it bear that load, which alone grants it the intensity of full communication, avowal absolves from sin and, by the same stroke, founds the power of discourse."[15] Confessional language, with its intention of clearing out the soul until it is pure, is never innocent itself.

Annual confession, Chloë Taylor writes, allows the emergence of our contemporary sense that confession is "psychologically necessary," and never complete; that we have to keep talking more and more about ourselves.[16] Though Luther sought to limit confession, with its hierarchical intervention between the confessant and God, "The Counter-Reformation Catholic church," Taylor tells us, "was quick to respond to these heretical claims which endangered its will to know."[17] With the obligation of annual confession, this will extends into the world of the laity.

Confession verbalizes the willingness and resistance of the spirited flesh. It is at once a species of obedience and another practice related to obeying and to the abasement of the very self that both also help to create. By it, the confessor endeavors to approach knowledge of the confessant's interior processes, and of the flesh where thought could be hidden; the monk attempts to make obedience audible, as obedient behavior strives toward visibility. The truth most sought is most potentially humiliating, a point upon which erotic recreations of confession and interrogation may seize.

The words a body makes are meant to reveal its truth, even as they create it. As Mark Jordan writes, the "speech act" of confession is "also a body's speaking."[18] It is a body signing the truth of itself, with or without a blush. The body's speaking constructs a special interiority, out of which truth is spoken, and to which meaning is given by its speech.[19] The interior revealed, though, may also be veiled over by the very speaking that is so central to creating it: "Studying Christianity before modernity, Foucault is ... concerned with how bodies manifest truth or how they continue to conceal it under regimes of endless verbalization."[20]

As Jordan points out, the transformation in power, as it comes to emphasize subjectivity, is likewise a transformation in philosophy—in the love of wisdom, in the desire for truth, "in the philosophic transformation by which bodily love becomes love of the true, redirecting erotics toward truth."[21] To tell the truth of the body becomes its own desire as it comes to be construed as a new form of freedom, a resistance to repression. "The obligation to confess," Foucault reminds us,

> is now relayed through so many different points, is so deeply ingrained in us, that we no longer perceive it as the effect of a power that constrains us; on the contrary, it seems to us that the truth, lodged in our most secret nature, "demands" only to surface; that if it fails to do so, this is because a constraint holds it in place, the violence of a power weighs it down, and it can finally be articulated only at the price of a kind of liberation.[22]

The demands and delights of social media have enhanced (or exacerbated) the validity of this observation: we perceive freedom in full expression and immediate, widely shared self-revelation. We perceive ethics, too; we think ourselves good if we have nothing to hide. But there are still "truths," movements and desires of the body, that demand to be kept rather than "liberated," that resist publicity. It is these resistant truths that pastoral confession especially engages, that bind discourse most tightly to the flesh, and that carry the strongest charge of power in both their revelation and their concealment. This play of veiling and displaying, construction and revelation, truth and make-believe, keeps confession paradoxical—and so interesting, too, in its susceptibility to failure.

Learning to confess entails training in the self-scrutiny that can become self-revelation: one must examine oneself for every confessable act and thought, even those outside conscious responsibility, and must push oneself to accuse, and to reveal, the body in meticulous detail. The practice of confession carries flesh, piece by piece, into word, moving the body toward the illusory clarity of speaking. The abbot, who instructs and interprets the flesh, must also draw it into words, most particularly where words emerge with reluctance. That early monastic concern with "nocturnal pollution" fits here—one is compelled to tell what exceeds both modesty and the will, to tell of the flesh where it seems to be most clearly in excess of "mind" while retaining, and implicating, "self."[23] Confessional speech tells especially the erotics of flesh, pulling eros and truth toward each other. Sexual acts and desires become central items of confession. Jordan points out that Foucault writes "of an explosion of sexual speech in the modern period (even if confessors were also cautioned against lurid description)."[24] Worrisomely to the confessors, their listening may enhance the confessants' desire. Taylor notes that in Medieval confession, "theologians recognized that by inquiring in such suggestive detail, and with such leading questions, they ran the risk of teaching sinful behaviors to penitents who had not previously been aware of the full range of sexual possibility available to them."[25] The problem reemerges after the Reformation, when "[s]exual interrogations in particular would create and fan the flames of erotic desire, implanting new fantasies in the minds of confessants, as Counter-Reformation doctrine itself came to acknowledge, which desires were new sources of anxiety over one's sins."[26] It is here that, as Foucault understands it, "the modern West's imperative to speak sex is imposed as a general obligation," writes Jordan; "The old monastic practices are generalized for all—at least, all who would be saved."[27] Sex becomes central to identity as the obligation to speak truth becomes the obligation, and then the urgent desire, to speak sex. And both come about as the obligation to speak serves the construction of an interior self to be spoken. The obligation to hear confession may become desirous as well. In the imperative to speak sex, the anticlerical sense that there must be something prurient about confession seems to have a strange cultural reality, however unlike the version portrayed in bawdy early modern novels.

Both monastic and erotic confessions have their strange pleasures and frustrations, their modes of resistance. Marking a distinction between modern confessional practice and ancient self-examination, Taylor says that the pleasure of modern confessants "is more perverse, erotic, and less calm, often followed by displeasure, accompanied by predictable claims about the difficulty of the discursive act involved, the courage required, denial of masochistic, narcissistic, or exhibitionistic pleasure, and so forth." She notes the contrast with the serene daily reviews undertaken in the ancient world, aimed at self-mastery and unconcerned with condemnation and exposure.[28]

However predictable, the claims of difficulty are not altogether dishonest, because it is crucial to confession that there be a challenge to overcome in speaking, a persistent tension. We are, however, more interested here in those who would not deny the pleasures, whose displeasure is not a simple rejection. As Burrus writes in *Saving Shame*, confession "is neither simply coerced nor simply voluntary." Both aspects *must* be at work: "One must want, at least a little, to be broken, to be exposed, or the confession is sterile: it makes no truth; worse still, it forces stillborn lies. One must also resist, at least a little, being overcome by this desire, or the confession, rendered glib by the promise of cheap grace, is equally fruitless."[29] Confessional desire is this wanting, the double pull of secrets on pleasure and power, of discursive knowledge on recalcitrant flesh. Its perfection will silence it; like obedient behavior, confessional transparency can only fail.

SPEAKING INSIDE OUT

> Secretly before the gaze of everyone.
> As if pain's proper dimension were thought.
> —Maurice Blanchot, "Awaiting Oblivion"

Because what is secret does not appear, the inquisitive (even inquisitorial) search begins with the presumption that something is hidden *within* the speaker; interiority is not merely elsewhere, but concealed. As Peter Brown notes, monastic spiritual guidance is aimed at exteriorizing the "inner world," until the monk can speak that inside without the hesitation that shame might provoke.[30] This imperative depends upon an anti-Augustinian transparency, upon the belief that the internal world can be wholly externalized, that the self constructed on the flesh of the monk can, though it rarely does, accord perfectly with the demand that there be nothing to tell. All shame stutters; all that merits confession is worthy of shame. The perfection of flesh is not-telling, an exterior expression of interior purity: purity from sin means purity from speaking. We tell and tell, until the flesh ceases to display and the words fall silent. That means, too, that the will has ceased to desire, ceased to connect itself to lust and carnal events.[31] Confessional speech begins in a reluctant and desirous creation of inside and out, at once finding and making an interior truth and placing it hesitantly before the listener; its final aim is the empty interior, which is to say, the interior without secrets, the wholly known self—no interior at all, and so no hesitation that breaks into speaking. As perfect obedience leaves no will, perfect confession leaves no self of which to tell the truth—yet, like Blanchot's writer, the confessant is compelled to keep on with words. Responding to the demand from another desire, another will, the self stands exterior to itself to take a less flattering view than our egoism generally allows, so that we can tell what we would rather not—and yet what we, in some strange twist, nonetheless want to tell, offering "testimony to the desire to make truth."[32]

Truth is made in company, to a confessor, a physician, a television audience—another distinction, as Taylor notes, from the private affair that was ancient self-examination.[33] The extent of shame cannot be realized alone; giving voice, we find that we must admit to ourselves the reactions we provoke in another.[34] Even the solitary desert ascetics had to write imagining an audience. Confession is a making and a reading; we are exegesis of a text made for interpretation. David Brakke points out that the chaste and transparent self that is the ostensible aim of confession requires constant disruption and division by speaking; one must divide oneself in order to observe and speak the self, to impose upon and construct.[35] The subject is never one, but doubles back upon itself in order to give itself over to the confessor. As it is doubled, only some part of it is given; there is, always, a remainder beyond speaking. The confession stretches itself paradoxically between hiding and revelation, between two incompatible desires at once paired and fractured by shame, between the self that is made and the act of self, making.[36]

The tense, intensifying stretch that emerges in monastic and sacramental confession, and reemerges in psychoanalytic and publicity-seeking confession, is provoked more deliberately by perverse desire. "Lazy Domme" writes, "Another simple humiliation trick is to get your sub to admit he enjoys something very submissive or humiliating. . . . If someone gets off on doing something humiliating, such as eating their own cum, then making them admit it is also humiliating." As she points out, this works better when the verbalization is more complete— "None of this, 'Yeah, I do' crap. Have him tell you in a convincing manner, and in his own words."[37] That is, to give voice to a claim, rather than simply acknowledging it, constructs it more deeply: the power to know, as we've seen, belongs to words. If the sub speaks in his own words, he creates the truth of himself in the speaking. Lazy Domme even suggests the possibility of getting the submissive to lie in the construction of a new truth—to beg for something he dislikes, creating a curious new shared truth of its desirability. In a related point, Taylor notes that the truth of confessional speech can be one of pleasure rather than of content. Using Rousseau's *Confessions* and Dostoevsky's *Underground Man* as examples, she writes that it is "masochistic pleasure" that matters; "not the content of any particular lies, but . . . rather the way in which masochistic confessional desire produces the need for lies precisely because the propositional truth or falsity of what is said is less important than expressing and providing an outlet for the [confessant's] pleasurable shame and guilt."[38] The truth of the self is produced, but it might not be a truth in the manner of facts, nor a self that was there awaiting discovery prior to its creation.

Our thinking about the risk and fear of confessional language may be assisted by Bruno Latour's meditation on "the torments of religious speech," in which confession begins. For Latour, prayer has become outmoded, because we have forgotten how it functions: sacramentally, which is to say constructively, and intimately, rather than referentially or analytically.[39] "The relationship is not that of ... a phrase to what that phrase is trying to say, but the skewed, twisted, quirky, warped, polluted relationship of an utterance to the person trying to say it."[40] What is this particular relationship? "Either we're dealing with information content ... or we're carrying containers, and causing individuals to emerge."[41] Like prayer, confession (which is sacramental in Christianity) is not about the "objective" truth of its content, but about what is made in speaking it.

In the puzzles of prayer, Latour points out, it is not only the praying selves who emerge: "How can the existence of real and helpful beings depend to such an extent on saying, on simple ways of speaking? What class of existents is this?"[42] Latour has in mind the "existence" of "God," particularly as it is created liturgically, repetitively—and in an outcry, too. But such speaking resonates considerably with the broader range of confessional speech; it has the form of information, but it is not data. It is creative. It makes itself true, makes its truth.[43] God, abbot, and dominant lose their roles if they are not addressed, if their questions go unanswered, their demands unmet; to meet them, the one confessing takes on those questions and makes answers in speech. The speaking repeats. It is bodily speech, evoking, to use Jordan's marvelous phrase, "the tongues behind ... words."[44]

The fractured self can be neither whole nor self-contained: I cannot establish my boundaries, the lines within which my self is constructed, except by crossing them. This too is a function of language. Bataille writes, "Thus I speak—everything in me gives itself to others. But knowing that, no longer forgetting it, undergoing the necessity of giving myself decomposes me."[45] In its very composition, to speak, as to obey, becomes a sacrifice of self—just as monastic confession demanded. Confession gives words: it gives words to the unseen acts and pleasures of the flesh; it gives words over to the one who asks. The truth of self, made in the telling, unmakes the possibility of self-possession. For Bataille, such dispossession is disentangleable from eros.[46] And confession, pulling at secrets, demanding the most reluctant admissions, is an endless source of the humiliating. The intimacy of eros is not least a sharing of secrets, up to the edge of the unsayable.

A scene from Bataille's novella *My Mother* tells of desire, pleasure, and the humiliating effects of enunciation as they are caught up together; it shows us, too, the ways in which words must fail.

> From within my fear, pitched to its extreme, I murmured, "From you I
> want the unutterable pleasure you offer," calling it by its name.

And I borrowed the words that had come from Rhea's mouth, I articulated them, and I savoured their turpitude.

I realized once I had pronounced those words—my face was aflame—that Rhea proposed the same thing to my mother; I realized at the same time that my mother did likewise.[47]

There is a marvelously apophatic quality to this passage. The pleasure is "unutterable," and apparently uninscribable; like God, it is named as unnamable, and though the narrator tells us that he "call[ed] it by its name," as a writer he does not do so. The effect is to convey a sense of a pleasure even more salacious and transgressive than any named perverse proposal could be. Whatever has been proposed among this unholy trinity, it is too secret for language. It is as if this mysterious practice is one that will get at the very unnamable of flesh, its "depth" that evades all telling and knowing alike. Confession, so commonly accused of being pornographic, is also a sort of inversion of pornography. Both genres attempt a full telling of what propriety leaves untold regarding the flesh. In both we find the same relentlessness of detail, the same biological insistence—and ultimately the same resistance to completion. They are inversions in the sense that confession aims impossibly at its own silence, pornography with equal impossibility at completion in language, at words that reveal the flesh all the way down, or all the way in, and yet keep speaking. Where the confessional aim is to silence irrational physical sensation and so the words needed to say it,[48] pornography aims with equal impossibility at a fully expressive language and an indefinitely extended sensation, at words that reveal the feeling flesh stripped bare, at images that reveal the perfectly articulate body. What both forms tell us is that the body keeps secrets whether we want it to or not, whether we tell it or show it, and that we may come closest to saying these secrets when we admit the failures of words.[49] *My Mother* suggests not only an impossible practice of knowing but an impossibly perfect fusion of language and flesh, one that cannot be passed along to the reader—a fusion that is likewise the impossibility of confession.

Confessing, I hear myself speak. Returning to me, even in the echo of silence, my words are not quite my own, not me nor even quite mine: they have been given. We already know that I cannot be wholly given over in words any more than in will, that some remainder eludes the telling. Neither, however, do I come through obedience and confession to the perfect governance of my own action or speech. Confessional speaking remains in question. To speak madness, as Huffer writes, is an impossible attempt to put the unspeakable into discourse, in which "experience becomes ... the opening of a question, an approach that 'interrogates the processes of [a subject's] creation'."[50] So, too, the widespread madness of eros, with all its violent and exhibitionistic demands, speaks answers that interrogate us further. This self is constructed as already disrupted, formed as already tending to dissolution, made on the foundation of a fracture. It can be neither located nor named properly. The proper self, as Bataille would argue, is useful. But Bataille, like the prurient confessor, loves impropriety: a strong objection runs throughout his work to the ways in which usefulness and productivity have overtaken our other values and our passions, not least those of religion and all sorts of sex. He turns to Nietzsche as well as to particularly vivid medieval figures (such as Angela of Foligno or Teresa of Avila) for a sense of danger instead, for the edginess that Maitland reminds us to value. He prizes the risk posed by "sensuality and pain," which may project us beyond "the demands of utility."[51] The confessionally constructed subject might turn out to be useful (if never only that), but the willful and verbal struggles of confessing are not. They cannot be made altogether productive, not even of subjectivity. Nothing stable is produced in confessional truth, because either the subject made is altogether undone in purity, or the rite is repeated. Jordan writes of *exagoreusis,* Christian verbal confession, "What distinguishes Christianity, Foucault says several times, is not the invention of the fall but of its repetition. Christianity is the religion of backsliders."[52] Over and over, under and after pastoral power, we ritually betray ourselves into being, trying to make the secret into truth, trying to make ourselves without secrets. But no truth arises in confession that does not fall again, no self is made that does not keep on keeping secrets: lapsing into knowing, speaking, it cannot tell the truth before itself, nor do other than lie by omission to the query from its God.

OUT OF BOUNDS

I've been wondering what it takes to destroy you.
I found out yesterday: all you need is humility.
                              —Swans, "The Center of Your Heart"

People are said to have "boundary issues" if they regularly tell more than others are quite prepared to hear, or engage others with greater intensity than those others find comfortable. Such people embarrass us; the question of boundaries, as we've seen, touches necessarily on that of shame. Shame shares the eros and the doubleness of the sacred, both characteristically out of bounds. When confessional speech exposes, risking humiliation, it too pushes the issue of boundaries.

In "Sex, Shame, and Disability Identity," Tobin Siebers remarks, "Shame is terrifying because it relies on public exposure: the etymology of 'shame' derives from a pre-Teutonic word that means 'to cover oneself,' covering being a natural expression of shame." Exposure is disclosure; it removes a boundary that can form a barrier around oneself, such as clothing, or silence. "But shame," he adds, "is also a sumptuous emotion. To stand out in public has its own delights. The feeling of shame, then, turns on the movement between the private and public realms."[53]

Shameful pleasure belongs not simply to the problematizing of these layers, but to the sense of boundaries and their crossing. The very act of discursively constructing a private interior is an act of sumptuous shame.

In his influential work on liminality—that is, on thresholds, boundaries between—anthropologist Victor Turner takes up the thinking of ethnographer Arnold van Gennep regarding what the latter labeled rites of passage. The passages run from separation, through liminality, to incorporation or reaggregation. Like the remainder, the liminal is neither of nor other than; it is between separation and unity. Liminality is characterized by betweenness and transition; it is a movement rather than a condition, and liminal "space" is less literally spatial than temporal and affective.[54] (The same can be said of "sub space," into which a submissive enters as submission emerges.) To be between places is to be at once at the boundary and out of bounds, out of place. As Ana-Karina Schneider points out, the liminal is "a transitional phase, characterized . . . by humility, heteronomy, self effacement, divesting oneself of one's possessions, sexual continence, acceptance of pain and suffering, etc. Incidentally, [Turner] notes, these are properties that we also associate with 'the religious life in the Christian tradition[s].'"[55] We associate them too, if more temporarily, with perverse humiliation. The liminal shares with the abject: "[T]he figuration associated with liminality . . . belongs, on the one hand, to the physiological processes of death, decomposition, catabolism, menstruation, and, on the other, to gestation, birth, and anabolism. . . . Moreover, the ambiguity of the liminal state is frequently represented as unclean or polluting."[56] At once abject and transitional, the confessant, the subject of interrogation, or the "passenger" in Turner's language (the one within the ritual passage) slips into the space of the sacred, and is exposed to "Knowledge that is usually sacred and secret,"[57] knowledge in a strange and elusive sense. The knowledge brought to speech in the backslider's recurrent confession is secret as well, ambiguous, unclean, and unstill. Its status as barely sayable is reinforced by the seriousness with which the confessional, even now, keeps its secrets. Concupiscence evades every admission. Rites of penitence or reconciliation are intended to transfigure, to take one from sinfulness to grace, but in the continuous fall that Christianity sees as the human state, a continuous transformation is required. The between itself, where questions and answers occur, may be valued as the unstable and moving place to which to return, again and again, to find oneself other than one is.

Small wonder the confessant eludes. "Scatter, spoil, destroy, throw to the dogs all that you want," taunts Peignot in the persona of Laure; "I will never be where you think you find me, where you think you've finally caught me in a chokehold that makes you come."[58] Captured in these taunting words is something else too— the elusiveness both of confessional revelation and of pornographic possession. For all her rush of words, for all the despoiled flesh of her fantasies, the fictive Laure like the real Peignot confesses incompletely; she hints, she submits, she resists, she retreats. She offers in her text the seductive shimmer of the submissive surface and the ultimate (necessary) refusal of the interior, no matter what we do with the image of the body or the words that make the pornographic scene—neither surface nor inside truly holds. Like the confessor or the dominant lover, the reader and the viewer find, just when they think they've got hold of the object, just when the revelation is complete, that speech has stuttered, and flesh eluded. At the threshold, at an edge, desire is drawn.

The confessional subject is exegetical, resistant, compliant, conversionary. Its language is the language of the sacred, with its pairing and fracturing of depth and height. I have suggested that it is not unlike the evocative language of prayer. Prayerful language is given to God as confession to the confessor, drawn out of the speaker: "Prayer," writes Certeau, "consists not in receiving from God, but giving to him."[59] Of course, one cannot tell God anything God does not know. The submissive seeking humiliation may speak desire already known, but altered in the speaking, drawn out so that it resonates with the secret, so that it speaks its own resistance to being said; it may make desire against its own resistance. The dominant will, like God's will, like the abbot's, draws speech, making truth from it by hearing.

Such speech is not given without expectation and desire—only without certainty. Certeau's account continues: "God must be there and 'attentive' to the discourse addressed to him. Prayer counts on that expectation of the other. But it is not sure of it." What if all that one has to offer in address is insufficiently captivating? "The I appears in its dependency on the other. I cannot express itself except in the desire emanating from elsewhere (rhetorically transformed into obligation on the readers' part). I speaks only if it is awaited (or loved), which is the riskiest thing in the world."[60] The desire to speak must meet with the desire, even the demand, to hear.[61] It must, but it might not. This risk sustains in confession a fine edge of anxiety, beyond that attending already to the telling of flesh and of shame. But here too is the beauty of the secret's infinitude: if the listener does not turn away, there will always be more for the other to hear, more than I, even without withholding, could ever give.

And yet, in another parallel to obedience, the urges of speech may exceed the demand. Connolly writes of Peignot, "[T]he speaking subject of Laure's poetry is always, at least in part, beyond the law in submission to the law."[62] Just as one might obey beyond any command, seeking a humility deeper than crucifixion, so too one might speak in excess of the truth, tell more than the confessor knew how to ask. In cooperating more fully than the demand ever imagined, Laure, like other perverse subjects, eludes any will that might think itself in command of hers—even as she eludes self-mastery, too. Indeed, any speaking-shame eludes complete control. In some contexts, confessing to humiliation, telling an embarrassing tale of oneself, "momentarily deactivates the disciplinary power of confession and turns isolation into something like a membership card."[63] Exposure, even humiliating exposure, has strange effects: it may form a subject and divide it from itself; it may isolate or invite into membership; it sets apart while being profoundly contagious. Exposure in speech (or, as I'll argue in the next chapter, sight) is necessarily incomplete: we are never wholly exposed, though we are always, more or less, vulnerable.

Ultimately, whatever we babble on to reveal, the secret is not said: it is of the saying. "Everything speaks of the word but this word says nothing. It doesn't say the nothing, it doesn't speak of the void, it doesn't address nothingness—which would still be a way, if completely negative, of turning us towards the distant, of referring," writes Latour.[64] Prayers call; they don't point. Confession circles; rather than seizing on truth, it takes hold of the confessant and confessor alike. Rather than referring into the distance, such language entices into proximity.[65] It cannot make-present, but it makes, nearby. As we are drawn near, we are drawn out, too. The penitent does not master language or self, but allows words, moving against resistance toward the confessor, to make-present the truth that speech constructs only for a moment—present, like time, only in the mode of slipping. This language stutters, leaves the spaces where its saying echoes with the unsayable. "Not unutterable through distancing, but through proximity. Too close, too intense to be looked in the face."[66] Too close for us to be sure of our bounds.

The connections among eros, shame, and the sacred in speech recur in Bataille's work as well. *L'Abbé C* offers a particularly clear instance. Charles, brother of the Abbé Robert, pays one Madame Hanusse for information; he pays her to talk. And he pays Madame Hanusse's daughter Eponine for sex. In fact, though, Eponine also speaks. Hers

> was the language of a prostitute, but it was infused with such fanatical
> determination, with such intense emotion, that it was impossible for
> anyone to be misled by its undeniable crudity. It was, at the same time,
> the language of passion, which put on that vulgar face in order to elimi
> nate not only any obstacle, but any delay that might have been set up
> against it. It was the plenitude of audacity which took the whole world
> for its own, measuring its violence on an infinite scale, and no longer
> admitting to any appeasement.[67]

A truly infinite violence would only destroy, eliminating the desire along with the obstacle. Eponine's speech is impossible. It is the speech of passion, which stutters and screams. Charles pays twice for speech—once for information, once for audacious passion. Both, it turns out, keep their secrets.

The highest reaches down to the depths of our shameful secrets; the lowest exalts itself to the heavens. Confession, a foundational and still essential means of control, is stubbornly unboundable.

DRAMATIC SPEECH

It pains me to record this,
I am not a melodramatic person.

—Anne Carson, "The Glass Essay"

As the most intimate sense of "self" is created in its very intimacy by its exteriorizing, a truth made proximate, so too the exterior questioning reaches in until
that inside is opened out into an immense extension. Speaking, troubling the very
boundaries that it makes, creates this intimate immensity, this impossible closeness,
too near for saying. The "inward" search, for impurity and divinity alike, struggles
to put the sacred into speech. It never quite fits. It cries out, instead. Jordan says
that for Foucault, "exomologêsis is not verbal. In it, 'the word has the value of a
cry, an expressive value.' Like the cry of the mad or the vivisected criminal, like the
murmur of subterranean insects."[68] The subject, as Foucault argues, however made
in words, cannot be wholly caught in language, but is found in the space of an
"anonymous murmur . . . without beginning or end."[69] I suspect that the declara-
tions of both sin and desire harbor more than a hint of this murmurous madness,
in words that may express, make almost-present; cries that do not tell reason, but
slip by and leave traces of secrets, of language cut improperly close to the flesh.

The attempt to perfect abjection, that is, may move the flesh as well as words.
Public confession has often included a corporeal lowering as well as an abasement
of will. Sarah Hamilton describes an Italian medieval ritual of public penance
from the outset of the twelfth century, by which time confession was largely between the penitent and confessor alone; the public rite had come primarily to be
reserved for "truly scandalous sins."[70] In this ritual, "as the priest sits in front of
his altar, with the cross of the Lord next to him on the right hand side, each of
them should come to him individually, and humbly kneel before him." While the
penitent kneels, the priest asks questions—about beliefs, about thoughts and out-
ward behavior, about the desire to repent and amend. At the end of the rite, "the
priest prostrates himself with the penitent on the ground" while both pray.[71] The
hierarchy raises the priest above the penitent for the interrogation, but the relative
lowness of all humans before God must remain clear. The speech that is weighted
with sin moves between penitent and priest, pressing both downward.

Whether the confession is public or private, meaning is brought under considerable tension. In both confession and the greater drama of exorcism, Jordan
writes, "'Convulsive flesh is the effect of resistance to this Christianization at the
level of individual bodies.' The official demand for endless speech is contradicted
by a dramatic interruption, a somatic refusal of the script."[72] Interruptive resistance
multiplies and recurs, as we might expect in this realm of repetitive speaking. We
may even view ourselves as resisting our own resistance to the irresistible, as Teresa

of Avila does: "[W]e have to do what [God] wishes; and here he reveals himself as our true Lord. This I know from repeated experience, for such was my fear that I put up a resistance for almost two years; and sometimes I still try to resist, though with little success."[73] This movement of resistance resisted is enfleshed. The flesh resists speaking, and resists the resistance to speaking. And the flesh is made words, and we dwell among them. Sometimes, we cry out. Sometimes, words fail.

We must be careful not only in what, but in how, we say. As Burrus writes, "While hagiographers regularly insist that it would be a sin not to sing the praises of the saint, writers of holy lives also often betray awareness that their praise may place not only the saint's humility but also their own at risk." In evading that risk, hagiographers may not only proclaim their own humility, but write in a "lowly style"; they "not only showcase the submission to humiliation that is part of the holy one's discipline but also augment this discipline in the very act of publicizing the saint's shaming by the demons of temptation."[74]

Notice how the complications multiply: not only is humility a temptation to pride, but the "lowly" attempt to appear unstyled is adopted as a stylistic choice, and the humility of the saint is both a temptation to and augmented by the humility of the hagiographer marveling at it. Hagiography is strangely akin to confession; both multiply humiliation by forcing it into words; both tempt the speaker to pride in the display of humility. When we get to the Middle Ages, hagiographers are not infrequently confessors, and the power play of hearing and telling, the exaltation of their own humility through that of those who confess to them but whose superior humility they in turn confess, may further exaggerate these twists.

Nor, again, is this movement restricted to the saintly. Peignot's commentators and translators emphasize her pride, even "insolence," which her translator Jeanine Hermann insists is her salvation.[75] Peignot herself declares that she must "Denounce all that BACKS AWAY/ narrows/ diminishes."[76] Pride appears not merely *in* her texts, but *as* those texts' very existence: surrounded by creatively brilliant but deeply self-centered men such as Bataille and Leiris, she nonetheless speaks, and writes. Peignot is profoundly and proudly masochistic, and no one else speaks for her. Hers is a pride that seeks intensity in tension, in the uneasy pull that does not drag it down but makes it proud of its very capacity for submission.

It is important here that pride, unlike the "self-esteem" that holds that one is extraordinary by virtue of existing, is falsifiable; this is what allows it to play in tension with humiliation. William Ian Miller notes that humiliation (like confession, like the secret) entails a sense of conflict between what one is and what one purports to be. "It is the presumption that enables the humiliation and justifies it.... [H]umiliation depends on the deflation of pretension."[77] Where humiliation is sought, however, matters become more complex; one's pride may be less the source of humiliation than both the ground for seeking it and the result of

experiencing it. What's more, the notion that there is a truth of what one is, an inner core, is fractured in speaking it. Confession undoes both the pride that comes
with a poor match to external judgment (arrogance or vanity) and that which
would hold to a sense of the private. But it still retains the pride that curls in on
itself to slide more deeply into shame.

"Confession," says Miller, "involves ritualized humiliation, which if voluntarily entered into can function as an act of self-abasement, or if imposed by an
authority, can be assimilated to shaming rituals.... Confession reveals that what
one appears to be is not what one is and as such it declares one's unconfessed self
to be a pretension to a dignity not deserved."[78] The telling redoubles the shame—
exposes the low sacred in speech—even if we do not assume a self unconfessed.
In Bataille's novel *Blue of Noon*, the narrator tells "the story of my entire life"
to a prim, virginal listener. "My telling it to a girl like her ... was so impudent
that it made me feel ashamed.... Each sentence was as humiliating as an act of
cowardice."[79] Something gives, some measure of pride, easily or against profound
resistance: and something is reinforced, the pride in overcoming that resistance,
itself a new sin for confessing. Masochistically, shame may add itself into the spiral
of pleasure.[80]

There is always something to resist: telling or not telling, truth and lie and
construction that is neither and both; constructing one as the other. When we
think well of ourselves, we would like public opinion to measure up; more dangerously, we might assume that it does so. We might try to hide what shames or
embarrasses us. If we cannot, our pride suffers. So pride, despite (or because of?)
its connection to the private, responds to a shared reality, to what is or could be
public, what can be dramatically abased in speech or bodily motion. The saint
and the pervert put humiliation into the place of pride, or give it pride of place,
exposing shame to (undo) public admiration—for which admiration may nonetheless emerge.

COMMUNICATING VULNERABILITY

> I have many strange confessions to make, obviously—I don't necessar-
> ily want to make them, either. So I make them in a dark tongue, in the
> confusion of speech. This is how I defer them.
>   —Carl Watson, "To Be Blessed with a Nightmare of Angels"

Something resists, something gives, and something opens: some secret seems, only
ever almost, to be revealed. The shameful secret meets the secret that is the secret
of saying and cannot be said: the sacred murmurs through sacrilege and sacrament
both, and shame through the subject impure at heart. This impossibility inheres in
the exchange of words, rather than preventing it. Indeed, Jean-Luc Nancy argues
that such a secret is essential to human connection:

The unavowable designates a shameful secret. It is shameful because . . . it engages a passion that can only be exposed as the unavowable in general: confessing to it would be unbearable while at the same time it would destroy the force of this passion. But without it we would already have renounced any kind of being-together, which is to say, being itself. . . .

Unavowable is thus a word that here mixes indiscernibly modesty and shamelessness. Shamelessly it announces a secret; modestly it declares that the secret will remain secret.

The one who is silent about this knows in this way what is not said. But this knowledge is not to be communicated, being itself the knowledge of communication.[81]

Nancy draws here on the work of Bataille, for whom "communication" has a rather different sense than it has in most contexts. Because the subject must be opened in order to communicate, Bataille links communication to laceration or wounding: it "only takes place between two beings at risk—lacerated, suspended."[82] The knowledge of communication turns out to be the knowledge of an open space, a gap: a non-knowledge. It is necessarily a mode of boundary breaking itself, perhaps closer to our model of a communicable disease crossing the boundaries of persons than to the simple imparting of information. Insofar as beings are beings—whole and discrete—they are safe, and they cannot communicate. But then neither, Nancy has reminded us, can they be; insofar as beings are whole and individuated, they are illusory. Kristeva links the communicative risk to the end of the self: "Communication brings my most intimate subjectivity into being for the other; and this act of judgment and supreme freedom, if it authenticates me, also delivers me over to death. Is this to say that my own speech, all speech perhaps, already harbors in itself something that is mortal, culpable, abject?"[83]

Bataille links the risk that communication demands to eros and to crime (breaking the bounds of law), and in both cases to the sacred, pulling like the secret between sanctity and sin. This is why Bataille puts the crucifixion at the heart of Christianity—"A night of death in which the Creator and the creatures bled together, lacerated each other and in every way put themselves in question—to the extreme limit of shame—was found to be necessary for their communion. Thus the 'communication' without which, for us, nothing would exist, is assured by crime."[84] From this, he concludes, "'Communication' is love and love defiles those it unites."[85]

Bataille's possibly startling take on the Christian crucifixion once more draws eros to humiliation, shame to intimacy, flesh to both poles of the sacred. For Simone Weil, who is probably the basis for the virgin to whom Bataille's narrator confesses in *Blue of Noon*, "God can be present in creation only under the form of absence."[86] Weil, too, turns to the crucifixion, as William Robert notes: "[F]or her, the cross involves a violent 'tearing to pieces' [*ecartèlement*], a 'supreme laceration, suffering that no other approaches' since the death of Christ, insofar as he is divine, tears God from God. . . . in the crucifixion, God self-lacerates."[87] The sense of necessary rupture or disruption that we have already found in confessional speaking and at the decentered heart of self-construction is essential to these conceptions of divinity as well.

Part of what makes these readings seem strange is that the Christian God is so often linked to the *healing* of wounds instead, including those remitted by absolution once confessed. Robert writes of medieval confession, "In determining a penance, the priest acts as a doctor. He treats sins as wounds. A priest, Canon 21 states, 'shall be discerning and prudent, so that like a skilled doctor he may pour wine and oil over the wounds of the injured one, [and by that discernment] use various means to heal the sick person.'"[88] Wounds here are the breaks inflicted by sin, to be mended by care and repentance. But other medieval and early modern sources invoke wounding with greater enthusiasm. Julie Miller offers several examples:

> Beatrice [of Nazareth] elaborates on one specific means by which God assaults her, stating, "At this time she also feels an arrow piercing through her heart all the way to the throat and beyond, even to the brain, as if she would lose her mind." . . . Angela of Foligno speaks of both the "arrow" and the "sword" of love, and Hadewijch anguishes over both the "sharp arrows" and "strange hatred" with which Love "transpierces the depths of my heart with storm." Catherine of Siena urges her readers to let themselves be pierced by the same double-edged sword and arrow of love with which Christ and his mother were wounded for our salvation. And Catherine of Genoa believes that the "rays" of God's love encircle humanity at all times, "hungrily seeking to penetrate" it; indeed, if allowed, these rays will penetrate "as deep as hell."[89]

One could go on: Rose of Lima is pierced with the arrows of Christ's love; the Baroque sculptor Gian Lorenzo Bernini immortalized Teresa's vision of penetration by a cherub's spear, the most famous of many saintly transverberations.[90] The anonymous author of *The Cloud of Unknowing* urges his reader to beat ceaselessly upon the divine cloud with the dart of love: wounding can go both ways.[91] Though Miller characterizes these experiences negatively as penetrative assaults, those who speak of them bring delight and wounding more closely together, as communication does—whether by spear or by speech.

Confession demands and creates an immense vulnerability, and even more, a realized susceptibility to wounding It attempts Bataillean communication in words. In an introductory note to her work, Bataille declares that Peignot "tore herself on the thorns with which she surrounded herself until becoming nothing but a wound."[92] A wound opens like a window; through it, the broken sacred heart beats visibly. When there is nothing but wound, we peer eagerly or anxiously or just voyeuristically in, wanting to see more—but there is only more wounding to see. The deepest secret conceals itself, or refracts only onto more secrecy, or hides within the visible and the spoken. L. Bernd Mattheus, who translated Peignot's work, writes of this passage, "Laure herself as something sacred, untouchable and incomprehensible?"[93] The untouchable is kept pure, uncontaminated by whatever contact might impart. But, as Milo Sweedler's commentary on the same passage reminds us, the untouchables are also the lowest of castes; what they touch becomes contaminated.[94] Purity is absence, emptiness, or silence. By the abjection of untouchables, their exteriorization from the rest of human collectivity, impurities are removed and kept away. Purity and danger intersect in what is not touched, what may not be touched, what is kept carefully from touching—even if it is glimpsed, perhaps through a wound. But they may be at their strongest in what is never quite glimpsed any more than it is quite heard, in the mystery or the secret, the unavowable or unsayable that is nonetheless the "knowledge" of communication, toward which confession asymptotically speaks. The secret, impure and dangerous, as unavowable and communicable as shame, remains untouchable by senses or words. Secrecy is kept by desire. By its own elusion, secrecy also keeps desire. Secrecy itself arouses.

Our exhibitionism and voyeurism come together here, or rather their auditory equivalents do: speaking aloud, we perceive ourselves heard. And we listen, never quite finding, for the sound just on its way to speaking, for some truth before truth is made, for the murmur of a secret. For what in speaking eludes speech, for the knowledge of communication itself. As Jordan reminds us, this search both belongs to and evades religion: "When [Foucault] approaches the joint (tendon, membrane) at which speech enters into skin or issues from it, he often reverts to religious terms or examples, to ritual analogies or instances. He does so especially when there is a question of what cannot be spoken. Religion tries to regulate how bodies sound. That sound—Foucault wants above all to hear that sound, in the moment when it refuses to become speech."[95] The regulated speaking of confession is always on the edge of the inarticulate sound of exorcism, of the convulsive cry—even the scream of the sacrificial victim. Language harbors its own incompletion, a finitude that allows it infinite desire, because it will never be fulfilled, never rest in an absolute meaning. The imperfect, impure subject keeps on speaking, giving words and self away, trying to hold on to the meaning never reached.

This too runs against the explicit healing intent of modern confession, which we already saw in Robert's citation of Medieval canon law. After early modernity's fascination with wounds has faded, crucifixes become less gory,[96] and in some post-Reformation Christianity the cross is laid altogether bare; divine wounds are denied and human wounds mended without scarring. For Bataille, as for Weil, the

Christian crucifixion is the ultimate in breaking and wounding precisely *because* theology has been so insistent on completion, so intent upon refusing brokenness. But the two pulls of fracture and mending exist with one another, both desired and resisted. On the one hand, the monk aims to speak fluently toward the absence of speaking at all, to speak a self that flows without stuttering into the perfect silence of its own absence—the unresisting purity of having nothing to tell. On the other, the speaker and the interrogator both struggle to bring into speech the secret that is too intimate and too immense, too deeply embedded in speaking, to be said at all—and they continue the power play of humiliation in their questions. The speaker struggles to satisfy the interrogator, fearing at the same time the cessation of interest, of questions, of desire. No confession is so thorough as to touch upon everything, but even every thing would be eluded by the unavowable secret.[97] Erotic confession builds upon this desire by deliberately intensifying both control and shame—and by counting upon the inexhaustibility of making truth about the self, even if we have to lie. Constructing the confessed self, confessional speech must sustain a wound at the heart.

DIRTY LITTLE SECRETS

> Oh, it's all about power baby
> You know what I'm sayin', oh it's all about power, baby
> It's all about sleepwalking through
> This endless night
> Tell me all your dirty little secrets
> —My Life with the Thrill Kill Kult, "Dirty Little Secrets"

If language comes in confession to bear the weight of sin, as Kristeva argues, so too it becomes a sacrifice—indeed, it gives away the very subject it works to create. Kristeva writes to Catherine Clément, "All religions, using the trenchant effects of language . . . celebrate the sacred as a sacrifice." In Judaism and Christianity, she adds, the sacrifice "inscribes language in the body," with a violence that few care to admit.[98] In the Christian context, as Bataille notes, God is sacrificed to God; the devout seeker of theosis, then, can strive with equal impossibility for divine completeness, or, "At his leisure, he can become humble, poor, enjoy his humility, his poverty in God; imagine God himself succumbing to the desire for incompletion, to the desire to be a man and poor, and to die in torture."[99] As ascetics have long known and we have already seen, this is just as impossible an identification; the deeper one's mortifications, the more one risks the temptation of outdoing God, mirroring the desire for a kenosis deeper than the abandonment of divine sovereignty.[100]

Such abandonment is as impossible as it is desired. Most of Bataille's writing, as Shannon Winnubst points out, "is consumed with the attempt to do the impossible—to . . . articulate that which surpasses us, 'to realize one's ends [by carrying] out a movement that surpasses them.'" This is the draw of sacrifice, "inviting and provoking us to undergo this exquisite jouissance—this intensified pleasure that is finally indistinguishable from pain—that marks the breaking forth of this excessive energy into our restricted lives."[101] For Bataille, as for Kristeva, a religious sensibility links this sacrifice to language. Not only is the speaking self made, drawn near, and wounded into communication by words, but it may also be sacrificed in them.

We want to be heard, and heard more; loved, even, and desired, in the selves that we are giving (up) by speaking them. To sacrifice the self completely would be, in the Christian imaginary, to love entirely (the sacrifice of Christ is understood, particularly in the Johannine version, as manifesting a divine love of the world). But we have already seen that we cannot be fully heard, fully known, or even entirely trusted when we speak. Impossibility sustains the possible, keeps stretching it further.

Bataille suggests, "Maybe the desire to know has only one meaning: to serve as motive for the desire to question."[102] Incompletion is built in to desire; when we want to know, it is in order to direct the next interrogative. Obviously this is not always true; if I ask for directions to the train station, I am unlikely to be grateful if I am led into an indefinite series of questions. But it does seem to be true of the more intense and puzzling desires that especially interest Bataille and that are my subject here. Derrida claims, "If confession is guided by a teleology, it is not confession."[103] It goes, it opens, it speaks—it does not aim; or, if it can be said to aim, it is at impossibility, at its own undoing.

Yet "language is an organ of will (of action)," says Bataille; "I express myself as a mode of will, which pursues its path to the end."[104] This will is connected to work; it intends results—action, self-expression. How, then, could it be sacrificial, as Bataille insists—how, especially, could it be a sacrifice of will, just as obedience is—to speak oneself? And the answer must be, I think, that to some extent speaking is sacrifice, is sacrificed, wherever it becomes that which is read or heard by another (thus, it invariably eludes the project and purpose one had in mind for it), but it is most vividly, most intensely sacrificial where it turns around upon itself to willfully sacrifice the very self it constructs: when it speaks under the perverse imperative of confession. That is: when speaking and what is spoken are not led, at least not entirely, by one's own will, but are drawn by the command of a will with which one finds oneself nevertheless in complicity or collusion, a will that one wills to obey, a question that one divides oneself to answer. One must be drawn in and resistant. One must be drawn, in part, to that very resistance, and to the chance that what resists can break. The break is a sacrifice of will (as an act of obedience), of language (given in answer), of the self (as constructed by language). But like all sacrifice, it is a making of the sacred: it pulls us toward mystery, and mystery toward our hearing. Sustaining the openness of communication is an aim oddly against an end. If there is freedom in not having to speak too long, then what becomes of one whose confession is drawn without end?

Endless questioning feeds back to the endless desire to know, sustainable only by what cannot be known or answered. As Blanchot writes, "[T]he fact (it is not a fact) of wondering whether the secret is not linked to there being still something left to say when all is said; it does suggest Saying (with its glorious capital), always in excess of everything said." The secret is not the said, yet it suggests, not particular things-said, but saying, even Saying, itself. The secret is "that which withdraws, hides in the demand that all be disclosed: the dark of the clearing or the error of truth itself—The un-knowledge after absolute knowledge which does not, precisely, allow us to conceive of any 'after.'"[105]

Blanchot's language lends itself to mystery, but he is cautious about sacralizing the secret, though his resistance is chiefly to a more traditional sense of the sacred as fixed and transcendent.[106] Bataille, for his part, is generally ready to desecrate anything, which is impossible without a lingering sense of the sacred. The disruptiveness of the sacred and the unsayableness of the secret link both to silence, which both does not say and disrupts saying. And which is disrupted by it, when the speaker has strength enough for the confrontation with shame. A brief dialogue in L'Abbé C highlights the proximity of this confrontation to that with the sacred. Robert, the first speaker, holds on to a secret that he does not wish to reveal.

> "I've been in the habit of lying, but now I couldn't do that, and I don't
> have the strength to talk."
>
> I was so ridiculously annoyed that I replied:
>
> "You didn't have the strength to say Mass, either."[107]

One presumes that in Mass, too, some secret would remain unsaid; after all, the Eucharistic liturgy proclaims "the mystery of faith." Perhaps the abbé knows that if he is trying to tell the untold truth, to tell his secrets, no measure of strength will suffice.

Through confession, intriguing connections emerge between the unspoken truths of the flesh and the unspeakable secret at the edge of knowing. Certeau describes secrecy as a strategic play, one actor trying to keep the secret that the other endeavors to discover.[108] This play may occur even when the one "keeping" the secret is working valiantly to give it away. The play requires a duality, an ear into which one may speak. That the strategy is a play of resistance does not undermine what is confessed; Foucault even argues that "the truth is corroborated by the obstacles and resistances it has had to surmount in order to be formulated."[109] The difficulty in bringing to language increases the demand for speech. Taussig describes a distinction, which he draws from Walter Benjamin, between truth as "a matter of exposure which destroys the secret," and as "a revelation which does justice to it."[110] Mystery can be revealed only as mystery, secret only as secret, which is to say that in no easy or everyday sense can they be revealed at all. Yet there may be a revelation that, without displaying the secret, tells us of it.

We may recall here Latour's claim for a sacramental, constructive quality to prayerful speech, which may extend to the confessional as well. He offers a Thomist definition of sacrament: "Words that do what they say . . . are called, for this reason, sacramental."[111] But what is *sacramentum* in the Latin church is *mysterion* in the Greek: the mystery, whether to be shared only among the initiated, or concealed by its very nature from comprehending knowledge.[112] Sacramental words speak mysteries, not to reveal what they are, but to give us a seductive hint *that* they are, made in the speaking, murmuring under words, even as sacrificial. The liturgical effect is the making of the truth that it says, the conversion of those who say and hear—not least in the liturgical sacrament of the Eucharist, where words make flesh of bread and divinity of flesh, both sacrificed, both remembered. The confessional effect is the making of the truth that it says, the conversionary shame of those who say and say again. Both make the shift from flat fact to felt secret. Neither is a speaking that stays said. Latour emphasizes that religious speech is not obscure, not even complicated—only, as he says, fragile.[113] "It isn't a mystery in the sense of an obscure message hidden from the common run of mortals but, yet again, the mystery of a sequence, a subtle sleight of hand, an extremely simple savoir-faire that draws out the reality in talk whose operating conditions alone allow us to speak properly."[114] It *is* mysterious, but in a way different from obscurity, because it is different from factual knowledge itself. It is different, even, from the performative speech to which we have long been accustomed; this speaking makes a mystery. In sacrifice, flesh may enter words: "Like a group of monks living in solitude but unified in God," Sweedler writes, "the hypothetical laura formed among the community of readers of Le sacré would be unified in Laure's 'glorious body': the one resurrected, as Mitsou Ronat's apt phrase would have it, in language."[115] Peignot dies very young, leaving her community with her carnal texts.[116] Language must be communal; it may even make communities, and yet it cannot quite tell the secret, the secret of the body that inhabits language, that language inhabits; the word made glorious and desecrated flesh.

This secret, inseparable from any said, is what we reach for most urgently in confession, interrogation, the search for the heights and depths of the sacred, the poetic communication of the stripper's text at an open mic. All speech desires, even (especially) speech barely exteriorized past resistance. Certeau declares, "This volition does not have speech for its object (as would be the case with a desire or a decision to speak). It defines the act of speaking. It is what all speaking says: to say is to want."[117]

The cry remains: all speaking confesses desire; all confession desires the flesh. The text and the flesh conjoin confessionally, secretly, infinitely. Confession is imperfect, as necessarily so as any other act of obedience, because the flesh cannot wholly be told and language's meaning is never fulfilled. What Huffer calls the "stuttering voice" of eros is, she argues, also a "voice of resistance . . . that can be useful to queers and feminists alike. It is a lyrical and ironic voice that both ruptures and amplifies those dominant voices of rationalism and bourgeois values. It is easy to mishear it, emerging as it does in the gaps of the pervert's silence or the hysteric's delirious babble."[118]

Bataille's novels are filled with his own struggles to capture these ruptures in language, where it tries to tell the pleasures, the desires, and the shames of the flesh. We read of the Abbé Robert, "He began to speak. . . . If it is true that his remarks, in a certain sense, eluded me, it was due to the nature of what he said: it was the sort of thing that can rob you, if not of your memory, at least of your attention: the sort of thing that can destroy it, reduce it to ashes."[119] Hearing these words is like gazing at the sun: not only do we not understand them, but the effort to attend toward understanding, to remember in order to hold onto the meaning, is destructive of attention, understanding, and recollection alike. Robert's speech, like Eponine's, is too dangerous to hear: the priest and the prostitute speak the extremes of the sacred. Bataille knows better than to try to present them; he speaks only of speaking, and in that way tells us about words that try to tell secrets, like the "unspeakable act" left unnamed in *My Mother*. Bataille's clerical and whorish figures are in the tradition of Sade, but they work against that tradition too. Sade seems certain of the iterative possibilities of language, and of its rationality. He never manages to say everything, to try everything, or to see everything as his characters peer into the bodies they so gleefully destroy—but the realization that it might be *impossible* to do so, while it quite probably drives him, does not seem to register fully. The impossible is where Bataille begins as much as it is what he seeks. And part of his impossibility is the effort to merge language and flesh; further, to merge them so that they tell and show their secrets.[120] It is as if one spoke the strange non-language of which Certeau writes, "The sounds, resembling fragments of remains, form an uncanny memory, prior to meaning. One would be hard put to say what it is the memory of: it recalls something that is not a past; it awakens what the body does not know about itself."[121] The truth of confessional saying is failure, a deep un-knowing of the body that sounds.

On the other side of the scream, where meaning gives way to the fleshy cry, is silence. Language, like the penitent who speaks it, is self-divided, is beside itself. It is divided by madness or vivisection, splitting reason or flesh as the voice cries out; it is divided by the silences that break the flow of words as the speaking voice falters. In confession, even a moment of silent hesitation before the confessor becomes a sign, the speaking voice resisting out of willfulness or shame. However, it is also silence toward which the penitent, especially the monastic penitent, speaks. The stuttering moment reveals a flaw in the heart, but utter silence, if it told the truth, would tell of perfection, precisely by not-telling at all. Only sin can speak. Struggling to give the truth of the self that it makes, speech under confessional interrogation is both the most intimate speaking (the stripped, the confessed, the humiliated: the revelation of shame) and not-intimate at all, because the speaking I eludes, because the I stripped bare is no core of self but pure elusion, the remaining other: because there is no core, only the secret of speaking. We approach its limit, and still it pulls us. No length of speech can quite extroject the remainder.

There remains the penitential option: insist upon my speaking; *make me*. We must not only be susceptible to temptation (we must experience it in order to resist it); we must also be tempting. Otherwise, the one who hears will cease to ask, and the confessant is always demanding: ask me again. Confession is sustained by a mutual desire to know, beyond whatever information might be confessed; to communicate, but not simply by exchange of data. To communicate is to undo the self constructed by the confessional act of communication. It is to bring language to its somatic edge, where it loses meaning. It is to humiliate the strong will that speaks sacrificially. Against the production of the truth, we use its own will to knowledge: we consent not to lies, but to mysteries.

FOUR

Uncovering

THE FAILURE TO SEE

ENLIGHTEN ME

I am sending you to them to open their eyes and turn them from darkness to light . . .

—Acts of the Apostles, 26:17–18

In obeying, one seeks and fails to make humility known, sometimes breaking through into humiliation held tautly in tension with pride. In confessing,
sin-weighted speech circles, shatters, stretches between those who try to force it to
make a knowable truth. But the West has long associated knowledge most strongly
with vision. As Augustine observes, we use "seeing" of all sorts of perceptions: "we
say not only 'See how that light shines,' which only the eyes can perceive, but 'See
how that sounds, see what smells, see what tastes, see how hard that is.' . . . other
senses claim the word for themselves by analogy when they are exploring any
department of knowledge."[1] "I see" means not merely that I have been presented
with information, but that I understand it. Knowing en*light*ens us; information
sheds light on problems.

And sometimes, we are drawn to see what also pushes us away. In an important
early discussion, Aristotle connects the attraction of repulsive things—more exactly,
of artistic portrayals of such things—to knowledge. We "delight to contemplate"
very faithful representations of "objects which themselves we view with pain . . .
such as the forms of the most ignoble animals and of dead bodies."[2] Given the
revulsion that such objects generate, however, a revulsion not entirely negated by
the representational distance, what could the source of pleasure be? "The cause of
this . . . is, that to learn gives the liveliest pleasure, not only to philosophers but to

men in general."[3] After all, for Aristotle, the universal human desire for knowledge is the beginning of philosophy. Though more Platonic and Stoic than Aristotelian, Augustine makes a similar claim. We read in the *Confessions* of "a vain inquisitiveness dignified with the title of knowledge and science. As this is rooted in the appetite for knowing, and as among the senses the eyes play a leading role in acquiring knowledge, the divine word calls it 'the lust of the eyes' (1 John 2:16)."[4]

Vision may show us what we wish to learn, including what we later wish we hadn't. Yet sometimes vision, too, may show us a mystery, and one of its ways of showing is in the frustration of the demand to see all things, that we may know them. Both Aristotle and Augustine are very much in favor of knowledge and query, but both also believe that we may *want* to see, literally and figuratively, what we *should* not. Might we also desire to see what we *can* not?

Certainly, we may desire to see shaming, and visible displays of degradation appear to precede auricular confession within Christianity. Foucault reminds us of the story of Fabiola, a fifth-century Roman matron convicted of remarrying while her first husband was alive. "The bishop, the priests, and the people wept with her. Her hair disheveled, her face pale, her hands dirty, her head covered in ashes, she chastened her naked breast and the face with which she had seduced her second husband. She revealed to all her wound, and Rome, in tears, contemplated the scars on her emaciated body."[5] Still earlier, we find a third-century Christian penitent "rolling himself under the feet not only of the clergy but also of the laity" and "showing the weals of the stripes he has received."[6] Such display "speaks," or rather renders visible, the truth of the new, penitent self, replacing the embodiment of the sinner.

The change to auricular confession does not simply replace the desire to see; however, the site of seeing may shift from penitence to liturgy. In the Middle Ages, William Robert notes, "Visual liturgies became . . . 'the very sacrament of the pious.' They did so especially among Franciscans and the laity they affected."[7] Franciscan piety is strikingly visual; Francis is often credited with setting up the first manger scene to celebrate Christ's nativity, and Franciscans were especially prone to getting dramatically naked in more or less public locations. At the Fourth Lateran council in 1215 (where annual confession became imperative), transubstantiation became dogma, so that those who saw the elevated host were officially seeing as well the body of Christ. "Eucharistic piety escalated, throughout the thirteenth century. It became increasingly visual," Robert writes, tracing this visual history. Yet as visuality intensifies, so too does a kind of concealment: "By the thirteenth century, priests turned their backs to congregants during mass. This turn performed, Sara Lipton writes, a 'desire to control and direct the gaze.'"[8] As visual interest increases, so too does concealment, defying the gaze but drawing desire.

The desire to direct the gaze is at work in asceticism and in perversity too, in a manner not exactly liturgical, but not so distant from it as we might expect—both sets of practices may be highly ritualized. The directed gaze must, however, be highly controlled. To look too long, or too longingly, is not only temptation, but sin in itself. And to look in this way slides easily into a look that searches for secrets, beneath the body's surface and in its intense sensations.

Thus, restraint of the eyes—keeping the gaze lowered, or avoiding eye contact with others—is, though increasingly less often, commanded by some monastic orders, and perhaps more often in relations of erotic submission. (As a common alternative to the downward directed gaze, submissives in the latter group are often blindfolded.) Nancy observes a similar ocular restraint with respect to the law that must be obeyed: "Prior to all other determinations, and as the origin of all other determinations (fear and trembling, submission, veneration, imitation, compliance) respect is a gaze, a regard (*respectus*).... It is a regard that does not raise its eyes, and perhaps does not even open them."[9] The downward gaze draws the self with it. Looking down (or not looking at all) is subservient, submissive; it is not just the animal eye-to-eye confrontation that it evades, but any imposition upon the exterior world, and any temptation to look not just on, but into.

Around looking and showing, as around hearing and speaking, pleasure and shame twine together, meeting in the humiliating desires and failures to show and to see. There is power as well as risk, pleasure as well as shame, in naked display; directing and manipulating the gaze is no small part of it. Bataille's characters, for instance, are not above flashing their genitalia in a show of power, as Madame Edwarda does, her "thin voice, like her slender body, . . . obscene" as she opens her labia to expose her "old rag and ruin," declaring herself "GOD," in all capitals.[10] This story, evoking sight, seeming to present us with a picture, somehow is not much less elusive than the unspeakable speech of Bataille's other narrators.

WHAT LIES BENEATH?

A naked man has few secrets; a flayed man, none.
                              —Roose Bolton, *Game of Thrones*

In most circumstances, a body's bounds of propriety extend well beyond the skin. The interrogating gaze, seeking what exceeds propriety, may look first beneath clothing. Naked skin is so closely linked to shame, in fact, that the connection is mythical: we recall that the disobedient human couple in the garden of Paradise, having eaten the fruit from the tree of knowledge, "knew that they were naked; and they sewed fig leaves together and made themselves loin coverings" (Genesis 3:7). Derrida, in referring to this "original shame," speaks of being "naked as a beast," with the knowledge that other beasts lack, the knowledge that one appears, shamefully, uncovered.[11] Other beasts, unashamed, may still shame us with their gazes. Under the skeptical gaze of a cat, Derrida writes,

I have trouble repressing a reflex of shame. Trouble keeping silent within me a protest against the indecency. Against the impropriety [*malséance*] that can come of finding oneself naked, one's sex exposed, stark naked before a cat that looks at you without moving, just to see. . . . It is as if I were ashamed, therefore, naked in front of this cat, but also ashamed for being ashamed. A reflected shame, the mirror of a shame ashamed of itself, that is at the same time specular, unjustifiable, and unavowable.[12]

In this impropriety and unavowability, we recognize the visual variant of the unavowable secret. Perhaps we are no less shamed in the mirror of another person's eyes—or a god's—but cats, with their sleek elegance, graceful strength, and absence of excess, may be especially good at the judgmental gaze.

Augustine's reading of this first shame, we recall, links it directly to disobedience. For him, nudity itself is less at issue than the new recalcitrance of the flesh, its insusceptibility to voluntary control. The parts of the body that relatively few human cultures hide, such as the face and hands, are those subject to quite a bit of rational control—though control is never complete. What makes the lack of control humiliating is not simply that it happens, but that it can be seen—that is why the people cover their loins. Our flesh becomes embarrassing when it becomes irrational, and able to flout the will. Of course, shame may multiply when it hits the face, causing a bright blush that feeds upon itself in the very site of reason's control.[13]

J. David Velleman offers an intriguing alternative version of Augustine's reading. Exposure, he argues, can only be shameful if concealment is an option; publicity humiliates only where privacy is possible. "Privacy is made possible by the ability to choose in opposition to inclination," he writes. For an instinct-governed creature, "impulses are legible in its behavior. Whatever itches, it scratches (or licks or nips or drags along the ground), and so its itches are always overt, always public. By contrast, our capacity to resist desires enables us to choose which desires our behavior will express."[14]

For Velleman, the private, which we understand as our own inwardness, is made by the fracture of the will—that is, by the tension between desire and resistance, by the fact that resistance is even possible. Humiliation entails stripping away the front that we have constructed, revealing those desires we have attempted to conceal or even to eliminate, whether by fig leaves or through self-discipline.

Shame, Velleman argues, belongs to a person whose self-presentation is thwarted, who cannot or does not present to others the impression she wishes them to have.[15] For Augustine, pure rational harmony is the idealized, Edenic contrast to the moment of shame. For Velleman, the contrasting term is instinct. Nudity is not enough for shame; even being seen nude is not enough. Rather, being exposed *without control* of the presentation is shameful. In this way, though Velleman's argument is importantly distinct from Augustine's, both come down to an insistence upon control of the presentation, whether that control is in the obedience of the flesh or in the accord between the presentation one desires and that which one actually makes.[16] And both modes of control are second best to what has been lost: perfect accord of reason and desire, or of instinct and visible behavior.

Emmanuel Levinas, on the other hand, argues that shame occurs in nudity not when the flesh is uncontrolled, but when it is intimate. "It is . . . our intimacy, that is, our presence to ourselves, that is shameful."[17] In shame we are unable to distance ourselves from the body on display, while at the same time we cannot easily or gladly claim and hold close what shames us.[18] A body treated altogether as an object is not shameful, and may well leave one (relatively) unashamed, as in the context of a medical examination or modeling for a drawing class. Nudity may be conceived as objectification, but it cannot be shameful unless it is exposes the body of one who is aware of that exposure *and* feels it as improper; one who is an agent too, and not just a thing. Though control is not central to Levinas's sense of visual shame, his instances of nonintimate nakedness are the boxer and the music-hall dancer, two exemplars of corporeal control and self-construction; the body is not shameful when it is nude (or nearly so) and presented according to one's will, nor when it is so divorced from subjectivity that the tension of a resistant desire does not appear. The tension felt between object and agency is not sufficient for shame, but it is necessary. At either end, when (almost) completely objectified or (almost) completely in charge, we are less likely to find ourselves humiliated. The tension in the distinction we try so hard to hold, of an inside and an out, is what threatens to humiliate us.

Nakedness, with its subject-object tension, may be courted by ascetics seeking out shame. The saintly body may, however, be transfigured beyond intimacy, particularly in the desert, an environment especially harsh on bare skin. The famous fourth-century Mary of Egypt was beautifully ornamented in her youth. After her conversion, however, she wanders the desert clad only in her own long hair, a sort of saintly Godiva, and it is thus that she catches the eye of the monk Zosimus. The fascinated monk is unsatisfied with skin or the draperies of hair, perhaps because Mary is so well hidden by the latter, perhaps because she is so far beyond desire that there is no intimacy left in her display. Zosimus demands her confession as well, trying to pull out an inside self, which would alter the nude body into a shameful nakedness.[19]

We also find saintly ascetics denuded in obedience. In Palladius's *Lausiac History* we read an account of Serapion the Sindonite, a wandering ascetic who spends much of his time reforming others. Hearing of a virgin much devoted to God, he insists upon meeting her; she makes the mistake of telling him "Order me possible things, and I will do them." First he insists that she appear in public, already a challenge for her, until she comes with him to a church. Then he demands that she disrobe and walk through the city, dismissing her concern that others will think

her "mad and possessed by a demon." The conflict that Velleman describes is vivid
here, in a scene that is very similar to the popular pornographic trope of forced
public nudity. She asks that he make a different request, "for I do not profess to
have reached this stage." Serapion again translates her apparent modesty into a
manifestation of pride, "Then having left her in humility and broken her pride, he
departed."[20] The tale leaves us not liking Serapion much. But what happens if her
pride has been in her humbling, or if she herself has sought to be broken? Matters
then are more complex, as indeed they may have been in her case.

Some of the best-known scenes of ascetically erotic nudity, thoroughly con-
founding the saintly and perverse, come from Angela of Foligno. The first is a
conversionary scene, which occurs as she stands in a church before a crucifix.

> I was given such a fire that, as I was standing near the cross, I stripped
> myself of all my clothes, and offered myself completely to Him. . . . I also
> accused every part of my body, one at a time, before Him. And I asked
> Him to make me observe the chastity of all my body parts and all my
> senses; I was afraid to make this promise, but at the same time, that fire
> compelled me, and I could not do otherwise.[21]

There she stood, and could not do otherwise, though one doubts that Luther
would have approved. Angela's desires and her actions reveal to us the continu-
ities of the pornographic and confessional, each with its imperative to tell all the
truths of the flesh, carried now to the realm of the visual.[22] Part by part, the body
is accused in confession; part by part, it is exposed to the gaze of the all-seeing
God, who indeed provides the *only* hope of being fully, and always, seen. It is also
exposed, not incidentally, to the gaze of other people, many of whom one suspects were somewhat startled. Even in the humility of her self-accusation, Angela
is certain that she is worth the perfect gaze, worth the slow enumeration of her
parts; she is certain that the body thus dedicated, accused though it is, will be
received as a gift. The impossible completeness of display, of being-seen entirely,
drives pornographer and saint alike. Like confessional speaking, a deliberate visual
display constructs us as subjects while revealing us as objects, and in this tension
its paradoxes, and its pleasures, emerge.

Later in her *Book*, Angela explicitly links nakedness to humiliation, with a
relish that may astonish us now.

> I was plunged into an abyss of deep humility . . . I saw so clearly the su-
> perabundance of my malice, iniquity, and sins that it seemed impossible
> for me to disclose them and make them known. . . . I was not ashamed,
> however, to confess in front of everyone all the sins I had committed.
> I even enjoyed imagining how I could make public my iniquities, hy-
> pocrisies, and sins. I wanted to parade naked through towns and public

squares with pieces of meat and fish hanging from my neck and to proclaim: "Behold the lowest of women, full of malice and deceit, stinking
with every vice and evil."23

Angela's vision of public nakedness continues the proud Franciscan tradition
of visuality. Francis himself outraged his wealthy father, a cloth merchant, by sell-
ing silk from his father's warehouse and donating the proceeds to a local church.
When his father demanded that Francis return everything that was his father's,
Francis, with his flair for visual drama, stripped on the spot (before not only his
father, but the bishop and the gathered, gossipy townspeople as well), handed back
not just his cash but all his clothing, and began a life of asceticism. Robert notes
the description of another Franciscan, in which "A brother asks a hermit what
he should do to be saved. . . . Without a word, the hermit stripped himself of his
clothes . . . and, girdling his loins and outstretching his hands, said: 'Thus ought the
monk to be nude of everything worldly, and to crucify himself against the temptation and struggles of the world.'"24 The famous Franciscan holy fool Brother
Juniper denuded himself so often that he aggravated, and perhaps embarrassed,
even his fellow Franciscans.25

Franciscan nudity is one of the most striking visual presentations of the order's general vow of poverty, a vow that becomes widespread among monastic
orders, and is itself not disconnected from secrecy. Certeau writes, "Individual
poverty was but the precondition of mutual exchange. It divested one of any asset
or held-back secret. It was essentially epiphanic. . . . The point was to create transparent bodies."26 Bodily transparency begins at the skin. Deliberate dispossession
as nudity can be hostiley presented as licentious exhibitionism or antinomianism,
helping it to play into the quest for humiliation. It is the dispossession or loss less
of objects (such as clothing) than of a state of self-containment. It is the loss of a
boundary, and a literal revelation. By it some small secret is exposed. Asceticism
seeks many things, not the same for each who undertakes it, but in those whose
asceticism takes this stripped-down form, it seeks some truth of corporeality—a
truth that sustains the will to know precisely by being unfindable. Bataille writes
of nudity, "In the end everything puts me at risk, I remain suspended, stripped
bare, in a definitive solitude: beyond the impenetrable simplicity of *what is*; and, the
depths of the world open, what I see and what I know no longer have meaning."27
The risk and the baring and the depths become part of non-knowing—or they
may, at least, when the self and the object remain stripped in tension, without the
desire for either quite giving way.

Yet with sufficient familiarization, even naked bodies become unremarkable,
losing their intense visibility. As Angela's fantasy suggests, we must sometimes layer
(meat with more meat, words upon words) to reveal. We might think that the
body is at its most fully displayed, and potentially most pornographic, when we
see all of its skin. But the nude in itself may be innocent, aestheticized, clinical,

or just plain dull. Conversely, what covers the body may function to reveal—its desires, its beauties, its secrets—rather than to cover bodily shame, as we see with Angela's bits of meat and fish. Pornographically, covering works in this same way, but less subtly. Clothing conspicuously failing to serve its purpose, dropped or tucked just under interesting and intimate body parts or revealing them through sheer fabric, is imagistically popular, as are jewelry and a wide range of revelatory undergarments such as gartered stockings, shoes, chaps, and, depending upon the nuances of one's genre preferences, gym socks. What "properly" functions to guard the most affectively intense bits of flesh from the exterior gaze here draws sly attention to its own failure.

Ornamentation, of course, slides into the kind of counter-ornamentation, the deliberate layering-on of the shameful and ugly, that Angela enjoys imagining. In a fragment from *The Sacred*, Peignot writes of being pursued by "a laugh ... that hung from her neck like a little bell and pulled her back ... on a leash."[28] The bell both ornaments and reimagines her animal flesh. As the excerpt goes on, the character rolls in the gutter, until, "Her hair full of excrement, her eyes crazed, her mouth soiled and yellow at the corners but still eager, she raised two hands."[29] Like Angela, Peignot layers the body's shame, its rejected and abject soil, as if to display the flesh inside-out, to show its hidden secrets—but those secrets remain. Laure remains elusive: pile on the ornaments, soil the flesh, bare it, open its orifices: however compliant, it resists. And its resistance must not, in the end, be altogether overcome; the only perfect overcoming is death, when the flesh becomes object alone.

OH BEAUTIFUL

> Your heart was proud because of your beauty; you corrupted your wisdom for the sake of your splendor.
>
> —Ezekiel 28:17

Ornamentation, however perverse its purpose, draws our attention to beauty, to enhance it or even to demonstrate that is missing. Beauty in the flesh may be a source of pride; classical myths, folk stories, and fairy tales even tend to link it to moral goodness. With Christianity, however, the temptation that beauty poses creates new problems, and the link to moral goodness is broken.

The break is far from simple. Hagiographies and popular stories of humiliated ascetics often place particular emphasis on the saints' attractiveness, which may sometimes, in the pre-Christian manner, be connected to God's goodness (how great a God to make such beauty!) and thus read as a sign of holiness. When the late ancient ascetic Pelagia first appears as a stunningly beautiful actress, for instance, the local bishop believes that "the woman's 'carnal beauty' ... is the manifestation of her actual spiritual power."[30] Pelagia's biographer, ostensibly the deacon Jacob, not only specifies many details of her clothing, but emphasizes her attractive power: "Thus it was that her beauty and finery lured everyone who saw her to stare at her and at her appearance."[31] Even the bishop is impressed, and he urges the other monks to be impressed too: "To be honest, fathers, did not the beauty of this prostitute who passed in front of us astonish you?"[32]

But beauty in a saint is always tricky. Many saints, particularly women, are said to have been beautiful in their youth, and many of them enjoy that beauty and the attention that it brings. If not naturally beautiful, they may enjoy wearing fine clothing and attending to appearances. St. Veronica notes in her autobiography that she enjoyed public display of her beauty and fine clothing, as well as the cross-dressing considered quite sexy in her seventeenth-century heyday—"With this transvestism I was enormously satisfied;" she declares; "it made me noticed by more people."[33] Likewise pleased with her own youthful beauty is Margaret of Cortona, a thirteenth-century Franciscan tertiary who later becomes conspicuous in her asceticism instead, begging her confessor to be allowed to cut her face with a razor, "because with the beauty of my face I did harm to many souls."[34] We recall again Fabiola, who is not a saint, but who displays as penance the public shame that is the destruction of her seductive beauty.

Even saints who are not naturally pretty, such as Catherine of Siena (who had facial scars from pox), may adorn their faces and dye their hair. Like Angela of Foligno, they may wear impressive finery that marks their nobility. An intensely focused attentiveness to the flesh as it appears, as it is visible, is vital in all these instances; beauty may not be necessary to it, but it often proves useful in enticing that initial awareness. Ascetic women resist beauty as a temptation to pride and a sign of attention to worldly matters, even as their hagiographers insistently draw our attention to it. Pornographic depictions of degradation almost invariably begin with descriptions of highly attractive people, though the variety of communities from which the stories and images emerge does at least present some variation in what constitutes beauty. Something must draw the eye to begin with, giving us an excuse to start looking.

Ascetic women who enjoy their beauty early on, however, come to regard it more warily later. Catherine joyfully cuts her bleached blonde hair to the roots as a sign of her religious devotion.[35] Angela, we have seen, strips bare and imagines substituting fairly revolting substances for her finery. Others go farther—the fifteenth-century Franciscan nun Eustochia burned her face and discolored it with herbs.[36] Late in the sixteenth century, the Dominican tertiary Rose of Lima (she of the arrows to the heart) "became afraid that her beauty might be a temptation to someone, since people could not take their eyes off her. Therefore, she rubbed her face with pepper until it was all red and blistered."[37] Even when it is not so deliberately directed against visual appeal, a harsh ascetic regimen can hasten the loss of beauty. The beautiful Pelagia lived so long in the desert that her body and even her gender became unrecognizable to those who knew her as a dangerously beautiful woman: "Her astounding beauty had all faded away, her laughing and bright face that I had known had become ugly, her pretty eyes had become hollow and cavernous as a result of much fasting."[38] Shadowed with lost beauty, Pelagia "continues to entice the gaze," Burrus writes. She becomes bewildering, even more seductive to the eyes than she was when she was beautiful: "What we behold when we view this disquieting figure ... is, as [Patricia Cox] Miller suggests, a grotesquerie: a *holy woman.*"[39] The escape from beauty provides no respite from the gaze; the grotesque may pull at the desire for knowing, the will to see, still more strongly.

Beauty is shifty aesthetically as well as morally. We may register not only its loss, but its excess, as ugliness—"the 'intensification' of beauty actually propels it toward its opposites,"[40] Carolyn Korsmeyer writes in her consideration of aesthetic disgust. Ugliness is humiliating; its acceptance, a form of humility. Yet Velleman argues that beauty itself can lead to shame by drawing attention: "[S]hame is more likely to arise in someone who feels all too attractive to an observer, such as the artist's model who blushes upon catching a glint of lust in his eye."[41] Donald Nathanson argues in his work on shame and selfhood that such shame in attractiveness is intrinsic to femininity: "Women must learn how to handle the effect they make on men [the context makes it clear that Nathanson has men's sexual arousal in mind] lest that effect cause confusion, embarrassment, and anger. Many women will later develop the skills that allow the use of this knowledge in a program of allure, but only after they have taken control of a system otherwise capable of producing shame."[42] It seems more likely to me, however, that any shame in these instances is in the intensity of an observation insusceptible to the will of one viewed, and that to be stared at for ugliness has the potential to be more humiliating still—though if that humiliating ugliness is deliberately delighted in, made a source of the viewer's pleasure, it too is well complicated. (It also seems to me that to place the responsibility for the gaze and its effects entirely upon the one seen, and to make that one always a woman, is ethically as well as aesthetically problematic. But this, I hope, is obvious.)

Like the nude, the disgusting body is more readily and more often evoked as female, as tending toward abject overflow and liquidity. Male artists have delighted in the female nude, but feminist artists have played upon its terrifying unboundedness. For instance, the work of Jenny Saville "defies the standard norms of the nude with her portrayal of bodies overflowing their garments with bulbous extrusions of fat. . . . Some commentators stress the extended angle of beauty; others note the power that disgust holds within her work."[43] Too much beauty is ugly again, fearfully excessive, like the too-long speech, the overflowed boundaries. The failure of proper containment is thrilling, like the telling of a secret. Shamed and attracted by the surplus, we cannot look away.

Nathanson argues, contrarily, that shame attaches to smallness. Pride is linked to "the acquisition of each moiety of normal growth and development," shame to "any failures along the way."[44] Thus it is, he says, that "height [is] a source of pride, and lack of it a source of shame," and "Bigness is associated with power—the ability to accomplish tasks—and therefore efficacy."[45] This seems reasonable enough in the development from child to adulthood, but afterward, it becomes a largely masculine claim. Men may be insufficient, but women, and still more those outside binary gender, are always and shamefully too much, a point that Nathanson does not seem to register—always taking up too much space, whether in height, in weight, in the volume of the voice, or in stance or demeanor. Social unacceptability attends to a woman who is "too large," a differently gendered person who is "too visible," as to a man who is "too small." The play with desire moves too much into not enough; *more* may be desire's most primal statement.

Too much, perhaps, because female desire is *supposed* to be lack, an emptiness awaiting full-fillment. This association, along with that linking women to vulnerability and penetrability, leads to interesting results among those who take humility as a positive: women are better at being worse, and so they have a sort of head start on both humility and exhibition. Though this positivity is not universal even among the ascetically devout, it can provide the material for a dizzying set of layers awaiting revelation. In analyzing the vision of the martyr Perpetua, who sees herself as a nude male wrestler, Burrus links gender, shame, and the exposure of skin: "Expecting to see a female body humiliated by its exposure to the public eye, we see instead the shameless display of the oiled body of a male athlete. Or, rather, we see both. . . . [T]he spectating eye is itself challenged and transformed, trained to see the shamelessness inhering in shame and the shame inhering in shamelessness."[46] As this shows us, both the masculine and the feminine have certain advantages in shaming; women are inherently "inferior," but men can be shamed as womanish.[47] "Misogyny is very nearly imploded," Burrus points out, "as the lowliness of the female sex opens onto a bottomless capacity for the very humiliation that is most ardently courted by ascetic practitioners."[48] Smart, powerful women such as Teresa of Avila or Hildegard of Bingen make extensive use of the trope of the weak and inferior feminine, not infrequently in the midst of quite strong theological and political moves.[49]

Sometimes it's tempting to uncomplicate the search for degradation, perhaps by pathologizing, as Léon Wurmser does: no one, he assumes, would go so low as to wish to be a woman. "The masochistic position is reexternalized," he writes,

in the form of shame: "I am ridiculed, mocked, despised, humiliated." The sexual nature of all this is massively repressed and appears only in an all-pervasive fear of being intruded upon and penetrated. The shame is displaced onto appearance, generalized "weakness," stupidity and unworthiness, the dread of being a woman and of being essentially

incomplete. . . . The masochism itself, of course, . . . is a poor defense
against intensely competitive, envious striving, a defense by regression
from a phallic to an anal-masochistic drive organization, or, as it were,
from "castration shame" to "masochistic shame."[50]

In other words, shame is not sexy, and we, necessarily being Men, worry
about being seen as feminine. If we embrace that possibility, accepting or even
seeking shame, it is as a sad and last resort, the only way out of a sense of utterly failed masculinity. Neil Bartlett, however, makes quite different sense of this
gender-tangled shame:

And the femme response, the radical gay liberation movement response,
the radical drag response, was, "I love to get fucked. I'm like a woman—I'm the one who gets fucked socially, politically, and physically. I'm
the one who gets fucked." That tactic of saying, "Don't give up your
shame," . . . by performing your own shame to *excess,* you heal yourself.
Empower yourself. And for me this is not a theory, this is an absolutely
physical sensation.[51]

For Bartlett, one does not heal oneself into freedom from shame, does not
become moderate, masculine, and proud, but rather complicates shame and pride
in a glorious mess of "absolutely physical sensation." This physicality connects,
like confessional words, back to a tradition of secrets. A longstanding notion holds
that feminine (and femme) sexuality is somehow secret, both anatomically and
psychologically. In this secrecy, in its gaze-drawing ability, in its vulnerability, femininity itself is held to be shameful. Of course, it is a commonplace that histories
and theories of sexuality are in fact those of male sexuality alone. Such inatten-
tion can help to create a sense of hiddenness, of something unknown, of a secret
enfolded in feminine flesh. That secret is then opposed to masculine rationality,
and so we find the tensions of control reinscribed: reason gives us control, while
what is secret and hidden cannot be controlled because it cannot be known; we
must figure out some way to see it. Another part of the line of thought, however,
seems to be based on anatomical difference, traditionally female genitalia being
less clearly or fully on display than those traditionally regarded as male. This sense
of the secret coincides with the demand to see. Derrida remarks upon "all those
(males and not females, for that difference is not insignificant here) . . . for example
Descartes, Kant, Heidegger, Lacan, and Levinas [whose] discourses . . . [go] on as if
they themselves had never been looked at, and especially not naked, by an animal
that addressed them."[52] Indeed, he rightly adds, "It is as if the men . . . had seen
without being seen, seen the animal without being seen by it; without being seen
naked."[53]

We know that sexes and genders neither divide nor line up so neatly as the
reason-versus-secret, pride-versus-shame divisions suggest. What matters is a sense

that what is not knowable, what eludes the light of reason, must be inferior to what is rational and visible. In this sense, woman is joined to other elusive categories, particularly to the "natural" and animal—who is, in Jean-Christophe Bailly's description, "outside in an exteriority more external than any open, and inside in an intimacy more internal than any closedness." He adds "The zone of nonknowledge—or of a-knowledge—that is at issue here is beyond both knowing and not knowing, beyond both disconcealing and concealing, beyond both being and the nothing."[54] This rather perfect description of a mystery connects both terms, feminine and animal, to the elusive sacred.

OPEN (SECRET)

> Who cares why these people have found themselves in this banal, suburban tract home in Burbank? He is not a delivery man; she is not a bored housewife. They are not the stars—their orifices are. Let them open.
> —Maggie Nelson, *Bluets*

A gaze that seeks bare flesh will often seek to push beneath the skin, to penetrate and to communicate, particularly if confronted with a sense that the body might harbor a secret, a mystery not yet seen. "So," Bataille declares, "what attracts desire in the being of flesh is not immediately the being, it is its wound: it is a point of rupture in the integrity of the body, . . . a wound that puts its integrity at stake, its rupture, which does not kill but desecrates."[55] Despite Bataille's authoritative tone, we know that often as not, wounds do nothing of the sort; it is more likely that they make us turn away. They intrigue only when they are in tension (wholeness disrupted is interesting; the altogether broken is sad) or when, like those of whose curiosity Aristotle and Augustine disapproved, we are overcome by our desire to know.

We approach again a communication that is not an information transfer but a bleeding-over at the site of wounds, the importance of vulnerability now literalized in the flesh laid out before inquisitive eyes. Boundaries must be broken for communication to be possible—but not all breaking is equal. A being can only communicate, Bataille writes, "if that being consents, if not to annihilation, at least to risk itself, and in the same movement, to risk others. . . . By destroying in myself, in others, the integrity of being, I open myself to communion."[56] We cannot connect and remain within ourselves. "Beings, human beings, can only 'communicate'—live—outside of themselves," writes Bataille. "And as they must 'communicate,' they must want this evil, defilement, that, placing being at risk in themselves renders both being and themselves penetrable to one another."[57] The wound that integrity demanded out of strength pulls us toward it; the wound inflicted upon the weak calls on us to mend it.

A wound is no definable something; it is a place in which something is not, an opening. While Bataille points to the desire for evil, Burrus reinforces the association of wound and holiness: "Because the saint is radically open to the need of others, she is endlessly vulnerable to need herself (she will give everything, again and again); and because she is endlessly vulnerable to need herself, she is radically open to the need of others. The appeal of the saint is that we make ourselves as vulnerable as she is."[58]

Like confessional interrogation, the penetrative gaze seeks not only communication, but *truth*. There are things it wants to know. Page duBois argues that "the logic of our philosophical tradition, of some of our inherited beliefs about truth, leads almost inevitably to conceiving of the body of the other as the site from which truth can be produced, and to using violence if necessary to extract that truth."[59] From the earliest traditions of Western thought, the purpose of torture's violence is to create the truth *as exposed*—from within. DuBois goes on to analyze Martin Heidegger's influential notion of truth as an unveiling, which rests on his interpretation of Plato, of whom he writes, "At first truth meant what was wrested from a hiddenness. Truth then is just such a perpetual wrenching-away in this manner of uncovering."[60] Nor is this a benign revelation; "Truth (uncoveredness) is something that must always first be wrested from entities. Entities get snatched out of their hiddenness."[61] Through "the gaze of the spectator," writes Diane Prosser McDonald, we seek "objective thought." To uncover or wrest out from is to make available to sight, in a way not subject to the prejudices ostensibly interior to the subject. But she too notes the corporeal violence: "This gaze violates the body by attempting to confine or fix its meaning according to inner structures or essences."[62] In general, alternative conceptions of truth, conceptions not so dependent upon nonconsensual violence, would be preferable. But like so many workings of power, this one can be pushed to turning upon itself, to failure, with its strange attendant and humiliating pleasures, its not quite inadvertent modes of resistance.

However determined the unveiling, mystery has ways of remaining.[63] "Defacement is like Enlightenment," writes Michael Taussig, bringing this violent uncovering fully into the light of knowing. As he notes, however, the dis-covery runs into the impossibility of clarifying everything. It encounters a secret that remains. "It brings insides out, unearthing knowledge, and revealing mystery. As it does this, however, as it spoliates and tears at tegument, it may also animate the thing defaced and the mystery revealed may become more mysterious, indicating the curious magic upon which Enlightenment, in its elimination of magic, depends."[64] Reason, as much as the rational subject, needs what contradicts it, some otherness that keeps it from quite being whole, from being entirely successful; an otherness that emerges all the more stubbornly in the effort to undo it.

The ostensible objectivity of the natural sciences does not elude this practice of wresting and unveiling, as duBois points out; as early as the Hippocratic tradition, medicine attempts to interpret the body's interior, and so too we continue to diagnose.[65] Here, again, the precise and rational truth is infiltrated by the untidiness of desire. Chloë Taylor reminds us of a less acknowledged effect: "Doctors, like priests, become objects of desire through their interrogations into the desires and pleasures of their patients, and the whispering subject produces a desire for herself in her listener, and in herself pursues a desire for this desire of the other in her speech." This confessional whisper, however, is not only aural: "The medical gaze, not despite its objectivity but because of it, is sensualized, and the 'spirals of pleasure and power' of confession are multifold: exhibitionist, voyeuristic, masochistic."[66] We presume that the "objective" gaze can stare like a god, unblinking and thorough. A fully objective medical gaze might not shame us, but because no objectivity is pure, because the rational gaze is embodied in a curious human, we may be reluctant, or both reluctant and eager, thus to expose ourselves.

The desire to know, to see the secret beneath the skin, is unsatisfied by the sight of the nude body or the meat dress. It keeps going, motivating a deeper stripping, or an opening, of the skin itself—both through its given orifices and through created cuts. We open the body to extract the truth, as if truth were tumorous. Saints slash or blister their skin, cut it open with whips or scrape it off with hair shirts. To ameliorate "his own persistent desire, Ammonius 'heated an iron in the fire and applied it to his limbs, so that he became ulcerated all over' (11.1–4)," while Elfpidius "reached such a high degree of mortification and so wasted away his body that the sun shone through his bones" (48.3)—revealing his body's interior to those who gazed at it in the light.[67]

Eros too seeks to deepen the intimate gaze. Both overtly pornographic depictions and erotic practices of humiliation focus frequently upon the body's orifices—not always the expected ones—and upon opening them as widely as possible, as if to display and detail the interior of the body. Consider not just the spread legs of even the most vanilla pornography, but such imagistic practices as ass or nostril gaping, too. Vaginal and anal specula, dental retractors, and urethral sounds are all used as erotic toys as well as medical instruments, while nose hooks offer up nostrils for their own perverse purposes. In the arts as they flirt with pornography, we might make note of Sarah Lucas's "Chicken Knickers," which takes Angela's meat-draping a step farther, placing the split-open body of a plucked chicken carcass at the crotch of a woman in demure white panties,[68] or the bloody performance pieces of controversial Austrian artist Hermann Nitsch, featuring cruciform animals in the position of Christ. These meat-on-meat visuals tell us what even the most blunt *Penthouse*-style crotch shot cannot. They remind us that the intimacy—the interiority, the inwardness—of the body is carnal; its inside is opened or openable flesh. And they remind us that intimacy, once we get over pretending that it is invariably sweet and supportive, is at once violent and funny.[69] Our bodies are both sublime and a bit ridiculous, and while we could argue that their absurdity, like their filth, detracts from their arousal value—as it certainly can—the arousal, the absurdity, and the violence might just turn out to be inseparable. Humor is not far from humiliating derision. Ours is the absurdity of being agents who cannot be divorced from our physical objectivity, ours the violence of being unknowable unless we wrench ourselves open—to find what is never quite us, to find that there is an elusive remainder. We risk absurdity in revelation—we might be laughable or boring rather than desirable—and we create a kind of violence whenever the interior is revealed.

The flesh need not be blistered and sliced to have its limits crossed. Bodily fluids may also cross the boundaries that establish propriety, being made visible or public when we think they ought not to be, because they properly belong inside and so must be hidden away; perhaps because they are, as Jonathan Sawday asserts, "a prognostication of death, but one which, no matter how quickly dismissed or forgotten, holds the attention and, briefly, dare not even be named. The interior of the body is perceived by a trace which may also become a token, a harbinger of dissolution."[70] Thus, blood flows, but not only blood, out of the skin, across bodies and centuries. Liquids refuse to follow paths or hold to forms; they wash clean but flow with filth. Divinity emerges in impurity; the blood of a sacrificed lamb rinses the monk's heart free of night's concupiscent fluids.

Small wonder, then, that Bataille's fiction is so full of these liquids—in *Blue of Noon* alone we find tears, sweat, blood, urine, and vomit, each repeatedly.[71] *Story of the Eye* is so fluid-filled that the first question my students asked me, when I dared to teach it, was, "What is it with all the peeing?" At the limit, filth and purity flow together.

Here too, gender plays its part, though Bataille's male characters do shed their share of fluids. Elizabeth Grosz asks, "Can it be that in the West, in our time, the female body has been constructed not only as a lack or absence but with more complexity, as a leaking, uncontrollable, seeping liquid; as formless flow; as viscosity, entrapping, secreting . . . a formlessness that engulfs all form, a disorder that threatens all order?"[72] Catherine Clément, for her part, muses that "In many regions of the world, the feminine share of the sacred is tears."[73] So it is perhaps unsurprising that our saintly tales of bodily fluids, for all that they may originate in the image of a crucified male whose side gushes water and blood, are frequently stories of women. Consider the possibly fictive fourth-century saint Thaïs, an unusually desirable Egyptian courtesan. When a suspicious monk visits her to see who has caused so much quarrel and bloodshed among those seeking her favors, he asks if she does not fear for her soul, "as well as those of the young men she has led to damnation." Suddenly overwhelmed, Thaïs begs the monk for a suitable penance. Obligingly, he burns all of her goods and seals her into a small monastic cell, "and when she asks the monk where she is to urinate he charitably responds, 'In the cell, as you deserve.'"[74] Thaïs accepts this, along with further humiliation, in a sort of late ancient predecessor to all manner of water sports. Because the positions in these matters are never uncomplicated, urination may also be an act of domination, particularly when it is performed upon another. Not only may this put the other into the receptacle position of a disrespected object, the toilet, it may also put onto the exterior body an improper, interior fluid, a waste.

Besides expressing both dominance and submission, exteriorized fluids may be unexpectedly beneficial, and may, in flowing out of bodies and even across the bounds of subjects, abruptly reverse the humiliated position. We read of the third-century Anastasia: "When they stripped her naked, to humiliate her, she cried to the judge: 'Whip me and cut at me and beat me; my naked body will be hidden by wounds, and my shame will be covered by my blood.' She was whipped and beaten and cut about. . . . Then her breasts and tongue were cut off. . . . She was finally beheaded with the sword outside the city."[75] Here the display of the flesh is covered by what is more commonly held in, kept concealed, by that flesh, the blood from the newly opened wounds; her humiliating failure seems to become a chaste triumph. But it is a triumph in failure; where her humiliation fails, that of the torturers emerges. Their desire to know what is under the skin is frustrated, in no small part by the blood that would seem to be an answer, but proves to be another veil.

Anastasia's wounding ends in death, without the secret of carnal life having first been revealed: how can each inhere within the other? Abjection is our reaction to "the interlacing of life and death," writes Zeynep Direk, and religion "signifies the general movement of life, in which life and death pass into each other."[76] The saints may be humiliated or they may evade humiliation, passing it on to their interrogators, highlighting the prurient interest that the latter would wish to deny. In fact, hagiographic accounts often end abruptly after the body is humiliated, wounded, or opened as much as possible (even if opened and healed). Sometimes an interval of years is noted, but no events occupy it; the narrative may skip straight to death, where the body itself hovers at the boundary—and begins to leak, bleeding through the boundary of death and life (though saints' bodies sometimes signify their holiness precisely by refusing putrefaction).[77] There is no completion. Blanchot links the secret not to death, but to the impossibility of knowing-dying, as "the inevitable accomplishment of what is impossible to accomplish—and this would be dying itself."[78] But the secret, which is always in excess, exceeds dying too.

Fluids appear in visions as well as in martyrdom. When the medieval devotions to the Passion and wounds of Christ emerge, many saints-to-be pay particular attention to the spear wound in the side, entering into it or drinking from it as from the breast. Catherine of Siena is among those who envision both, entering Christ's body through the wound, and declaring that God "showed me from far away his holy side, and I cried with great desire to place my lips on the most sacred wound."[79] She will attempt to fulfill some measure of this desire by drinking the fluid from the sores of lepers, themselves both abject and wounded. Lepers are harder to find these days, but perverse pleasures may be found on either side of golden showers, urine drinking, or the ingestion of newly shed blood (some of the fluid in *Blue of Noon* is ingested, too, as when the narrator "press[es] two lips to her thigh and swallow[s] the few drops of blood I had just drawn.")[80]

In the marvelously titled *Yuck!*, Daniel Kelly tentatively offers some "candidate universals" for disgusting substances:

> [F]eces, vomit, blood, urine, and sexual fluids ... corpses and signs of organic decay.... Bodily orifices—and via contamination, things that come in contact with bodily orifices.... More generally, artificial orifices or breaches of physical bodies such as cuts, gashes, lesions, or open sores ... are also good candidates ... disgust appears universally sensitive to the boundaries of organic bodies and in many cases is activated when those boundaries have been, or are in danger of being, breached.
>
> .... Items and substances once within those boundaries, which were once inside or part of the body, but then exit or are detached from the body, constitute a related class of potentially universal elicitors of disgust. Severed limbs and externalized innards ... the waste products mentioned earlier ... blood and saliva.... Fingernails and hair are other good examples of body parts that are innocent enough when still attached, but become aversive once separated from a body—especially when they are in danger of reentering via the mouth.
>
> In this sense, disgust not only polices the boundaries of the body but also enforces a "no reentry" policy.[81]

Confession and display both risk disgust because they play with interior and exterior, courting their confusion and thus risking the violation of this policy. Opening, voiding, and reclaiming the flesh, whether in hagiography or pornographically, violates the policies of purity. Even the genres may fluidly blur. In Pelagia's tale, the element of dirt and bodily fluid becomes explicit: she soaks a monk's feet with her tears, wiping the muddy dirt onto herself. She calls herself debased and debasing names: a "ravenous vulture" a carrion eater, a consumer of loathsome rot; "a disgusting stone on which people have tripped up"—but upon which they must first be walking, with those dirty feet. "A deep ditch of mire," which scarcely needs our elaboration. "O I am a destructive moth," she says, "and I have gnawed into many bodies," feeding upon the flesh not meant for food; "I am an abyss of evils." She then begs the bishop to strip her of her dirty clothing, so that she may be redressed for baptism—but knowing as we do how struck he is with her beauty, we cannot help wondering if he might hesitate (or proceed too eagerly). It is a scene, as Burrus notes, so loaded with terms of abjection that it risks self-parody.[82]

The desire to know, to be able to say, "I see," is a desire to know more, to find the remainder of flesh that intermingles death with living, to find the site and the source of what leaks and flows—to find the humiliating, to abject the object and keep the subject intact. Yet in seeking to see, it always fails; the frustration, depending upon the rules of the game, may drive the participants farther into pleasure or lead them to end the frustration by ending the play itself, in a martyr's death.

INTIMATE DISTANCE

Immensity is within ourselves.

—Gaston Bachelard, *The Poetics of Space*

Abjection marginalizes, pushes away, spits out. For any of these to be possible, the abject must first be intimate—proximate, at least, or even interior, reminding us that our margins are not the fixed barriers for which we take them, that inside can harbor pushed-without at the same time. Gazing, we find that some distance remains. "'The unique appearance of a distance, no matter how close it may be,' . . . could also be a definition of the gaze, of what is raised in any gaze that is raised up toward us,"[83] writes Bailly. Yet there is, always, the unseen, invisible just as it might be "unutterable . . . through proximity."[84]

This is a strangeness about gazing: it is proximate, even when dispassionate; when passionate, it is intimate, but it relies upon the very distance it might try to overcome, the space-between that might reverse the gaze without closing the gap. Burrus reminds us that shame, which seems so necessarily public, "is also the most intimate and internal of emotions." Shame marks the place where "the limits of mutual exposure" meet.[85] The play of distance and fusion invokes proximity, a nearness that is not a unity. And proximity by itself may elicit disgust, as Aurel Kolnai writes, describing "the peculiar phenomenon whereby an object that of its nature would not be disgusting can under certain circumstances appear to be so through proximity—as in the case of satiety in regard to the associated pleasure, or of an abominated sexual approach in regard to the associated taste or body."[86] To gaze demands the intimate, proximate, uncloseable distance between the outside and us. We stare, we are ashamed, we cover, we uncover, we pry open, and we fail: to see, and to show, and to connect so perfectly that we are fused and ourselves and omniscient besides, all at once. "There is not one glance that does not hide a secret," writes Peignot.[87]

Peignot's quasi-autobiographical Laure offers the most intimate speech and details imaginable—the stripped, the confessed, the humiliated, in her revelation of shame and the shameful. She is always-revealed, like Angela, watched by the jealous God who follows her hands under her dress.[88] And yet she eludes: "I will never be where you think to find me,"[89] she declares. She remains arrogant, and mysterious. Like Angela, who strips before God, Laure could only open to the perfect and unwavering gaze; who knows what the voyeur might miss when blinking? She imagines such a gaze in human terms, but still finds that she has to include God to be certain: "[A] man made invisible by the famous ring watches me every second, God 'who sees all and knows all thoughts' watches me, severe."[90] And when "Laure had found God again," Peignot writes, "He was not a human being, she made him a hero, a saint, then she wanted him to hurt her, she imagined being beaten, thrashed, being wounded, a victim, humiliated, and then once again adored and sanctified."[91] Laure is on to her lovers; she knows *she* remakes them as God, and she knows her ever-gazing Gods to be of her own creation. She eludes, not caught (unaware or by surprise) after all; in her elusiveness, she seduces. She is never there where one thinks to find her.

The fictitious Laure is an abject ideal. Even God or a divinized lover can see only that abjection, as Bataille long ago told us, cannot be seen, any more than it can be named in description—thus, it remains stubbornly secret. "It is impossible to give a positive definition which is both general and explicit, of the nature of abject things," Bataille declares. We can only list or describe them, or offer a negative definition of them "as objects of the imperative act of exclusion."[92] What is more, human abjection "is simply the inability to assume with sufficient force the imperative act of excluding abject things (which constitutes the foundation of collective existence). Filth, snot and vermin are enough to render an infant vile; his personal nature is not responsible for it."[93] But there is an important distinction between this inability and irresponsibility on the one hand and perversely desired abjection on the other, he adds. Such general abjection as the child's "is formally distinct from sexual perversions in which abject things are cultivated and which derives from subversion."[94] To *cultivate* the discarded is a search for failure, a quest to be found vile or lacking in force. If perverse eroticism subverts, it is in some measure by refusing to value success.

In the embrace of the abject, we find the sacred. William Burgwinkle and Cary Howie explain: "Both pornography and hagiography mobilize this distinction between the subject and the impossible object in order, temporarily, to undo it. The body on display, when fused with the viewer's desire, can appear extra-human: paradoxically invincible or utterly abject."[95]

This paradox is not a simple fusion of a dual body and the spirit, nor a denial or overcoming of one or the other. It is, rather, a carnal mystery. Milo Sweedler, who may not much approve of Peignot's perversity, tells us that she is "undoubtedly irrecuperable to a feminism that wishes to propagate positive images of women." After this discouraging pronouncement, however, he acknowledges that there is "another current in feminism." And it is a current of mystery: "The twist by which Laure's degradation leads to her sanctification inscribes her fantasies—and perhaps her life—in a long tradition of French mystics, recently claimed by a number of French feminists. Indeed, this mystical tradition is . . . itself feminine."[96] Not necessarily female, to be sure; like male masochists, monks and male ascetics may be feminized or exceedingly masculine, or may play with the relations and identities between them. Sweedler cites Luce Irigaray's description of the woman "chaste for having faced the worst perversions, for having prostituted herself to the most disgusting acts, the most filthy and excessive acts."[97] Purity and danger not only meet, they commingle, in the mystery or the secret, in what remains after we would swear that there is nothing left to see, to say, to show, in "what cannot ultimately be touched, rejoined, repaired or redeemed."[98]

Mystery is not immaterial. But in an understanding that dates back at least to Aristotle, matter is always in synthesis with form; we can think neither unformed matter nor immaterial formation. Bataille links abjection—though in an indirect fashion and in an (appropriately) incomplete and posthumously published text—to what he calls the *informe*. What most nearly appears as the truly monstrous, the form that cannot even be comprehended, is the unformed: materiality itself. Recall the formlessness that Grosz attributes to femininity; neither quite deformed nor simply malformed, the *informe* threatens the order of forms themselves. The unformed is the elusiveness of matter, the unstable betweenness of knowable formations. In Bataille's *informe,* all parts are dis-placed; all space becomes space between, but there are no stable subjects and objects to mark the limits, and the monstrous unformed always seems to overflow into a disturbing proximity.

Abjection is not merely displaced or out of place, but troublingly unplaceable, refusing inside or out. I abject the remainder that is nonetheless the trace of myself, matter that impossibly escapes from stable form. Blood, tears, and urine—all of them more or less shameful—flow liquidly out of flesh, harden and evaporate, are washed away or eagerly left behind. What we struggle to see is not only the traces of matter's motion. It is, rather, the unplaceable movement and space of the incarnate mystery, always seeming to be nearby, never quite *here.* We seek to make the resistant into the speakable, into the knowable and properly conceptualizable, not into this irritatingly slippery and fluid confrontation with what eludes us. We gaze avidly, or avidly draw the gaze to, shame and remnant and the very interior of the flesh. Yet only further questions open. Shame remains. We peer in, and our monstrosity peers back at us.

THE DOUBLE ENTRY GAZE

Why did you put mirrors in their eyes?
    —Detective Will Graham, *Red Dragon*

Among the ways in which boundaries are troubled, the reversibility of gazing is one of the most intriguing: if one sees into another's body, perhaps the secret of flesh will show up after all, even as the secret of one's own. The knowledge-demanding gaze of the one who stares and asks and demands seeks to go beyond the limits of vision not only by invading the known body, but by reversing and thereby doubling the seeing gaze: seeking the secrets of the bared and opened body, the body at the margins rendered abject and monstrous, the voyeur looks into the heart of the flesh. Howie and Burgwinkle write, "[I]n the case of the ecstatic or pornographic body . . . we are encouraged to view the image more from a myopic point of view, using a kind of surgical gaze that tries to touch the surface or even invade it, all with the intent of opening up the viewer him- or herself to potential invasion."[99] Rather than maintaining a disinterested aesthetic distance, vision may be pushed and pulled toward a double penetration—most of all before the flesh. Perhaps, if the desire for knowledge is strong enough, it could overcome the necessary distance of proximity, and get all the way inside?

In much of early Christian and pagan thought, to know the divine is to be known, until the very terms of knowing, the differentiation between knower and known, come undone. There are even visual metaphors: "The eye with which I see god is the same with which God sees me. My eye and God's eye is one eye, and one sight, and one knowledge, and one love,"[100] writes Meister Eckhart, carrying this claim into the fourteenth century. As optical theory develops, the Middle Ages present us with a more "scientifically" grounded reversibility. In a combination of ancient theories of intromission and extramission—visual power or force traveling from object to eye or vice versa—theorists such as Al-Kindi and, much later, Francis Bacon hold that both have elements of truth;[101] thus, Howie and Burgwinkle can remind us of the "medieval sense that visual penetration always goes both ways."[102]

This sense of the dual gaze returns in the work of Jacques Lacan, for whom gazing is at once anxious and pleasurable, active and passive: the object seen, without ceasing to be object, nonetheless gazes back, tells me of my self (it makes me self-conscious). Lacan associates this reversible gaze with both the voyeuristic will to see and the exhibitionistic will to be seen.[103] The voyeur looks into the heart of the flesh—but cannot quite see it, after all.

Bataille in his fictions even goes so far as to place eyes into orifices—*The Story of the Eye*'s Simone inserts the eye of a dead priest into her vagina, as if to show it directly the secrets that it was forbidden to see in life.[104] But of course, only an eye freed from one body can go into another body, and those eyes are no longer seeing. The penetrating gaze runs into something, no thing, not quite a barrier, not quite a limit, not even, quite, a deflection, but the nonvisible, the unpresentable. Seeking oneself in the sight of another body, one cannot quite see or know what refuses inside or out, the remainder that is nonetheless the trace of oneself.

Gazes cross even when the positions of subject and object seem to be clear (I am surrounded by a world that gazes back). Sedgwick notes that the protoform of shame—the physical response that later links with the feeling—first appears in infancy as "the moment when the adult face fails or refuses to play its part in the continuation of mutual gaze; when, for any one of many reasons, it fails to be recognizable to, or recognizing of, the infant who has been, so to speak, 'giving face' based on a faith in the continuity of this circuit."[105] Framed in only slightly different terms, this is the Freudian moment of ego-emergence; the infant begins to sense its own, bounded self when nurture and nourishment are unexpectedly absent. Things, it realizes, have edges; this is how we come to pick objects out of the blooming, buzzing confusion of the world.[106] We seek ourselves not only in other bodies, but in the surfaces of mirrors and the mirroring gaze by which we know ourselves seen. To know the secret would be to reflect it, or at least to be capable of reflecting it. But there is a mystery in the mirror, too, the breakable gaze of an imperfectly integrated body, ensuring the imperfection of self-knowing— and of knowing the selves of others.[107] Lacanian thought links abjection directly to the return of the world's gaze; the child who gathers together her image of a whole and bounded self while gazing at her reflection may feel that more than this reflection gazes back. "I see only from one point," Lacan writes, "but in my existence I am looked at from all sides."[108] He draws upon Merleau-Ponty to add, "We are beings who are looked at, in the spectacle of the world. . . . Is there no satisfaction in being under that gaze of which . . . I spoke just now, that gaze that circumscribes us, and which in the first instance makes us beings who are looked at?[109] Satisfaction and vulnerability, pride and humiliation, entangle. I cannot quite see myself being seen. By acknowledging the inwardness of another, the invisibility of the remainder, secrecy dispossesses vision.

NOTHING TO SEE

> You're invisible now;
> You've got no secrets
> To conceal.
>
> —Bob Dylan, "Like a Rolling Stone"

Shame may be linked not only to being seen, but to going unseen. The will to know is also the will to be known, to turn upon oneself as the object of knowledge, and this demands that one be *worth* knowing, much as confession demands that one be worth listening to. Both the hypervisibility of the bared and opened body and the invisibility of the insignificant body can shame us. Though both can enter into the play of pleasurable humiliation, the latter is perhaps more difficult. There are those who are aroused by being conspicuously ignored, as Severin is when Wanda dines without acknowledging him. Usually, for arousal to emerge, the one ignored must know that the neglect is itself intentional (and thus has its own tension built into it); this complicates the shame of being so uninteresting or disgusting that others turn away.

Otherwise, we pass less pleasurably from one form of shame to another, even a greater, especially when the transition from fascination to disdain or shared embarrassment is clear. Our desire to hide is provoked when others try not to see us.[110] In her *Autobiography of a Face*, Lucy Grealy is pleased at first with her dramatic surgical scar, but "soon becomes schooled in the pedagogy of mortification. Although at first when people stare at her she feels that she is special and that she has a kind of power because other people notice her, she also becomes aware that when she catches adults staring at her, they get embarrassed and quickly look away."[111] They react to her hypervisibility by quickly rendering her invisible instead. Any body that is socially disapproved—over or undersized, disabled, "inappropriate" in movement or pigment or dress—can turn away gazes. "If hiding is a classic defense against shame . . . a fat woman [] is hypervisible and cannot 'hide' her fat,"[112] writes J. Brooks Bouson, but people may also turn quickly from fat women, and there is a mainstream denial of any desire to gaze on fat flesh (though of course the desire is not unusual). The goal of hiding as part of the shame affect is to prevent further exposure and with that, further rejection, but hiding also atones for the exposure that has already occurred. In fact, punishment coming from the outside may consist not only in further exposure, such as derision and public humiliation, but also, or instead, in the demand to expiate by hiding, to fulfill the desire expressed as "I don't want to see you anymore." (Or at all: "shameful" traits must not be "flaunted.") Extremes of hypervisibility and invisibility alike are shaming. If the voyeur is embarrassed and turns away, the possibility of pleasure is broken—truly shared shame is not usually pleasurable, nor is genuine disinterest.[113]

Bouson describes the shame of invisibility as it appears in Toni Morrison's *The Bluest Eye*: "[I]n the vacant gaze of the white store owner, Mr. Yacobowski, Pecola senses racial contempt. 'He does not see her, because for him there is nothing to see.'"[114] Here, no one turns away, but the failure of one's appearance to register can be as shameful as any appearing. As Wurmser has it, "If it is appearance (exposure) that is central in shame, disappearance is the logical outcome of shame."[115] One struggles to avoid both: an appearance that puts an end to the need to know more, and a disinterest that keeps knowledge from being desired.

This doubleness keeps pride pulling on shame, keeps the paradox open and alive. We desire both to be seen and to harbor further mystery, to be unseeable and to be before the eyes of all, to fascinate the viewer endlessly and to keep our secrets. "Shame is primarily exhibitionistic," says Paul de Man, and this exhibitionism need not be unintended.[116] Exhibitionism and voyeurism, like the revised liturgy, direct the gaze—but this time to what is "inappropriate," to what is not conventionally given for seeing. Yet here, as at the moment of the elevated host, the viewer strains to see a mystery, and the exhibitionist to show the same. The double desire to stare and to turn aside is further complicated when we want to display what shames—and to keep the other from looking away or feeling ashamed as well. We want to display, and to blush, without shame's contagion. The gaze that disdainfully or embarrassedly slides away and the gaze that never registers are failures of the gaze that feeds our knowledge. Like the too-intense stare, they can play into shaming. As with other humiliations, this may in turn feed a perverse pleasure, or it may simply be saddening. If pleasure is to be possible, the demands of desire must be especially strong.

LOOKING AT A MYSTERY

I'm convinced we're all voyeurs. We want to know secrets, we want to know what goes on behind those windows.

—David Lynch

The complex of hyper- and in-visibility, of seeing and being seen, of the search for reflection and the restraint of the eyes, has very old links to the secret. Classically, the *mysterion* is characterized by esotericism, not by genre (it may be text, doctrine, object, or rite). It is not to be revealed to the uninitiated, to those who are not members of the group or even those who are not members at a sufficiently high level. Sometimes it is concealed in plain sight by densely coded texts or visual symbols. We, most of us, are not supposed to look, not supposed to know.

As soon as we learn that we are not supposed to look, we want to do exactly that—as Aristotle knew. Where firsthand knowledge of mysteries proved unavailable, Church fathers were obligingly creative. In his exhortation to the Greeks, Clement of Alexandria extensively describes and condemns the practices of non-Christian mystery religions. Knowing full well that he isn't supposed to discuss these mysteries, he declares defiantly that he shall "thoroughly lay [them] bare" and "display them" for "spectators of the truth."[117] He will "tell openly the secret things"[118] Having done so, he immediately goes on to compare these mysteries, with considerable exegetical vigor, to orgies, in both the sexual and the more broadly frenzied sense.[119] Lest we assume that the rites he describes are purely symbolic, Clement assures us that "night is for those who are being initiated a temptation to licentiousness . . . and the torch-fires convict unbridled passions."[120] What is hidden from sight must be linked to the intersections of sanctity and lust. Why else, the accusers seem to wonder, would practices be kept secret, if not because they are shameful? Irenaeus, the famous chronicler of heresies, accuses several "heretical" Christian sects of both excessive secrecy and varied licentiousness. His invective against the Valentinians is exemplary: they "yield themselves up to the lusts of the flesh with the utmost greediness."[121] "Some of them, moreover, are in the habit of defiling those women to whom they have taught the doctrine. . . . Others of them . . . having become passionately attached to certain women seduce them away from their husbands, and contract marriages of their own with them."[122] Raynaldus assures us of the later Albigensians, "Those who were called believers of the heretics were given to usury, rapine, homicide, lust,

perjury and every vice; and they, in fact, sinned with more security, and less restraint, because they believed that ... they should be saved, if only, when on the
point of death, they could say a Pater noster, and receive imposition of hands from
the teachers."[123]

It is hard to tell, sometimes, if what infuriates the opponents of "heresy" is
a particular mysterious practice or just the very fact that it is hidden. Tertullian
writes quite remarkably of the Valentinians:

> These individuals care about nothing more than to conceal what they
> teach—if indeed anyone who conceals can be said to teach. Their duty
> of guardianship is a duty brought on by their guilty consciences. ...
> [T]he fact that they keep silent about these mysteries make them an
> object of shame. Consequently the mystagogues make entry difficult and
> perform long initiation rites before they accept the devotee; they put
> him on probation for five years in order to increase his anticipation
> by suspense and in this manner cause the awesomeness of their rites
> to match the desire which has been elicited. Their duty of secrecy is a
> natural consequence; they guard closely what they are finally to reveal.
> Then—the entire godhead of the sanctuary, the object of devoted sighs,
> the secret signed on all tongues: the image of a penis.[124]

That the Valentinians seem in fact to have been a little ascetic, deeply literate,
and poetically Christian holds little power against the notion that they worship
the image of a penis, the object of a desire cultivated and intensified by prolonged
anticipation, kept secret only to heighten the desire, and consequently emphasizing the shame. Somehow alive, detached from the rest of the body, the penis presents a monstrous picture: no wonder, Tertullian implies, that its obscenity is kept
so long concealed. Tertullian's link of secrecy to shame is intriguing because, on his
reading, it is not shame that silences the Valentinians, but secrecy that makes the
mysteries shameful. Shame attends to what we cannot see, as to what we cannot
say, or will.

The accused both conceal and reveal too much. Their accusers conflate two
senses of the forbidden—the naughty with the secretive—and then conflate both
with the unknowable divine mystery, the untellable secret. These conflations are
errors, but they might be less distant than we think from a genuine, incarnational
sense of mystery or secret—the intersection of the double sacred and the perversely erotic, the impossible pursuit of knowledge in its failure.

Like the abbot's ear and the heresiologist's mind, the pervert's gaze is greedy,
refusing to stop at a fixed or confined truth, demanding further openings and
revelations. In this refusal, in this demand for infinitude in the finite, the character
of the sacred is revealed. There are both shame and veneration in the peripheral

almost-glimpse of a mystery. The shameful is another pole of the sacred. Richard Burton writes that Peignot's

> life is torn between . . . on the one hand, the *sacré de droite*—the noble, positive sacred embodied for Colette in the images of Jesus and Joseph and all the other holy pictures around her, "blue, pink, gilt, surrounded by stars, silk-wrapped and be-ribboned"—and, on the other, the *sacré de gauche*: that which must be shunned and abhorred, bodily products such as mucus, excrement and sweat, the body itself, and above all its nether regions that God—who sees everything—must never see a little girl touch and examine, even in the attic in which she hides herself away.[125]

The good is wrapped up and properly enclosed, so that we know inside from out; the bad is abjection exemplified, poured out of the body. But neither quite holds without the other. In a religion for which the founding myth is one of divine embodiment, a sense of carnal mystery is not particularly bizarre—but it is quite difficult to regulate. Secrets in general are like that, and so are bodies. Derrida writes, "[I]t is not a matter of knowing and . . . it is there for no-one. A secret doesn't belong, it can never be said to be at home or in its place."[126] The secret of the gaze, like gazing itself, is reversible, unplaceable. Not only do we never see what we sought, but we never quite know what is seen. We can neither say nor show enough. Those hungry for humiliation seek the secret too; the abyss that gazes back seems always to be just one layer farther in. Such is the desire that Jean Baudrillard calls obscene, "when all becomes transparence and immediate visibility, when everything is exposed to the harsh and inexorable light of information and communication." He contrasts this with an older understanding, in which obscenity is "of what is hidden, repressed, forbidden, or obscure." Instead, this is "the obscenity of the visible . . . obscenity of what no longer has any secret, of what dissolves completely in information and communication."[127] But here I would suggest again that seeking the unknowable through the forbidden, the improper, obscene, or scandalous, is not (solely) a fallacious conflation, but an incarnational sense of mystery or secret. Baudrillard's new obscenity fails before the old. Perhaps, even, the pleasure of the obscene is in its failure.

The new obscenity would put an end to the secret, publicizing it at the very surface of the skin. In this sense, though, the obscene will always give way to the seductive: secrets, not least those of the body, are far more stubborn than we think. In his essay "Whatever You Do is a Delight to Me!" Robert Mills writes, "'Queer wishes' is a phrase invented by Simon Gaunt to describe those textual repudiations of same-sex desire that, while professedly functioning as definitional markers of the heterosexual matrix, also 'fail to occlude what they seek to repress.'"[128] In the gaze as it functions for martyrs and masochists, there is a queer reversal of this queerness: what the viewer and exhibitor seek to show remains nonetheless in shadow. Angela might enjoy the thought of her walk of shame, but as a mechanism of revelation, it remains imperfect: the flesh she reveals by covering it with meat layered with words is hidden beneath them, too. The meat outside her skin never maps perfectly, even with labels, onto the meat within; never fully displays its shameful desires.

Both the one who exhibits, opening the body to scrutiny, and the one who looks, sideways at the heart through the window of the wound, are doing a great many things, of course, but one thing they are doing is trying, with the desperation of all impossible desires (which is to say: with the fervor of all of eros and all religion) to see and to show. To see the mystery, to show the secret: to know what cannot be known, to know that unknowing is. The body attracts the gaze; ears listen to its tales, eager hands strip it bare; assistive technologies and divine interventions alike serve to open it up—yet it eludes us. The urgent search for revelation reverses: in revealing the body, we seek to invite within us the mystery that the ascetic, mystic, masochist, or martyr seems to know so surely within her own flesh—only to find that the seeming is no more than that; this knowing is only in the elusive manner of the mysterious. It is easier just to ignore it. But sometimes easy is just too boring.

When it is, shame becomes shameless. Hungry for reversible seeing, touching, knowing, the humiliated and the humiliator alike seek the truth, as if we could find the mystery in the forbidden publicizing of skin, as if the interior were somehow a secret site, and not simply another shifting and changing and reversing layer; as if we could undo the wrappings of the good sacred and not lose everything in a mad flowing forth. In this very elusiveness, however, the body, always withdrawing its truth from even the most sadistically or lasciviously attentive gaze, the most persistent interrogation, is a revelation of mystery: not of the answer to the question, but of the infinite immanence, the deeply superficial indwelling, of the question itself. All people by nature desire to know—but some people by nature desire to want to know, possibly even more. Some desire is too strong to be satisfied by satisfaction. So it seeks failure, and fails to find it.

What we seek to see and hear, through that urgent reversible double gaze, through hearing our voices pulled out of ourselves, is not the urine in the cell, the blood on skin, the shame written, if not on the flesh, at least on a placard hung around the naked body. We seek, rather, to make the resistant into the properly conceptualizable, not into this irritatingly slippery confrontation with what eludes us. We want to be able to say, with satisfaction, "Yes, I see." We gaze avidly, or avidly draw the gaze to, shame and remnant and the very interior of the flesh. We keep asking questions, keep pushing for what will refuse to yield and to answer. Yet only further questions open. We depend upon it; the desire to know, too, may be bored by satisfaction. The secret that there is no secret, drawn to the flesh that speaks it, twists just enough to reveal the secret that there are always more secrets. In the play between the unsayable and the not-to-be-said, the unshowable forbidden and the invisible secret, a mystery is drawn out and it draws us in, in a reversible and no longer perfectly closable opening. Body displayed, flesh broken tells the very secret that it keeps. The body holds secrets—but it does not reveal them to the eye, or the ear, or the knife. Once more, what remains defies the stability of inside and out, and the desire to know gains power from its failure.

FIVE

Undignified

FAILURES OF FLESH

VULNERABLE DIGNITY

Have you ever tried to get to your feet with a sprained dignity?
—Madeleine L'Engel, *A Wrinkle in Time*

Dignity is always at risk in humiliation. As we saw in discussing obedience, the risk has usually been understood as a threat to the autonomy of rational and capable beings. Slowly, however, ethicists have come to realize that overvaluing autonomy at the expense of interconnection poses its own ethical risks. Our deep relationality suggests that there is more to dignity than just self-rule or the development of our own capabilities. Theorists such as Debra Bergoffen and Ellen Feder have argued in favor of grounding dignity not in sturdy autonomy but *in*—not despite—our fragile corporeality and mutual vulnerability. While neither discusses consensual humiliation, their more nuanced theories of dignity may give us tools for further exploring such odd pleasures.

In her analysis of rape as a war crime and a human rights violation, Bergoffen argues against predicating dignity on autonomy alone. Such a predication, she argues, is born out of "a desire to escape the risks of being vulnerable."[1] Instead, dignity arises *in* our shared "embodied vulnerability."[2] Fully embodied, we find dignity in sensuousness, in desire, in bodily connection.[3] Bergoffen makes explicit a potential paradox: "[M]y dignity belongs to me as a subject in the world," she writes, "and is in the hands of others insofar as I am an object in their world."[4] Because I am always and necessarily both, my dignity is inalienable and fragile at once. Like dignity, the play with shame and failure is grounded in this tension.

Working with delicate precision on the fraught question of care for inter-sex children, Feder extends Bergoffen's analysis into an important alteration of the Kantian grounding of dignity in freedom. Feder begins by noting that par-ents often want, even overwhelmingly, to diminish their children's vulnerability.[5] Such vulnerability is necessarily shared, familial; no good parent is indifferent to the possibility of a child's pain or sadness.[6] To accept a child's dignity, however, is also to accept a parent's vulnerability—not least *to* the vulnerable child. This acceptance must mean not only that parents accept their children and keep them safe—something most will do eagerly—but that they also accept and protect their children's vulnerability, even knowing that the parents may thereby be exposed to hurt. There is a dignity in remaining vulnerable that is lost if we try too hard to secure everyone in the name of an abstract autonomy.[7] Rather than attempting to secure in advance against every possibility of pain, we respect dig-nity by allowing the body and the future their genuine openness, their possible unfoldings—which will, of necessity, run sometimes into obstacles and harm. This embodied vulnerability does suggest the necessity of certain protections and modes of care, as in the ethical uses that Feder and Bergoffen make of it. But such protection does not shut off all risk in advance, or fortify boundaries against any incursion.

This respect becomes particularly urgent with an increasing caution and re-striction in discourse, meant to ward off discomfort and to make everyone feel safe and at ease. These are laudable goals, though they seem to be easy to respect only when one's own views might be threatened. They appear all the more laud-able when they are mocked by those whose intentions are hostile—those who want to make sure that safe spaces exist only for the groups who have least needed them historically. But this safety comes at the cost of vulnerability, as professor Laura Kipnis noted in a 2015 essay that was swiftly condemned by students: "The feminism I identified with as a student stressed independence and resilience. In the intervening years, the climate of sanctimony about student vulnerability has grown too thick to penetrate."[8] In the defensiveness on both sides of the fraught territory of protective rules and trigger warnings, we guard not only against harm, as we should, but against vulnerability too. Hostile approaches sneer at protection as an indication of undue fragility, suggesting that what is needed is not protec-tion but a thicker skinned and less vulnerable populace; sympathetic approaches risk allowing the skin to thin to the extent of letting nothing touch it. On both approaches—avoid all harm or become invulnerable—we forget to guard vulner-ability itself. Such guarding seems to require a depth of respect for human dignity that is too demanding for many people.

Kipnis's concern also reminds us of a particularly bewildering point: that we respect vulnerability and strength only together. This is nothing so simple as the claim that in being wounded we develop strength, or that strength is what keeps us from woundedness. It is, rather, that what cannot be wounded is in no intelligible sense strong, just as what cannot be resisted is in no intelligible sense powerful. Burrus describes the vulnerable dignity of the second-century martyr Polycarp: "Having been led to the pyre, Polycarp strips off his clothes, but it is less his shameful exposure than his poignant fumbling with his shoes that reveals the inherent vulnerability of dignity to shame, the dependence of dignity on the possibility of shame."[9] Someone with no dignity cannot be shamed by fumbling, by stripping, by anything at all. Dignity must be susceptible, vulnerable. "Shame thus clings to the vulnerability of flesh,"[10] Burrus writes. Conversely, to be shameless is undignified, though one might not especially care about it. It is hard enough to acknowledge that dignity is not respected in all protection, that we can actually disrespect capacities by making them unnecessary. It is harder still to make sense of the perversity of a desire that seeks out of strength the exploitation of one's own vulnerability.

The fragility of flesh echoes dignity's vulnerability to command, interrogation, or exposure. In shameful exposure, one is both publicized and isolated, as if presented from behind some sort of translucent barrier. We may respond to shame with indignation, and we often respond to indignity with shame. Dignity is likewise vulnerable insofar as it depends upon propriety, whether it is of conduct, place, or appearance. The dignity that demands the protection of vulnerability itself is, I would argue, respected in both asceticism and erotic play—because it is the strength of vulnerability that grounds both kinds of practices, and is stubbornly sustained in them. But this connection is no resolution; I do not want to claim that ultimately these matters are as simple as any other mode of respect, nor to assume the agreement of any of the ethicists whom I've cited.

Approaching dignity through autonomy, we encountered the peculiar freedom of obedience. If we follow Martha Nussbaum's ethical modification of approaching dignity as demanding the development of capacities, we must consider negative capability. As the term was first used by the Romantic poet John Keats, negative capability encompasses "being in uncertainties, mysteries, doubts, without any irritable reaching after fact and reason."[11] Keats's examples, Shakespeare and Coleridge, indicate that he has artistic abilities specifically in mind, but the willingness to be in mystery and uncertainty is certainly relevant to other practices motivated by unknowing, entangled in secrets and searching. That one does not "reach irritably after" does not mean that one fails entirely to reach; Keats goes on to admire Coleridge for "being incapable of remaining content with half-knowledge."[12] Social theorist Roberto Unger argues for an understanding of negative capability as "the empowerment that arises from the denial of whatever in our contexts delivers us over to a fixed scheme of division and hierarchy and to an enforced choice between routine and rebellion."[13] Such is the curious power of failure, where there is no direct resistance, only an impossible imperative. The resonance with dignity is perhaps even more intriguing here, as these negative capabilities refuse hierarchy, seeming to offer the option of dignity irrespective of position.[14] We must consider as well the active ability to undergo, so often seen as merely passive or even as an inability; that is, again we must consider the dignity of vulnerability itself. This ability is prized among many who submit to another's imperatives with the aim of humiliation; there is always pride in being able to withstand more shame. Valuing negative as well as more evidently active capabilities, valuing the ability to undergo, disallows a simple verticality or hierarchy of dignity—but not the possibility of playing upon it. In the play with propriety of place, we necessarily disrupt as well the rationality of autonomy; it is not from reason, but from desire, that the force of pleasures and pains arises, that the refusal of fixed schemes is made possible.

Hélène Cixous, in an interview with Mireille Calle-Gruber, points this out with typical grace. "With the person we love, we have a relationship of absolute vulnerability.... In love we know we are at the greatest risk and at the least great risk, at the same time."[15] Cixous resists the irreparability of the word *breaking*; "But there is wounding," she says, and for her the term has a fleshier resonance.[16] To play intentionally with wounding is risky, but the risk is never quite separable from eros. All shame is in interplay with vulnerability. It risks being purely destructive. We can only sustain the possibility of the paradox that begins in the multiple directions of desire, and pulls the wound open in order to regard its inexplicable beauty.

Vulnerability is the possibility of failure—the failure of boundary, of autonomy, of propriety. The priceless value of living things *must* be fragile: otherwise, it could, like a price, be fixed in sturdy stability. The notion that there is dignity in vulnerability is not simply a nicety, nor a cliché. The desire *for* vulnerability, the desire that emphasizes vulnerability and that even wounds, is not simply a destruction of dignity. But the relationship, as we repeatedly find, is deeply complicated. In the rest of this chapter, I want to explore ways in which a few further practices of humiliation undermine various conventions of dignity—especially those of propriety in hierarchy and order among classes, ages, genders, and more, through complex ways of playing with performance.

DISGUST, LAUGHTER, AND ASSIMILATION: DENYING THE THREAT OF SHAME

> There was no area of my mind
> not appalled by this action, no part of my body
> that could have done otherwise.
>
> —Anne Carson, "The Glass Essay"

Vulnerability is essential not only to dignity but, more self-evidently, to eros. Erotic vulnerability is proximate to disgust. There is something persistently intriguing about disgusting things, and persistently humiliating about our interest.

Kolnai writes, "There is without doubt a certain invitation hidden in disgust as a partial element. . . . [N]ot only is an aversion to its object characteristic of disgust, but also a superimposed attractedness of the subject toward that object."[17] Kolnai calls the disgusting "both invitation and deterrent, both inducement and threat," each provoking the other to greater extremes. Disgust pushes us away from what we would otherwise seize, but the urge to take hold does not disappear.[18] We easily recognize here the movement of interest and revulsion that both Aristotle and Augustine remark. Kolnai argues that "disgust sows itself substantially in the fact that the object signifies to the subject at one and the same time both life and death . . . and draws both tightly towards it."[19] The movement of blood over the skin has already shown us some of this strange doubleness. The paradoxical signification gives pleasure-in-disgust a strange sustaining power, allowing an unusual intensity of sensation and hinting at impossible knowledge of death in living. Kolnai notes, for instance, that we might seek out unfamiliar, possibly disturbing or strangely flavored foods, "as a way to increase the potency of the taste experience."[20] Our recoil becomes appetite without the revulsion disappearing.[21] Our very senses seem to respond more strongly when part of what pulls at them is pushing them away.

Kolnai also links this duality to what he calls "disordered sexuality," "all that is disorderly, unclean, clammy, the unhealthy *excess* of life."[22] By this standard, Peignot exemplifies such disorder. Milo Sweedler writes of her relationship with her lover Boris Souvarine, "One has the impression that Laure is neither repulsed by nor—and perhaps for that reason—particularly attracted to Souvarine. He, for his part, allegedly 'represses his disgust,' rather than, to Laure's implicit disappointment, converting it into attraction."[23] Her disappointment arises not because of revulsion, but because Souvarine's uncomplicated, unexpressed disgust cannot play into the surplus she seeks, into her desire for too much.

Our inability to turn away becomes itself a source of fascination. It is not that the desire for knowledge simply overcomes the desire to end the sensation, but that each desire, caught in the other, is thus frustrated and sustained, and thereby heightened. We are not seeking simple information: we look, listen, or taste because in the abject and overspilling, where life and death are drawn tightly, they also approach one another. We look, as if maybe in too much life we could know what makes living, as if in overripe decay we could understand death. We look for a mystery, and even just looking unsettles us.

We may seek out not only what revolts us, but that which is repulsed *by* us. Amalia Ziv writes in "Shameful Fantasies," "For a lesbian to want sex with a gay man means flirting with the possibility of being found unlovable, of being shamed by someone one desires and perhaps identifies with. This risk of rejection is also the flip side of the pleasure of transgression."[24] The long-troubled realm of identity politics (what is a proper lesbian doing wanting sex with any

man, anyway?) is troubled further by shame, further still by the deliberate shaming of humiliation.

The culturally valued stable identity can be shored up by defenses against
the contestation of our selves. Nathanson rightly argues that comedy is a fairly
reliable defense against shame, meant to secure the border between shame and
pride.[25] This safety is particularly threatened when we are exposed before those
with whom we already feel unsafe, where embarrassment becomes humiliation.
We might provoke laughter on purpose to avoid laughter that threatens.[26] Laughter, though, can also dismiss what the viewer does not want to see, a shame that
is demanding to be shown. Neil Bartlett writes, "There's a very dangerous thing
in current pornography ... where the bottom is always a kind of cheerful joke."[27]
This is a danger when one simply laughs at a particular role or position; it is dangerous, too, when one laughs to avoid the discomfort in which one is being asked
(or tempted) to dwell. Even cheerful laughter might conceal contempt, a sneer of
superior disgust that denies being enticed as well. There is even a genre of humor
in which laughter is deliberately evoked by disgust, the gross-out joke so beloved
of preadolescents.

It is humiliating to be laughed at, and yet we may seek derisive rather than
comforting laughter. Or we may struggle not to seek laughter, not to back away
from the intensity of the humiliation by making a joke of it. It is humiliating
to be found disgusting, to be abject, and yet we may seek abjection. That such
perversion will generally be rejected is necessary to it: in assimilation it loses its
disgustingness and its risibility, and without these resistances its pleasure becomes
nonviable. The resistance that perverse and ascetic pleasure requires should not be
confused with resistance for its own sake, most often encountered in the life stages
that demand distancing or differentiation, such as toddlerhood or adolescence. In
those more nearly universal stages resistance is part of the effort to establish an
individuated self; in the more complex versions, we lose the neatness of the self
in an engagement with failure that resists even failure's own completion. The particular indignities that I shall discuss below exemplify this distinction, even when
they include those infantilizing roles.

The careful unraveling of threat emerges in more theoretical and political
discourse as well. The feminist "sex wars" of the 1970s and '80s, taking on pornography and sex work as well as bdsm, were, surely, well decided by the 1990s,
giving way to a relaxed libertarianism, leaving us more easily jaded than shocked.
Yet when Nathanson pathologizes shame as a mode of masochism in 1993, he is
both more anachronistic and more timely than we might expect. "I know of no
episode of masochistic behavior that is free of shame," he writes. "What passes for
delight in the suffering of the masochist is the anticipatory positive affect mask-
ing the pain experienced during an activity that is intended to assure bonding."[28]
There is no real delight in this passing. Nathanson views shame as a failure of love

and communion, an "abject state of isolation."[29] Rather than a complex pleasure in the depths of failure, Nathanson sees masochistic shame as seeking to end itself. For Wurmser, as for Nathanson, the love denied by shame is of self as well as of others. Wurmser writes that "masochistic submission—as shameful as it is—is an attack on the horrid self that wants to take away from others what they own. It is thus a kind of reaction formation: I don't want to compete. Quite the contrary, I am groveling—and I even love it."[30] Again, that someone could grovel in complicated pleasure, could compete for a deeper humiliation, cannot fit this view of submission. The pleasure of shame is read instead as self-hating passive-aggression. There is not much way around such an analysis that cannot be made into support for it, but I am more inclined to accept Ellis Hanson's delightful description:

> "I like the kind of sex that's embarrassing," I said to my students in my most recent failure to come out properly in a classroom. "If you're not ashamed of the sex you're having, chances are you're not doing it right" (they wrote this down for the quiz). In the spirit of Leo Bersani, I have come to value sex, gay and otherwise, as a respite from pride, as a relatively pleasurable and reliable source of degradation, its success often predicated paradoxically on its failures.[31]

For more conservative theorists, this predication can only mean that the failure is sought by mistake, as a compensation for or a way around something that the seeker fears, and that the success is an end to the failure and the shame, even if there is no other positive result. For Hanson, the paradox is genuine: failure is sought, degradation pleasurable, good sex shameful.

Pleasurable failures are those of too little, too much, or the wrong sort—failures that we turn from and toward at once, and that insist upon our vulnerability. Too much is especially a matter of the too, too solid flesh, all the more where that flesh is alive with desire. Desire itself is embarrassing when it is too much to be readily and quietly met. To be too much or to want too much is shameful; we can be humiliated by our confrontation with our excesses as much as our deficiencies (the excess of our lack). This is especially so not just for fleshly desire, but for flesh itself, as we have seen in the overflowing bodies of Jenny Saville's art. As Lynne Gerber has argued, the excesses of flesh and desire that we associate with fatness arouse widespread horror and disgust, more moral than aesthetic—but she points out that in that horror is the possibility of something more powerful than disapproval, a sense of the sacred reclaimed in what is forbidden and out of bounds.[32] More powerful than acceptance at any size could be the embrace of excess, which resists a "subjectivity based on the fantasy of individual coherence and completeness."[33] This embrace realizes that there is no room for the shameful, no proper place, because it doesn't fit; there is no Goldilocks sizing for humiliation.

Excessiveness in flesh and in desire threatens the sense of dignity as propriety. It is what we would like to hide away in a closet, or sweep to the margins.

Too small, too limited, and yet too much—how dare we reach for the infinite, for the sacred and for the most profane, even for the scatological? While deficiency touches upon lack and its curious connections to desire, the too-much touches upon the excremental—and what could be more shameful than such a touch? What could be less dignified than being drawn to this displacement?

AM I THAT NAME?

He's pecked to death
But he loves the pain
And he loves it
When she calls him names.

—Joan Armatrading, "Call Me Names"

As reliable sources of degradation go, it's hard to find better than flesh—but some kinds of flesh are more reliably humiliating than others. There are at least two categories of humiliation that play with the subjectivity and subjection of these kinds. The first is less common, and plays upon the abjection of the self as it is perceived in the world, where that perception is particularly vulnerable to being marginalized and even degraded. The more common mode takes on an identity other than that of the perceived self, a role that is less culturally dominant, powerful, or central.

Identity is a complex source of play, its center held (shakily) by abjection. This is part of the incentive for pride: if an identity is abjected, pushed aside, then insisting that it deserves pride of place threatens the order that has marginalized it, and often that threatening is just what we hope to do. An embrace of shame troubles this hope. As Sedgwick writes, "Shame interests me politically . . . because it generates and legitimates the place of identity—the question of identity—at the origin of the impulse to the performative, but does so without giving that identity space the standing of an essence."[34] Shameful identities do not claim the status of essential, enduring selves, but rather perform themselves, making their impermanent truths.

The first kind of play, which will take up this section, makes use of identity as a resource for shame, in the manner that Ziv and Hanson do. It is particularly difficult because it contests not only our egalitarian sensibilities, but the intensity of those sensibilities in communities that have come only recently to a sense of pride. Janet Hardy and Dossie Easton call this "playing with cultural trauma," and note that it is controversial. They suggest that fresher and more recent traumas are more likely to provoke arguments than older ones, which might have had some time to heal: "[T]he scenes that are likeliest to cause problems are those from the more recent past—most often those that involve the Holocaust and Nazis, and those that invoke the racially based slavery of the American eighteenth and nineteenth centuries. Older incidents such as the Spanish Inquisition seem to push fewer buttons because they're buried deeper in our cultural memory."[35]

In a particularly thoughtful account, Mollena Williams describes "the lure of taboo role play," including play with race and racism—a taboo, as she notes, that may be even stronger *within* the bdsm community than outside of it, especially among those who are invested in "demystify[ing] kink by downplaying the risks and the danger."[36] That is, the more intensely we try to normalize perversity (assuming, perhaps, that pathology is our sole alternative), the less likely we are to accept degradation that plays with what people must endure every day. Assimilation and normalization can occur from multiple directions, and almost always with deeply good intentions.

Normalization, like laughter, can defend against the contestation created by shame. In these connections, we may also hear that the perverse is really just another guise of the very reassuring. Being bound is like being swaddled, a comforting absolution from responsibility. Such reassurance acknowledges that ceding autonomous control may be disconcerting, but asserts that it ultimately leaves us secure. These claims are too widespread, and sometimes too thoughtfully presented, to be dismissed; I would assert only that they are not universally accurate—and that we seldom find them for the pleasures of shame.

Williams emphasizes the need both for preparation and aftercare, not least for the "perpetrator," in such play.[37] Crucially, she notes, participants need clarity of desire—which annoyingly includes clarity about desire's often muddled, multiple, and contradictory nature. Though her focus is on race, she points out the possibilities for similar inhabitation of transgender, disabled, and other highly marginalized identities; others may put into play anti-Semitism, homophobia, or even biases about appearance and beauty.[38] The "wrong bodies" embraced by *Gay Shame* are all identities that could provide Hanson's "relatively pleasurable and reliable source of degradation."[39] In such pleasure seeking, humiliation is demanded, even as it is also imposed and resisted. These identities may be claimed with an insistence on the contempt that they can incur. Here too we find early antecedents, as Burrus reminds us: "[T]he existence of an identity that can be claimed and reclaimed—'I am a Christian!'—is secured in and through iterative spectacles of shame."[40]

It is unsurprising that such play is so fraught. We often feel that that justice, like dignity, demands undifferentiatedness because it must refuse to mark or stigmatize. Thus, respect for dignity seems to require that we can do what we can to diminish the effects of such marking, and that we refrain from deliberately drawing attention to it.[41] And here, of course, matters take a turn for the weird; it is not hard to see how such a refusal to notice can edge into the shame of rendering invisible. Small wonder that many such stigmata simply enter the realm not of apophasis, but of Matters One Does Not Discuss. To acknowledge them would unsettle the dignity of position, insisting on vulnerability instead. We might say more definitely that it is unethical to draw humiliating attention to a stigmatized identity in many circumstances—any, in fact, where there is no flicker of the contrary desire toward shaming. Luckily for pleasure, those flickers do sometimes spark.

Those who occupy marginal positions may also transfigure the mocking, the "degradation or exploitation of a participant based on their perceived membership in a social group, usually defined by race, religion, sexual orientation, disability, class, ethnicity, nationality, age, gender, gender identity, social status, or political affiliation."[42] They might even play with the very fact of an uncertain or fluid identity. Williams recounts a group discussion in which "an individual who self-identified as transgendered hesitantly revealed a fantasy they'd had of coordinating a scene that would enact a 'fag bashing.' . . . This was an especially nuanced exploration for them, they explained, as their affect is often fluid and they embrace a mercurial approach to gender and how they define it."[43] As Williams points out, however, the performance of one's own identity, so deeply that it becomes "depersonalizing," is available to anyone. "Are you a wealthy heterosexual white man? Then you might find yourself in a bad way if you fell into the clutches of a female supremacist bent on vengeance, full of disgust and scorn for your worthless, useless excuse for genitals and your grotesque white male privilege. Again, it is all about expanding your definition of what is risky, what is edgy, and personalizing the depersonalization."[44] Just as we begin with a play of desires, some of them subjectivizing, rather than with individuals who possess their own wills, so too we begin with the play and positioning of identities from which these desirous dances are choreographed, rather than from an assumption of persons slotted firmly into their appointed places. We begin, that is, with the possibility of undermining positional dignity altogether.

We've already seen instances of ascetic insistence on strongly claiming, and pleasurably manipulating, stigmatized identity, in the cases of devout women who use their gender as a head start on their ascetic self-deprecation. They are already low, degraded by their sexed inferiority, and they use that position in embracing humility and humiliation both. Nor, of course, have these associations disappeared. In *Unbearable Weight*, her philosophical analysis of anorexia and female embodiment, Susan Bordo writes, "Internalizing this ideology [identifying woman with body], which views the body 'as animal, as appetite, as deceiver, as prison of the soul,' women come to feel 'unease' with their femaleness, 'shame' over their 'degraded' bodies, and 'self-loathing.'"[45] Femininity remains an identity that can be claimed both by those in whom it is assumed (especially but not only among ascetics) and those for whom it is not (especially but not only in perversity).

Williams argues that the erotic manipulation of an already abjected identity may grant one the strengths of reclamation and survival.[46] Those against whom their own culture is biased can reclaim the strength of their own identities. (We may see some parallel here to other reclamations, such as members of marginalized groups reclaiming slurs that others have used to name them.) Williams asks, "What if you realized that these words didn't have the power over you that you thought they did? What if you were able to weather this abuse, this ugliness, and walk away unscathed? Or stronger? What if you were able to look upon your abuser thereafter with compassion instead of rage?"[47] Perhaps, she suggests, from "the ashes of such debasement," we "can rise and feel even stronger and more empowered than before,"[48] like her wheelchair-using friend who "shocked the hell out of a roomful of jaded perverts by enacting the victim in a scene where he was kicked out of his chair, dragged around, degraded, and humiliated with all manner of shocking epithets and completely inappropriate language."[49] All of this is possible—but with a Bataillean caveat, that if one simply aims toward power or even compassion, one will never quite encounter the debasement, having that reassuring goal always present in advance. As Williams is clearly aware, these pleasures are not only, often not primarily, about their beneficial results—not, at least, while they are happening.

What Williams calls "consensual nonconsent," beginning in a powerful desire in order to push the limits of subjectivity and will, is found in asceticism, too. Here, writes Burrus, many practices "seem to derive their signifying power from the blurring of the categories of self-willed and involuntary affliction and of chastisement that is apparently deserved and that which is seemingly arbitrary or accidental yet thereby no less part of God's providential plan."[50] Desire's direction and multidirection may be more important than the question of *whose* desire is in play; the ascetic's God works through the Roman official to fulfill the ascetic's desire for God's desire. Or rather, desire puts that "who" into question too, as consenting to nonconsent creates something impossible for the will. Truth, falsity, and the very distinctions or correspondences between truth and appearance tangle dizzyingly.

As I've noted, this first kind of play with flesh and the loss of dignity depends upon claiming for oneself what others have given. Whether a marginal identity can be occupied by others, though, depends upon a complex interplay of factors, and I am far from certain of them. Some boundaries are fairly often crossed, as we'll soon see—men to women, people to animals, adults to children—but it is much more rare for Caucasians to play as people of color, or the able as the disabled. It is easy for such play to feel like mockery. We know that we are less comfortable drawing attention to race or disability than to gender, the nonhuman presence of an animal, or the fact that a person is a child. Though gender play, for example, may seem from the outside to verge on parody, it seems to be undertaken with great sincerity, real consent to nonconsent. In fact, men who play with the humiliation of being dressed and treated as (highly stereotypical) women most often prefer that women humiliate them, rather than seeking to mock female inferiority. It may be, as Easton and Hardy's reading suggests, that such contemptuous traditions as blackface are still too alive and culturally potent for role play across race to be a pleasurable option. I propose this only as a possibility; more certain, however, are the pleasures found in other roles of devalued flesh.

FLESH LESS WORTHY: LITTLE BABIES, BIG WOMEN, AND ALL THE BEASTS OF THE FIELD

> Between the body and the body there is nothing, nothing but me. It is not a state, not an object, not a mind, not a fact, even less the void of a being, absolutely nothing of a spirit, or of a mind, not a body, it is the intransplantable me. But not an ego, I don't have one. I don't have an ego ... what I am is without differentiation nor possible opposition, it is the absolute intrusion of my body, everywhere.
> —Antonin Artaud, *To Have Done with The Judgment of God*

In modes that may be more common and are certainly better known, humiliation plays not with, but against perceived identities. Here, one inhabits not the role of what one already "is," or is perceived as being, or is said to be, but rather a role that one by all such evidence "is" not—a play made possible by the strong element of performance in these identifications. This occurs particularly when the initial, everyday role is distant from degradation, as when men with social or financial power play as servants or women, or adults as infants, or people as other animals. William Ian Miller describes humiliation as the revelation of a truth contrary to pride.[51] "But what is truth?," this role play asks, and the answer will not stay still. The rest of the roles that I'll describe in this section play with the idea of capability by limiting it; the identities assumed are all seen as lacking, to some degree, the capabilities of a truly rational and autonomous subject.

Jeremy Waldron, writing of human dignity and against torture and inhumane punishment, lists "four species of degradation": bestialization, instrumentalization, infantilization, and demonization.[52] These may serve us as a starting point for our exploration of assumed identities, though we must alter the list a bit by including feminization, and by considering the demon a little differently, given demonization's relation to othering of many sorts.[53]

Instrumentalization, writes Waldron, may be "associated with the Kantian meaning of indignity: being used as a mere means, being used in a way that is not sufficiently respectful of humanity as an end in itself."[54] This is emphasized in forniphilia, wherein one finds pleasure by employing the human body as furniture—from the fairly obvious footstool or tabletop, through creative plant and drink stands, to the edgier human ashtray or toilet, where the abject excess of waste meets the indignity of becoming a thing that has a price (and perhaps a fairly low one).[55] That is, if we associate the abject with cigarette ash or human waste, there is a more intense abjection still in receiving that waste, becoming the unsettling place for it. In addition, objectification usually includes some visual element of exposure or display; fully dressed or modestly positioned human furniture is uncommon, though not unknown. Tension between subject and object status is required for such play to retain any force; undoubtedly, there is transgression is the employment of dead bodies as objects, but necrophilia functions as humiliation only for those who perceive the bodies of the dead as retaining subjectivity.[56] (It might also humiliate the living, if the bodies are those of people for whom they cared, as in the paradigmatic example of Hector, whose body is dragged carelessly about through the *Iliad*.)

Monastic life often demands impoverishment in terms of possessions, including useful objects, but it does not overtly demand that the monk substitute for such objects with his own flesh. However, early monastic manual labor, upon which most Rules insist, was labor that in many other contexts would have been performed by slaves. Slaves, following Aristotle's arguments, were highly instrumentalized. Aristotle writes in the *Politics*,

> [T]he manager of a household must have his tools, and of tools some are lifeless and others living.... [A]n article of property is a tool for the purpose of life ... and a slave is a live article of property. And every assistant is as it were a tool that serves for several tools; for if every tool could perform its own work ... if thus shuttles wove and quills played harps of themselves, master-craftsmen would have no need of assistants and masters no need of slaves.[57]

Insofar as the slave's body is highly, dehumanizingly instrumentalized, then, this mode exists ascetically as well, and presumably there is something humble, but potentially humiliating too, in being willing to work in this way. The degradation of objectification, though, is at least less obvious than in the case of perversity; the work, rather than the instrumentalization, seems to be the point, but the latter does sneak in.

Waldron does not mention feminization, but a focus on humiliation, both intentional and otherwise, makes it hard to ignore. If it is shameful, degraded, or socially marginal to be "properly" feminine in body—a body identified as woman and female—it is still more so for someone who identifies as male or even as butch to take on the trappings of femininity. That it is embarrassing for men to appear feminine has been a persistent notion in many Western cultures. Across two and a half millennia, Charles Taylor picks up on Aristotle to note that a shrill voice or "effeminate" hands may shame men by their perceived clash with masculine dignity.[58] This association of the feminine with the undignified and even degraded runs so deeply that the practice, and especially the pornographic representation, of female dominance over men—a quite popular genre—has sometimes been called "role-reversal," on the presumption that men enjoy the pretense of victimhood only because they know they cannot really be victimized, especially by women; that is, because there is an unassailable boundary between the actual and the appearance.[59] Though it has become outdated and was always, I think, a misreading, this interpretation does suggest that the stereotype of the degraded and powerless feminine is so strong that it appears to some quite intelligent people to be reinforced by its evident counterexamples. Play with gender for the purpose of shame is a better fit with Halberstam's "shadow feminism," which "take[s] the form not of becoming, being, and doing but of shady, murky modes of undoing, unbecoming, and violating."[60]

Even as, (we must hope), more women develop shameless comfort with their everyday physicality, the sense of the feminine body as animal and degraded is put to use for more pleasurable purposes in forced feminization. In these practices and fantasies, the person re-dressed may be transferred across levels of power as well, from employer to maid, executive to assistant, successful entrepreneur to fluffy sex kitten.[61] Of course, men can dress in women's clothing without shame, as the glorious pride of drag queens attests, though this is necessarily complicated by the history of shame that they have had to overcome. (There are also plenty of hipster men in skirts, though they too are playing on the idea that they *ought* to be a little ashamed.) Likewise, lesbians may sometimes dress as boys for their daddies, but any element of *diminishment* here seems to be related to age- rather than to gender-play. Masculinity is likely to be praised, particularly as a quality of mind. Ascetic women have even been declared masculine as a gesture of admiration from the outside or defiance on their own part, as when the harsh desert turns the beautiful Pelagia into the weatherbeaten Pelagios.[62]

In fact, women's attempted unsexing may be rejected by those with more power. It is culturally telling that there is no similarly widespread practice of women experiencing perverse humiliation in male garb; certainly, butch lesbians may be socially and even physically punished for their appearance, and we know that Joan of Arc's preference for male apparel proved fatal to her—but the male appearance is not usually adopted with the intent of exploring shame. As Leslie Feinberg notes in *Stone Butch Blues*, the legal requirement that one wear at least three pieces of "gender appropriate" clothing was used as an excuse to harass and harm both butches and drag queens, and they resisted the demand as not only inappropriate, but shaming, a punishment for daring to claim not only a nonstandard identity, but among women, the garb of cultural power.[63] Because masculine dress has that power, it is less likely to be shameful. Here too, we find long antecedents, such as the story of Paul, who rejects the determined Christian Thecla in her desire to join him in his work. As Burrus summarizes, "Thecla imagines herself a virtual man: 'I will cut my hair short and follow you wherever you go.' In Paul's eyes, however, she remains a beautiful woman, likely to be tested again and likely also to demonstrate unmanly weakness in the face of such testing. . . . Thecla, in Paul's view, is still the captive of her feminine vulnerability to shame."[64] For all his boasting of beatings, Paul does not seem to recognize the value that this shame might have for a Christian ascetic—or he may be worried by the power that Thecla claims with her new look.[65] As we know, it is not long before male saints, in their need for humiliation, are feminized by themselves or their hagiographers, as shame and vulnerability come to be still more eagerly desired. Having noted that "Un-manning (or even 'feminization') is also achieved through rituals of humiliating exposure,"[66] Robert Mills elsewhere writes, "Male martyrs get penetrated too, of course, and it is possible that their own torments occasionally possess a sexual resonance, when read from a certain angle: Lawrence, George and Quentin are all stripped naked before being beaten in *South English Legendary*, a humiliation that transforms their bodies into bare—albeit bloodied—flesh. Yet, in their exposure to the threat of rape, female virgin martyrs clearly possess a particularly vibrant symbolic potency."[67] As identity is bent, or even opened to turn itself outside in and bleed inside out, so too is gender. Even so manly a martyr as Sebastian of Fabiola may describe his impending martyrdom as a bride's eager anticipation of her groom's arrival.[68]

The feminized soul of the ascetic and mystic male may extend itself to the body. Catherine Clément writes, "[O]f all the bolts along the cleavages that the sacred gleefully blasts off, the distinction between the sexes is undoubtedly the most important. It is at this point that I shall introduce into the record the frequent bisexuality of mystics."[69] For representatives of this bisexuality (in the sense of a sexed ambiguity more than a sexual desire), she notes "a man who must dress as a woman to exercise the duties of the N'Doeup," echoes Certeau's remark that Teresa of Avila was nicknamed *il padrecito*, "little father," and describes an Indian man who renders oracles in a trance state in which he leaves his traditionally male roles to become "Mother."[70] It is not the feminine that is sacred here, but the crossing; as Clément has it, "Sacred bisexuality is not something one can move beyond, it is the movement itself. . . . Moving from one sex to the other is common currency in the history of mysticism, but the mystic does not stop at that difference: he passes, that is his act."[71] Once more it is the liminal passageway, the between, that is the troubling space of the sacred. Clément is struck by the power that saints acquire by their stubborn identity with disidentifying.[72] (We immediately recognize at least one version of queerness as identity refusal.) When the crossing moves over the border keeping high from low, valued from degraded, the mystical takes on the tone of humiliation as well. After all, as Kristeva notes in the same correspondence, for a long time, "women's familiarity with their intense and evasive body made their religious experience a confrontation with *abjection* precisely, and with *nothingness*."[73] A body always moving between identities is as evasive as that of a saint, or of a masochist who is never where others expect her to be found. It is easier to find pleasure in performing a degraded identity when the performer is in transit from another position.

The feminized body in perverse pleasure tends to delight in stereotypical clothing and behavior. An example comes from a story that is, its author vows, "absolutely true," a sort of assertion we have seen before. Prior to a long account of his own resistance, anger, and arousal as his will is gradually overcome by a dominant woman, he happily declares, "This is my story of how I went from a 230 lb man of muscle, hanging out with my guy friends nearly every night, drinking beer, full grown beard, and loving every minute of it, to a dainty, limp wrist, pink panty wearing, cum guzzling, fuck toy sissy, and loving every minute of it."[74] There is no declaration of shame here—but even here, every image evoked is strongly culturally marked as shameful. The transformation from attributes marked strongly as masculine is a commonplace in such stories, as well, as if to make sure that we notice the shaming due to the scale of the difference.

This bodily debasement is not only about gender, or rather, it is not about gender as if that could be plucked out of its complex of associations and inter- sections. Instead, those associations come deliberately into play. Among the most frequent is the connection of women to youth, even infancy.[75] Women and teen girls may dress in "Lolita" fashion, playing upon mainstreamed versions of this connection, but the "pink panties" of the happy sissy in the previous paragraph are still more girlish than womanly. There is not usually any intentional shame among women who aim at youth; that is, their desires do not seem directed toward humiliation, their own or that of those drawn to them. Perhaps because there is so much less transgression or friction in infantilized women than in infantilized men, a very high percentage of those who play erotically with infantilism (adult babies), are men—up to 90 percent, or even more by some counts. (Age play as adolescents or older children may be more evenly divided.)[76] This group includes a substantial subgroup of "sissy babies," men whose pleasure in humiliation comes of being dressed and treated specifically as infant girls. Waldron describes infan- tilization as a

> type of degradation [that] might have to do with the special dignity as- sociated with human adulthood: an adult has achieved full human status and is capable of standing upright on his or her own account, in a way that (say) an infant is not. So it is degrading to treat an adult human as though he or she were an infant or in ways appropriate to treating an infant. This is particularly important with elementary issues about care of self, including taking care of urination and defecation.[77]

Though to remain the receptacle of one's own waste might be marginally less transgressive than to receive another's, it remains a powerful mode of abjection.

While it may be that "[a]mong people who have unconventional erotic identities or practices, A[dult] B[aby]/D[iaper] L[ov]-ers are perhaps some of the most
misunderstood and denigrated,"[78] not all adult babies (nor the related group of diaper lovers) are interested in tense or difficult pleasures; not all are seeking humiliation. Many find security or relief in returning to the state of being entirely the
object of care; and like men who dress in adult female clothing, not all find degradation in it. In fact, Tristan Taormino suggests that those who do find pleasure in
humiliating infantilization "are perhaps the smallest niche-within-a-niche; they are
kinky folks who use diapers to dominate, discipline, humiliate, and otherwise play
with power dynamics." She provides some comments from this marginal group:
"'For me, the diaper can be like a collar; it's a constant reminder of my baby girl's
submissiveness,' explains Russ, [her interviewee]. 'The diaper puts her in her place,
and the ritual of changing it reinforces the dynamic again and again.'"[79] Ignacio
Rivera argues that such play "can involve an intricacy of domination, incest, rape,
and sometimes torture," making it "edge play for me."[80]

With or without an admixture of other roles, infantilization denies the pride
that Nathanson attaches both to age and to size, perhaps another reason for the
predominance of men among its aficionados (that is, to be a small woman is less
shameful than to be a large one).[81] Size-related shame is distinctly gendered in
other ways as well. A man may be shamed for being small in stature, but to be
genitally small is, while less readily displayed, more shaming still: the humiliation
of the "micropenis" is such that acknowledging that one is "hung like a toddler"[82]
is considered quite brave.[83] Though there are medical definitions as to what counts
as a micropenis, for the sake of humiliation the measured size of the penis is less
relevant than the commentary directed to it: in the most markedly manly of members, smallness is potently shameful.

To regress to the small and the childish is to push back into that shame, into
failure, into childhood, which is, "as many queers in particular recall . . . a long les-
son in humility, awkwardness, limitation."[84] The infantile identity may be sought as
well by saints seeking humiliating failure, as when the seventeenth-century Louisa
of the Nothingness, writes Kristeva, "adopted the attitude not of a nihilist but of
a child."[85] The canny innocence of holy fools is also much like that of children.
Intentional infancy is a state in which autonomy and capability are sacrificed, and
humiliation sought.

The scale on which we measure ourselves is not solely physical, to be sure;
height is placed not just along a yardstick but on the Great Chain of Being. A person may be scorned or dismissed as "less" than human, a status accruing to almost
anything other than us. Feminist artists have played deliberately with the elision
between women and nonhuman animals, and thus shown us something more of
shameful flesh. Lucas's *Chicken Knickers*, earlier mentioned, serves as an example. In
another, Saville's *Host*, "the identity of the body is in transition. It is neither human
nor pig but something of both—as such qualifying as a classic monster. The border

of human and animal is challenged, a border that . . . is patrolled by disgust."[86] This fascination, disgust, and transition make the human-animal border well suited to humiliating crossings. The Cynics were named, after all, for dogs, and medieval satire depicts Aristotle being ridden like a horse by his mistress, Phyllis, nicely displaying both animality and a reversal of the gender roles that Aristotle himself so firmly endorsed. Waldron writes, "The higher than the animals sense of human dignity gives us a natural sense of degrading treatment. . . . So for example a human is degraded by being bred like an animal, used as a beast of burden, beaten like an animal, herded like an animal, treated as though he did not have language, reason or understanding, or any power of self-control."[87] There is in every example an insistence upon inescapable flesh.

Playing-animal may, as Lee Harrington argues, be a mode of becoming-body, of reconnecting with a level of physicality that most of us abandon in our daily lives.[88] If shame is in flesh, then deliberately inhabiting animal embodiment, reconnecting with our fleshiness, may be a particularly reliable degradation. Like adult babies, some who play at animality may seek security (enjoying being cared for, or the absence of the responsibility to come to decisions), while others deliberately invoke the shame of a "lesser" status. Exemplifying the former, a young British woman cheerfully explains to the gossipy tabloid the *Daily Mail*, "I am a pet, I generally act animal like and I lead a really easy life. . . . I don't cook or clean and I don't go anywhere without Dani." (In a nice irony, her boyfriend, who leads her around on a leash, lashes out at a bus driver who refuses to allow them to board by "call[ing] him a fascist pig"; clearly this is no all-in affirmation of animal status.)[89] On the other hand, "Fans of erotic humiliation might be drawn to worm and bug roles," writes Harrington, "where a dominant partner can 'squish' their partner underfoot or treat them for the length of the scene as worthless and small."[90] Others might seize upon the humiliating elements of undertaking such human activities as eating and walking in clearly non- (or sub) human fashion, from dishes on the floor, on all fours, or on a leash: "Bambi Bottom" enjoys the fantasy of "being led on a leash and thinking about what other people seeing me would think about this person who's less than a person, who's owned by someone else."[91]

Peignot offers us vivid examples of the interplay of dehumanization in animality and the pleasures of shame. In her poem "Esmerelda," the title character is "kept in horse's stall" and instructed to "Get up/ the chain to the trough."[92] Bataille's biographical appendix to Peignot's collected writings takes these pleasures out of the realm of creative writing with a description that moves from animality to other abjective modes: "During her Berlin period, she dressed immaculately . . . black stockings, perfumes and silk dresses by the great couturiers. She lived with Wartberg, never went out, never saw anyone, stretched out on a divan. Wartberg brought her dog collars; he put her on a leash on all fours and lashed her with a whip like a dog. . . . Once, he gave her a sandwich smeared with his shit."[93]

Ornamented with bridles, ears, collars, snouts, couturier dresses, or twirly-tailed butt plugs, one may nonetheless remain naked as a beast.

Animal status allows some measure of willfulness while resisting full humanity. Miller even argues, "If what distinguishes humans from animals is the ability to feel humiliated, then to be humiliated and feel so is what humanizes."[94] To play at being inhuman, to obey the command to become-animal, can thereby accent the human sense of humiliation. Clément notes the animality of saints that so intrigues writers, such as Flaubert's St. Anthony, who "sinks[s] into an animal nature" and experiences revelation.[95]

Such humiliation may be sought ascetically too, in giving up the luxuries of human living. Early monks in the Syrian desert "ate grass, legumes and roots, wandered about on the mountain like wild animals."[96] These monks were called *boschoi,* meaning grazers; in the fourth century Ephrem the Syrian compared them both to animals who "graze . . . for roots upon the mountains" and to birds who "pick up dry vegetables from the heights."[97] He adds, "They wander through the haunts of wild beasts as if wild themselves, and with the birds . . . they perch from rock to rock."[98] "When it was time to eat," writes the historian Sozomen, "each one would take a sickle, go up to the mountains and feed on what grew there, like animals at the pasture."[99] (The sickle does seem a bit of a cheat if one is truly seeking animal status.) A wary monk describes the desert father Onophrius, whose "hair was spread over his body like a leopard," and who might be able to climb like "a mountain ass."[100] And our holy fool Symeon returns, drawing a fascinating comparison: "Trying to persuade a companion that they should leave their monastery to go off alone into the desert, Symeon explained that living off what they could find, rather than worrying about how they would survive, would make them more like the angels."[101] Like the Cynics, the hermit saints push the extent of human-ness to its sacralized animal depths, becoming more like angels. Though the grazers were chiefly a late ancient phenomenon, ascetic animality did not die out altogether; some monastic reformers in eleventh and twelfth-century Europe also spent time in the wilderness, living off of plants and tree bark.[102]

It is a common enough notion that to be animal is to lack dignity, on the grounds of unreason, displayed in the lack of language.[103] If only what is rational is dignified, perhaps too only what can be ashamed of being undignified is capable of dignity (especially if we rethink dignity as requiring us to be vulnerable). "Shame," writes phenomenologist Anthony Steinbock, "is evidence of the distance between the human being and sensuous life, something that is only accomplished from the perspective of spirit. It is for this reason, writes Hegel, that animals do not experience shame."[104] That distance is not always easily sustained, and other animals, gazing with feline censoriousness at our naked flesh, may remind us that a dignity based on being human is fragile. Insisting that our dignity come in being separate from our animality leaves us open to unpleasant surprise, as Giorgio

Agamben tells us in his description of feral "wolf children": "[W]hen confronted with these uncertain and mute beings, the passion with which the men of the Ancien Régime try to recognize themselves in them and to 'humanize' them shows how aware they are of the precariousness of the human."[105] We can play with animality because it is so present as a possibility—and this is why we have to deny it so firmly—or perversely confirm the pleasure when the denial fails.

For Hegel's interpreter Alexandre Kojève, Agamben argues, "the body of the anthropomorphous animal" is "the body of the slave . . . irreducibly drawn and divided between animality and humanity."[106] If dignity belongs to nobility, the animal-slave is the body undignified. For Heidegger, as for Hegel, "[t]he superordinate character of the human is established by excluding animality from the essence of man,"[107] writes Edith Wyschogrod. Dignity as propriety of place must sustain as immovable the human distance from the animal. To diminish the distance is to humiliate ourselves. Animalization performs deepened embodiment, vulnerability and all. In those depths of vulnerability, however, we find not only the animal, but the divine: like the inferior woman and the incapable infant, the ostensibly unknowing beast edges upon the unknowable god, and a deeper dignity is bizarrely affirmed in its failure. The return to dignity offers a crucial distinction: to exploit vulnerability is to damage or try to damage dignity. To engage vulnerability in a multidirectional, initially consensual tangle of desires and pleasures ultimately highlights instead not only the depths of the sacred, but the entanglements of vulnerability with strength.

ANIMAL (AND OTHER) TO GOD

> Thou didst create the nine gods at the beginning of all things, and thou wast the Lion-god of the Twin Lion-gods.
>
> —Hymn to Amon-Ra

Like many continua, that from animal to divinity may stretch so tautly as to meet again at its end points—though in this case, we must also suspect that the distance was not what we once thought. The particular case of animality may draw us back to the value of the failure underlying all modes of desired humiliation: the objectified, the feminine, the infantilized, the marginalized and disavowed, all pull up as well as downward, as the feminization and infantilization of saints reminds us. The history of thinking about animality in terms of this double sacred, though, is especially well developed. I follow it here with a sense that the connections will extend to other dehumanized or depersonalized roles as well. Edith Wyschogrod, turning from Heidegger's hierarchy, explicitly connects human animality to vulnerability, vulnerability to "transcendence," and transcendence to sainthood: "To accept corporeal vulnerability by divesting oneself of home and history so far as possible is to transcend the essence of man through its underside, by taking on sheer animal sentience."[108] Even while we enjoy theorizing our continuity with other animals, we can play with the history of the animal as other to our civilized selves. We abandon speech, with all its rights of rationality as well as its ability to demand. We abandon the uprightness that we connect to both dignity and power. We abandon human fashions of dining and drinking—so deeply associated with humanity that in *Gilgamesh*, our oldest written story, partaking in a human meal of bread and beer is part of the transfiguration of Enkidu from animal to human being.[109] The transcendence from human to animal is a leap not only down, as if into an abyss, but beyond our knowledge. A leap, even, into saintliness. Saint and animal alike are at the edge of personhood—and, in the vulnerability of their wandering bodies, of dignity, too.

Waldron's nearest equivalent to this sacred strangeness is demonization, of which he says, "[O]bviously one of the functions of the 'degrading' treatment standard [in law] is to limit the extent to which we can treat someone who is bad or hostile as though he were simply a vile embodiment of evil."[110] It is irrelevant, in political and penal torture, that the sacred stretches evil toward good; such torture is irredeemable. But it is not irrelevant here, where humiliation is sought.

In Bataille's early *Theory of Religion*, writes Direk, "[r]eligion is a mediated experience of primary intimacy with animality," with an intriguing twist, because animality "is the greatest value that man lost in subordinating his life to work and utility."[111] Religion is an attempt not to break free of our animality, but to find it again. Animals and gods are exempt from work, from laborious productivity. Objects, stereotyped and purely decorative women, and infants, like animals, don't have to work, either (unless they are instrumentalized—but even there, their work fails to carry forward their human projects). For Bataille, this "[break] with the servility of knowledge, individualism, and project"[112] is mysterious and sacred. It is a way toward our unworking. The art of failure breaks the possibility of successful result, the possibility of knowledge and of the well bounded subject to whom it belongs, the accomplishment so essential to labor. Bataille goes so far as to argue in *The Accursed Share*, his complex treatise on the economics of sacrifice and expenditure, that our cultural prohibitions are aimed at preventing a "return" to our repressed animal status. And that

> what is *sacred* is precisely what is *prohibited*. But if the *sacred*, the *prohibited*,
> is cast out of the sphere of profane life (inasmuch as it denotes a disrup-
> tion of that life), it nevertheless has a greater value than this profane that
> excludes it. It is no longer the despised bestiality; often it has retained
> an animal form, but the latter has become *divine*. . . . Thus, the *sacred* an-
> nounces a new possibility: it is a leap into the unknown, with animality
> as its impetus.[113]

This is a transcendence through the underside.

It is also a complicated set of moves. Unproductivity is cast out of human life. It is not dignified enough. It is uncivilized. It is unknowing, irrational. But cast out, unproductive and frustrated unknowing continues to disrupt in the form of the unknown, troubling the achievement of civilization. Halberstam reminds us that dehumanizing is an aspect of failure—to be animal is to fail at being human; so too all of the failures of dignity and position that might twist into pleasure. But this, like other failures, may be a queer art, a complication, a resistance. Halberstam points to the example set by the claymation film *Chicken Run*, which offers "scenarios of revolt and alternatives to the grim, mechanical, industrial cycles of production and consumption."[114] Halberstam adds, "The beauty of these films is that they do not fear failure, they do not favor success, and they picture children not as pre-adults figuring the future but as anarchic beings who partake in strange and inconsistent temporal logics." Age joins animality in this strange, unsuccessful resistance. The pairing, Halberstam argues, might help us to produce "generative models of failure," models that "remind us that there is something powerful in being wrong, in losing, in failing, and that all our failures combined might just be enough, if we practice them well, to bring down the winner."[115] We cannot practice them well, though, if we go in planning to win. The temporal logic of work is linear and teleological. The temporal logic of failure is far more scattered.

The sacred is cast out of profane life, as being undignified—yet before it, we are not and cannot be dignified enough (*domine, non sum dignus,* says the Latin liturgy). These two come together: the sacred transfigures our lowly status, but this is not the same as raising it. This is not an either/or choice, nor is it a zero-sum continuum, in which we are the more profane the less we are sacred, the more object, marginalized, abjected the less we are god. But like the animal—like the woman, the child, the ashtray, and end table; like the bodies despised for race or age or ability—we may fail. And once more, in a strange resistance, we may become divine in failing, like those monks whose failure was grounded "in the image of Christ, the eternally humiliated."[116] For Peignot, not the glory of the resurrection, but "the stations of the cross, the story of the spit exalts Christ."[117] We have already seen, more than once, that the demand for abjection is its own *imitatio Christi,* and it is one with a long history of queer enthusiasm.

We must recall, too, the difficulty of that imitation. Hanson writes,

> In his insistently Christian theology of queer shame, [Jean] Genet demands a mortification no less trying than the Passion of Christ, and the beauty of its abjection shimmers in the distance, vaguely, mystically, like some New Jerusalem in which we will find ourselves, one day perhaps, redeemed. He found it embarrassing sometimes that his shame was always receding absurdly into pride, the self-betrayal of a self-betrayal that cancels itself out. . . . He always ends up wanting to show us his good

side by showing us his bad side, which makes him immediately grow nostalgic for his "painful anxiety" and search for some fresh and more reliable embarrassment.[118]

It is not just that we are humiliated by our failures; we fail, even, to find the humiliation that we seek. A wholly successful degradation (a complete failure) can bear no remainder of pleasure, but we will not seek degradation without that remaining reminder. The temptation that faces those who try to deepen their humility, whether devoutly or perversely or both, is less often despair than success. And if avoidance of that pleasure fosters despair, this too keeps at bay the possibility of succeeding at humiliation.

In the emergence of Christian humility, writes Burrus, we also "detect the emergence of a shame that no longer desires honor."[119] Such humility, such humiliation, places knowledge stubbornly on the path of failure before the unknown upon which it insists. In the theosis of failure, shame becomes its own force. Burrus draws on the work of Edith Wyschogrod to suggest that a saint is exemplified by "an active passivity, a willfully embraced humiliation, that in turn demands a response, 'irrespective of cost.'"[120] That response is the exposure, she adds, of our own need. To bare one's need is a maximum of vulnerability, particularly to humiliation. "Shame organizes a whole range of affects that leave me and my students feeling vulnerable, even sexually exposed: ravishment, submission, confusion, helplessness, fear, anger, aggression, tenderness, love, and of course pride,"[121] says Hanson, reminding us again that we need pride for humiliation to work, and not solely in order that it may break.

Each of this multiplicity of humiliations—through vulnerability that grounds dignity, disgust that heightens attraction, degraded flesh that remains adored, the consecration of the desecrated—plays with the secrets of appearance and the slips within position. Its truth succeeds as a truth of failure: the failure of subjectivity, identity, gender, maturity, humanity suspended between nothing and god, as each fails to be true. These failures thwart knowledge not by hiding the truth, but by showing it as otherwise than true, always shifting, implicated more than layered; the failure of what we were once so certain that we knew.

SIX

Unfinished

THE FAILURE TO CONCLUDE

I think the modern age of the history of truth begins when knowledge
itself and knowledge alone gives access to truth.
          —Michel Foucault, *The Hermeneutics of the Subject*

All people by nature desire to know. The famous opening line of Aristotle's *Metaphys-ics* still strikes us as nearly unarguable, even when a particularly frustrating co-hort of students threatens to convince us otherwise. We have seldom been struck, though, by the tension already implicit in the statement, the paradoxes stretching between desire and knowledge. It is desire, *eros,* that takes Socrates up the ladder of knowledge, but ultimately desire must abandon even knowing as we know it, knowledge that can be precisely and properly said—so says Socrates, the one who knows, though he can only say it from the distance of a double fiction, the story of the cosmic ladder of loves told by a prophetess of Socrates's own creation, a *mythos* by which he reaches toward the truth, leaving even philosophy behind.[1] To approach a truth that is other than knowledge, argues Foucault, is to move from philosophy to spirituality—across a split that does not exist in the ancient world.[2] In the ascent of eros, even Socrates follows what Lynne Huffer describes as "a passionate thinking toward thinking's limit as something other than thinking," an ethical and erotic practice by which, I would add, the limit, the other or the outside, enters thinking itself.[3]

In the movements of desire that I have tried to follow in this book, there is always some movement toward an unknowable, some listening for the voice where it breaks. Let me review them here, just quickly, beginning at the beginning by going back to Genesis. Disobedience is implicated there in knowing and in shame, in the desire to know. Giving in to the desire for knowledge, humankind is faced with opacity and obstacle where it once found translucence and ease. The inherited struggle against sin is also an inherited struggle to know divine will in order to harmonize one's own with it, and so to know one's own will, and to control one's flesh. In perfect harmony, one would give pleasure to God, finding one's own pleasure entirely there. Teresa of Avila writes, "I do not love the world or the things of the world, and nothing seems to give me pleasure unless it comes from You; everything else is to me like a heavy cross." But the challenge is not only to know what comes from this divine You, what its desires are. It is, more immediately, our unintelligibility to ourselves: "Yet I may be deceived," she ruefully continues, "and it may be that my desires are not as I have said."[4] If I know what You want, and I show what I know in my action by obedience, then I will know what I want, because it is what You want, and You have said yes to my behavior, and there it is out in the world for us to see. But I don't know any of this. The edifice of obedient knowledge is grounded on a counterfactual, *if* we knew. . . . Postlapsarian existence closes off that option of mutual knowledge—leaving the desire that pulls us back toward it, nonetheless. It is here that Nietzsche's claim for the strength of the ascetic will may be strongest; most wills find failure far too easily, far too often, to need to find a force to make them bend. What Jacques Lacan calls "the one who is supposed to know," the analyst from whom the analysand presumes knowledge, becomes, monastically, the superior who is supposed to want, the God of mysterious ways and desires. The dominant who demands is supposed to be sure that her demands are fully in accord with her own desires. But nobody knows, really. The power to be obeyed is pulled into the paradox of obedience, straining to hear the voice that gives the imperative.

The delight and frustration of seeking to know another must also alert us to the otherness of ourselves. *Know yourself* is a commandment even earlier than the Aristotelian insight, inscribed over Apollo's temple at Delphi, where the oracle once said that Socrates was the wisest of men. This wisdom, Socrates slowly deduces, is that of non-knowing; he is wiser than others only because they presume that they know much more than they actually do know, while he makes no such assumption. Socrates, the wisest man and constant questioner, is stupid in Halberstam's queer sense of the word: "Stupidity could refer . . . to the limits of certain forms of knowing and certain ways of inhabiting structures of knowing."[5] "Know yourself," in other words, means to Socrates "you cannot know everything," and we can inhabit that knowledge by refusing to claim success. But you can try to know everything, still, because you want to. So we try by talking (even if we don't talk quite as much as Socrates) and by listening, by interrogation and answer, by a mode of obedience that draws out our speech and uses it to make us. When we run into that limit, however, we know something else: that there is an other than knowing, too, and that it weaves through us and our knowledge.

In confession, all of our words are made flesh, and some of our flesh is made words, made and remade by the truth of the descriptions we give. When inside and outside are making each other, though, there is necessarily some gap, some remainder, some failure to fit together at the edges, where "the formation of words leaves gaping wounds."[6] We cannot approach these wound-points without having them invert themselves before us, taking the meaning out of our words, or taking the meaning out with our words, leaving us stupid, or leaving us liars—failed, backslid, relapsing. Any bounded subject is risked by its own construction. But as it breaks apart, unbinds, the babbling voice might speak: no one's voice, saying no thing, whispering secrets, murmuring underneath all the answers we can give. We hear that we have failed, that the secret remains; it whispers nothing: fail again. But for a moment, though we could never say what it means, we feel that we have touched the lips of the wound, that we have nearly heard the voice at the edge of the self.

Language has its limits—but of that we were already aware. "I'll know it when I see it," we say, and so perhaps we can know through the exposures of flesh, where vision meets invocation. Art, medicine, and pornography have combined to strip much of the mystery from the surface of the nude. We restore some of it by interdiction, allowing us real or feigned voyeuristic pleasure in the sight of what we are forbidden to see. Where bodies continue still to withhold, as they always do, we look into them: the artistic imagination, the surgical scalpel, and the pornographic zoom lens all do their best to help us. But we can no more see the mysterious flesh than Roman officials could view the martyrs under their veils of blood. The fluid spillover veils flesh from the gaze that wants to see the precise distinction, the exact divisional line, between subject and object, between death and life. The flesh harbors secrets, not inside it, but in the manner of a mystery, as something other than that which knowing can find. The pleasure in its display would fail if we did not know that the display would fail too, that there would always be more to draw the desirous gaze, more that calls to us as that which remains unseen.

Maybe we have been seeking in the wrong places? We continue to search where we know we will fail; I seek to know my place, putting my dignity at risk. Reduced to a form of flesh I had thought other than mine, I become child, animal, furniture; the worthlessness of my own flesh affirmed, I become queer, crippled, ugly. Describing Bataille's sacred, Kristeva declares, "Paradoxically, in evoking the divine ... we evoke journeys to the opposite limit, where the human sinks into animality and nothingness."[7] Paradoxically, in sinking the human into animality and nothingness, we transcend from below into the absolutely immanent; we find once more the mystery of material beings. There is no place for it—I seem to be able to inhabit all sorts of displaced and despised embodiment, but none brings me low enough to know materiality itself. My hierarchical position destroyed, only my vulnerability remains.

In every case, failure entangles with knowledge, and knowledge with desire; in every case, something remains. Hélène Cixous also takes knowledge to be the object of eros, but like the knowledge of indescribable beauty in the *Symposium*, the knowledge that Cixous's lover seeks is impossible. It is the "drive to know what you feel on your side, when you jouis, this craving to know how what is good for you is good, without which there is neither desire, nor love, nor jouissance." That this is unknowable is not simply happenstance, but a matter of the secret made necessary by the very nature of erotic desire.[8] This desire to know seeks the unknowable, knowing it to be unknowable—perhaps depending upon that unknowability—yet seeks it no less. We are not trying to keep secrets; rather, what is secret keeps us from telling, and keeps itself however we angle to capture it. Cixous notes the strangeness of wanting to exchange, intimately, the "strange and invisible presence" of "the inexchangeable."[9] Bataille, trying to understand eroticism, similarly notes that the gulf of "fundamental difference" separates humans from one another and cannot be overcome. But, he adds, "we can experience its dizziness together."[10] Likewise, Cixous sees in the movement of impossible desire "a sort of paradoxical miracle . . . right where we are unable to share, we share this non-sharing, this desire, this impossibility."[11] Both suggest to us that we share only that we cannot share, neither know nor tell all, no matter how demanding the inquisition, how persistent the gaze, how flexible the will to abasement. Cixous's words remind us that if we have not thought much about the tensions between knowledge and desire, still less have we thought about the pleasures in those paradoxes, and the power in those pleasures—unsurprisingly, as they belong to frustration and failure.

Push this primal curiosity far enough, and we find perversity. In the introduction that I've just cited, Bataille tentatively defines the erotic as "assenting to life even in death."[12] This connects eros to the borderline that marks the abject and disgusting, where overflow and failed containment suggest both an effusive exuberance of vitality and the repugnant spillage of rot. Curious, impossible eroticism is perverse in the Freudian sense as well, which comes close to the etymology of perversion as turning about the wrong way.[13] In Freud's terms, the perverse is any pleasure turning away from a sexual teleology of climactic release—and thus, since there must be something *to* release, a necessary part of any sexual pleasure.[14] In Lacanian terms, perversion is particularly focused on the other's pleasure; a pervert is the "epitome of desirousness, and a man who pursues jouissance as far as possible"[15] following, as Cixous does too, an obscure trail that does not lead to a result—but following it farther than most.

The Lacanian pervert becomes, voluntarily, an object without *voluntas,* an instrument for another's pleasure, finding pleasure only in that instrumentalizing. An impossible pleasure, of course, as what is pure object or instrument is free of will, desire, knowledge—and pleasure. It is as if all that remains of will is the will to know, to know the other's desire in order to meet it, of course, but also to know the other's inexchangeable pleasure and—in order to be the instrument of that pleasure—to know both the other and oneself, in desire, in language, in flesh. If we take seriously the points that Bataille and Cixous have made, and for that matter the failure-destined desires that I have tried to describe throughout this book, then we realize that this perversity is eros affirming, seeking, and even stubbornly embracing impossibility.

Perversity may locate itself as the object of any of the various drives that Lacan proposes, but one of them is of particular interest. What he calls the invocatory drive desires the voice, as the scopic drive the gaze. This does not privilege confession over visual display, but rather pushes the limits of meaning—seeking not the denotation of words, but the sound beyond sense, where meaning collapses. The sadist or masochist, Lacan says, locates herself as the object of invocation.[16] Invocation is the call between desire and response, so entangled and intercorporate that Lacan can't even create for it one of his famous diagrams.[17] In his seminar on the invocatory drive, Adrian Price looks at tales of divine voice, such as that in the first book of Kings (19:11–13).[18] In these stories, as he points out, the "incarnation of God is both immanent and transcendent." So too is the invocational voice, paradoxical in its place and its displacement.[19] It "effectively does seem to awaken the other." Yet, "the Other is absent as a guarantee."[20] That Other, says Jean Charmoille, is "presupposed but not yet defined."[21] In other words, invocation proceeds without certainty, calling out of a desire to know and toward another's desire, without being able to know that desire, knowing its own desirous inability.

It seems odd that sadism and masochism would both entail the same subject-as-object location. Certainly, these descriptions seem more readily intelligible as belonging to the masochistic position, where instrumentalization is clearer. But we must recall the constant inversions of knowing and of desire, the urge to see into an other in order that one's gaze might finally penetrate oneself, the urge to hear oneself speak in order to know who one is, the desire to be nothing but wound, and still know. The desire to know the unknowable *as* unknowable, as mystery, belongs to all parties caught up in these peculiar tangles.

And invocation may be even stranger than it already seems, because its object isn't *words*, but *voice*. It calls out for the cry of inarticulate pleasure. To be sure, voices speak, and make sense; perhaps we are called by desire and desire to be called, to be invoked, without much caring how it sounds. But when it becomes persistent enough, invocation demands pure voice, in which knowing fails. The desire to know all the meaning that a voice can carry will greedily drain all the meaning from it, until it is not the abstract meaning carried by words that is desired, but the carnal, sonorous, sensuous voice. The voice that stutters, scratches, whispers, screams.[22] That granulates, crackles, caresses, grates, cuts, comes.[23] Or the neutral murmur, "hidden in what cannot be named ... the neutral ... which has about it nothing sovereign that has not already surrendered in advance."[24] Or the Word behind words, by which body beyond sense bears the possibility of anything we might know.

Listen, it whispers. Do you want to know a secret?

These are the voices for which perversity listens, the voices that inspire ascetic devotion. How does one speak, exactly and clearly, of the very fact of what
eludes saying? As Bataille has it, "[I]t is difficult for words to say that which it is
their purpose to deny."[25] It is difficult, too, for words to say that which was probably never their purpose, but toward which they seem to be irresistibly drawn, the
mysteries before which they fail, humiliating the speaker, the writer—any lover
of words.

The secret that failure seeks cannot be known; it is a mystery, not a datum.
It cannot be said; it is apophatic. It is invisible, untouchable, inaudible, beyond en-
actment. It can only be desired. We might suspect it of being simply absent—that
is, of being a fiction, indeed a lie. But the absence of the secret is not of a sort
that reduces it; rather, it is at the heart of its presence. "There is nothing secret,
anywhere," writes Maurice Blanchot, "this is what the secret always says.—All the
while not saying it. For, with the words 'there is' and 'nothing,' the enigma continues to rule, preventing installation and repose."[26] The mystery remains: in our
remains, in our remainder—the site and nonsite of our abjection, our introjection
of otherness, our extrajection of self, our own impossible divinity, our own place
in the *humus,* the dirt.

If the power and the pleasure of humiliation, deep shame, or abjection are
negation only, feeling them simply means desiring to withdraw or minimize. They
may lead to a loss of subjectivity, but without complexity and without the sense
of otherness tangled within—without remainder, and absent any joy. If they are
pleasure only—if they are just games, or even contests of machismo and endur-
ance that one can win—their attraction is easier to understand; yet once more,
uncomplicated, they fail to get at the tangles that characterize mystery and eros. It
is only in sustaining the paradox that we find these queer, failed, impossible pleasures that hold on as they discard, that attract as they repel, that shatter the bored
and bounded subject not by an imposition of irremediable violence, but by the
violence that complicates from within the bounds themselves. There is something,
abject and rejected, too much and disgusting, desirous but not for satiation, that
pulls at perverse and ascetic desire. There is something resistant. It is a limit for
knowledge, an edge for play, and a potent arrogance in the depths of humiliation.
"[S]hame and pride, shame and dignity, shame and self-display, shame and exhibitionism are different interlinings of the same glove," writes Eve Sedgwick.[27] If
there is no proper inside, only interlinings, one inside after another in shifting layers, then in deep shame we may nonetheless be caught up in a pleasure that seeks
what resists it, that takes pride in its own resistance, and that resists that pride as
well.[28] Shame can be reclaimed within an imperative to pride only insofar as one
also reclaims the perverse. Even then, perversely enough, it cannot be reclaimed
altogether without losing itself. Prideful, shameful failures still cannot be reduced
to successes.

Yet there remains a marvelous arrogance, even insolence, in so insisting upon reaching the place of failure, when coming under the law is too easy, too boring. Laure, exemplar of humiliation, may be exemplary for our arrogance too. Peignot's correspondence and her notes to herself eloquently exemplify the struggle not to give in to either side of the apparent binary between humiliation and pride. To back away from abjection, as most would, becomes its own diminution. She declares to her sister-in-law, "Perhaps I've been too arrogant, but I cannot be content with mediocrity any longer."[29] She wants insistently to embrace "[n]othing that is not a cry of joy or pride."[30] And she urges herself, "Do not accept what lessens you."[31] What would lessen her, and must therefore be avoided, is not the violent play of eros, but the ordinary. She writes to Bataille, "I understand that I need you terribly in order to live and this does not make my unbearable pride suffer, you know."[32] She describes what seems at first to be a reversal: "an invincible pride, and then ... abjection or the absurd trust of a little girl in a Confessional."[33] But her pride is genuine; it has not been conquered by abjection or misplaced trust, but complicated and strengthened instead. Likewise, at the level of the sacred, says Catherine Clément, "the freely chosen humiliation of the person before God" requires "a formidable pride, far from ... modesty."[34] Such oddly bent pride does not suffer, or rather, it does not only suffer: it transfigures.

And it disfigures. We should recall Rogozinski's description of kenosis: "the condition of this invocation allowing him to call him by his Name. It is indeed the ... story ... of a living flesh that is disfigured and transfigured, that dies and is resuscitated—and it is the story of *our* flesh, our life, the intrigue of the ego and the remainder."[35] Transfiguration is characteristic of sacred things. It is invested in a conversion not from one pole to its opposite, but from the everyday to the imminently sacred; not from pride to humility, but through humiliation that breaks into arrogance, and vice versa. Not everyone regards this conversionary possibility without skepticism, of course, and there are scholars who quite confidently assert that Peignot is psychologically unwell, particularly in the pleasure she takes in various senses of filth.[36] Yet Bataille declares of Laure that "she was obviously purity, pride itself, reserved."[37] Just as humiliation pulls at the strength of pride itself, so too filth tugs at the pure. The sacred is equally abject and exalted. Without abjection, without remainder, dignity is impossible. Without pride, there is no shame. This is a queer pride indeed—all the more so when it flips or transfigures again into queer shame, with its humiliating pleasures. For humiliation to enter into pleasure, the desire for it must be tangled with pride, allowing the two to pull upon each other, even to the extent of pride in the depths of humiliation to which one is willing, or able, to go.

Failure works not against hope or joy, but against their simplification, against reduction. It reminds us that tragedy, too, has its beauty; that ugliness, even, has its fascination. It reminds us to remember the sneaky pleasures of displeasure, the sheer strength of obedience, the secrecy of exposure, the power of shame, the arousal of abasement. Historian George Chauncey notes the assumption that all pre-Stonewall participants in underground sexuality "must have been heterosexuals or tortured, shame-filled homosexuals who crawled there and back." Of course, they were not, and of course that matters. But, "Some of them were and others of them did (some of them reveling in being so close to the mud)."[38] It is that last option, that reveling, that makes the shameful interesting. The inherent resistance of this interest foregrounds political complexity: politics, not least queer politics, needs what will fail it, what threatens it, what threatens the political itself and not just what threatens a given system: it needs the erotic, and the sacred. Derrida worries, "In terms of political ethics: if a right to the secret is not maintained, we are in a totalitarian space."[39] But politics in relation to these pleasures must precisely not politicize them, not make them into use value. To instrumentalize them is to get rid of the threat that they pose, substituting a threat that is more unilaterally destructive to living things. There is a difference between intsrumentalizing oneself for another's pleasure and instrumentalizing the pleasure itself. I have argued before that perverse delights such as those found in deep asceticism, sadism, and masochism seem so odd, and even sometimes threatening, because they undermine the goal orientation that makes products even from mysteries. This they do by their insistence on irresolution, by getting us nowhere—as failure does, as knowledge finds.

Flesh resists perfect knowing, perfect control, perfect construction. It resists perfection, with its necessary stasis. It may enjoy, even, the sheer intensity of its imperfection. What is possible, what is impossible, for a human will, a human body, a human, interhuman, transhuman desire? Everything, no thing, a mystery—something, mysterious. In finitude, it resists. In its finitude and its failure.

Flesh acts, and speaks, and means; in all of these, it may fail. Shame leads beyond self through the depths of self, beyond the knowable in the nooks of the body, beyond the will in the stutter to silence. Silence traverses the wordless invocative voice. "[T]he scream creates the abyss into which silence rushes,"[40] says Lacan, though we must remember that "the presence of silence in no way implies that there is not someone speaking."[41] We must suspect, even, that there is silence in all speaking, blindness in all seeing, displacement in every position. And in some speaking, frustrated, humiliated, and hurt, there is an abyss-opening scream. It speaks, it fades, it sustains. In the humiliation of rational, willful knowledge, in the inarticulate cry of the flesh, we fail to hear the secret.

Notes

CHAPTER ONE. UNWORKING

1. Elspeth Probyn offers an exemplary remark: "There is a shame in being highly interested in something and unable to convey it to others, to evoke the same degree of interest in them and to convince them that it is warranted. This is heightened when the questions you want to ask seem so large they escape any one authority." Elspeth Probyn, *Blush: Faces of Shame* (Minneapolis: University of Minnesota Press, 2005), 130.

2. Virginia Burrus, *Saving Shame: Martyrs, Saints, and Other Abject Subjects* (Philadelphia: University of Pennsylvania Press, 2008), 115.

3. Maurice Blanchot, "De l'angoisse au langage," in *Faux pas* (Paris: Gallimard, 1943), 11. Translated Lydia Davis and Paul Auster in *The Station Hill Blanchot Reader: Fiction and Literary Essays*, ed. George Quasha (Barrytown, NY: Station Hill, 1999), 345. Thus cited in Milo Sweedler, *The Dismembered Community: Bataille, Blanchot, Leiris, and the Remains of Laure* (Newark, DE: University of Delaware Press, 2009), 170.

4. Martha Nussbaum, "Replies," *Journal of Ethics* 10, no. 4 (December 2006): 489. In this passage, Nussbaum is responding to John Deigh's criticism, in the same issue, that she ought to distinguish humiliation from shame, objecting only to the former. John Deigh, "The Politics of Disgust and Shame," *Journal of Ethics* 10, no. 4 (December 2006): 383–418.

5. Judith Halberstam, *The Queer Art of Failure* (Durham: Duke University Press, 2011).

6. David M. Halperin and Valerie Traub, "Beyond Gay Pride," in *Gay Shame*, ed. David M. Halperin and Valerie Traub (Chicago: University of Chicago Press, 2009), 9.

7. Jennifer Moon, "Gay Shame and the Politics of Identity," in Halperin and Traub, *Gay Shame*, 360. Moon uses Nancy Fraser's understanding of "counterpublic" here: "Fraser defines 'subaltern counterpublics' as 'parallel discursive areas where members of subordinated social groups invent and circulate counterdiscourses to formulate oppositional interpretations of their identities, interests, and needs.'" Citing Nancy Fraser, "Rethinking the Public Sphere," in *Habermas and the Public Sphere,* ed. Craig Calhoun (Cambridge, MA: MIT Press, 1992), 239.

8. Jon Simons, "Power, Resistance," 311. Simons refers to Michel Foucault, *Power: Essential Works of Foucault 1954–1984*, ed. James D. Faubion (New York: The New Press, 2000), 330–32.

9. Lynne Huffer, "Foucault's Eros: For an Ethics of Living in Biopower," in Falzon, O'Leary, and Sawicki, *A Companion to Foucault*, 437. See also Lynne Huffer, *Mad for Foucault: Rethinking the Foundations of Queer Theory* (New York: Columbia University Press, 2009), 256: "[T]he life administered by biopower is the modern form of a bios Foucault describes in his ethical work on the Greco-Roman and early Christian worlds."

10. Halberstam, *The Queer Art of Failure*, location 117.

11. This point is central to most studies of the affect of shame, and is too widely disseminated for me to be able to provide an exact reference. However, Silvan Tomkins is widely credited with the idea. One presentation appears in his chapter "Shame-Humiliation and Contempt-Disgust," excerpted in *Shame and its Sisters: A Silvan Tomkins Reader*, ed. Eve Kosofsky Sedgwick and Adam Frank (Durham: Duke University Press, 1995), 133–78.

12. "[Diogenes the Cynic] used to say that it was the privilege of the gods to need nothing and of god-like men to want but little." Diogenes Laërtius, "The Life of Diogenes," in *Lives and Opinions of Eminent Philosophers: Including the Biographies of the Cynics and the Life of Epicurus* (New York: C. V. Ruisdale and Gottfried & Fritz, 2015), Kindle edition, locations 4225–26.

13. Ibid., location 3830.

14. Friedrich Nietzsche, *The Gay Science*, trans. Walter Kaufmann (New York: Vintage, 1974), §125.

15. Diogenes Laërtius, "The Life of Diogenes," location 4244.

16. Mark Jordan, *Convulsing Bodies: Religion and Resistance in Foucault* (Stanford: Stanford University Press, 2015), 188.

17. It may be worth noting that adherence to a similarly strange standard of truth appears in what Huffer calls the queer characters and figures of Foucault's *History of Madness*—"the leper, the fool, the pauper, the vagrant, the sodomite, the libertine (Sade), the prostitute, the homosexual, the hysteric, the poet (Nerval), the mad philosopher (Nietzsche), the crazy painter (Van Gogh), the suicidal writer (Roussel), or the antitheatrical playwright (Artaud). . . . along with others—onanists, *précieuses,* melancholics, hypochondriacs, nymphomaniacs, ad infinitum . . ." Huffer, *Mad for Foucault*, 50.

18. George P. Fedotov notes, "The Church, when canonizing a holy fool always presumes that the mask, the disguise, the point of departure of this kind of life is monastic-ascetical." George P. Fedotov, "The Holy Fools," *St. Vladimir's Quarterly* 3, no. 3 (Fall 1959): 8.

19. Francis's disciple Brother Juniper, among the best known of the holy fools in the Western church, appears in *The Little Flowers of St. Francis* as something of a simpleton. But he is calculating in his search for mockery. Encountering "certain wild young men, who began to mock him, treating him with great contempt and indignity . . . Brother Juniper was no way troubled thereat, but rather incited them to ill-treat him more and more." Nearly stripped and looking dreadful after the assault, Brother Juniper goes to the gate of a town where, as he had anticipated, he is taken for a murderer and "dragged . . . with great fury before the tyrant" (2.3)—where he continues to encourage the misconception. *The Little Flowers of St. Francis of Assisi*, trans. and ed. H. E. Manning (London: Burns and Lambert, 1884), 191.

20. Catherine Clément, in Catherine Clément and Julia Kristeva, *The Feminine and the Sacred*, trans. Jane Marie Todd (New York: Columbia University Press, 2001), 126.

21. Fedotov, "Holy Fools," 3. "The saint constantly commits disreputable and preposterous deeds, causes scandal in a church, eats publicly sausages on Good Friday, destroys merchandise in the market, dances with prostitutes and spends the nights in their houses. Of course, all these acts have a hidden beneficent sense. They work for the conversion of sinners. But the external scandal is great, and it was precisely this effect which was aimed at."

22. E. Poulakou-Rebelakou, A. Llarmakopoulos, C. Tsiamis, and D. Ploumpidis, "Holy Fools: A Religious Phenomenon of Extreme Behaviour," *Journal of Religious Health* 53 (2014): 98. Citing Lennart Rydén, ed., *Das Leben des heiligen Narren Symeon von Leontios von Neapolis* (Uppsala: Almquist and Wiksell, 1963).

23. Jordan, *Convulsing Bodies*, 188. With reference to Michel Foucault, *Le courage de la vérité: Le gouvernement de soi et des autres II: Cours au Collège de France, 1983–1984*, ed. Frédéric Gros under the direction of François Ewald and Alessandro Fontana (Paris: Gallimard / Seuil, 2009).

24. Fedotov, "Holy Fools," 7: "But an unethical and irrational root remains. It is: The need to lay bare the radical contradiction between Christian truth and both the common sense and the moral sense of the world in the act of ridiculing the world."

25. David Frankfurter, "Martyrology and the Prurient Gaze," *Journal of Early Christian Studies* 17, no. 2 (2009): 215.

26. Frankfurter, "Martyrology," 216. Citing Tertullian, *De spectaculis*, in *Tertullian: Apology and De spectaculis, and Minucius, Octavius*, ed. and trans. T. R. Glover and Gerald H. Rendall, Loeb Classical Library 250 (London: Heinemann, 1931), 274. Also citing Clement of Alexandria, *Exhortation to the Greeks*, in *Clement of Alexandria*, trans. G. W. Butterworth, Loeb Classical Library 92 (Cambridge, MA: Harvard University Press, 1919), §4. Butterworth translation amended by Frankfurter.

27. Frankfurter, "Martyrology," 218.

28. D. A. F. de Sade, *Marquis de Sade: 120 Days of Sodom and Other Writings*, compiled and trans. Austryn Wainhouse and Richard Seaver (New York: Grove Press, 1994), 496. Asterisks in original.

29. Ibid., 497.

30. Leopold von Sacher-Masoch, *Venus in Furs*, trans. Fernanda Savage (Digital: Project Gutenberg, 2011), Kindle edition, location 858. Regrettably, I have yet to find any means of eroticizing the experience of flying economy.

31. Ibid., locations 1601–06.

32. Ibid., locations 1114–17.

33. Clerical and monastic figures also appear in Sade's *Justine, or the Misfortunes of Virtue*, trans. John Philips (Oxford: Oxford University Press, 2012), and *Juliette*, trans. Austryn Wainhouse (New York: Grove Press, 1968), in which Juliette has a long discussion with the pope.

34. Michael Taussig, *Defacement: Public Secrecy and the Labor of the Negative* (Stanford: Stanford University Press, 1999), 13. Taussig argues that *sacrilege,* bringing sacred and profane improperly close together, is always implicit in *sacrifice,* meant to open a space for the sacred by emptying it of the sacrificial victim. Ibid., 146.

35. Burrus, *Saving Shame*, xii.

36. Anne Carson, *Eros the Bittersweet* (McLean, IL: Dalkey Archive Press, 1998), 30.

37. "This denial [*dénégation*] does not happen [to the secret] by accident; it is essential and originary. . . . The enigma . . . is the sharing of the secret, and not only shared to my partner in the society but the secret shared within itself, its 'own' partition, which divides the essence of a secret that cannot even appear to one alone except in starting to be lost, to divulge itself,

hence to dissimulate itself, as secret, in showing itself: dissimulating its dissimulation. There is no secret as such; I deny it. And this is what I confide in secret to whomever allies himself to me." Jacques Derrida, "How to Avoid Speaking: Denials," in *Languages of the Unsayable: The Play of Negativity in Literature and Literary Theory,* ed. Sanford Budick and Wolfgang Iser (Stanford: Stanford University Press, 1987), 25.

38. Carson, *Eros the Bittersweet,* 35.

39. Ibid., 30.

40. William Robert, "Performing Religiously Between Passion and Resistance," *Journal for Cultural and Religious Theory* 12, no. 2 (Fall 2012): 70–71.

41. Pascal Massie, "The Secret and the Neuter: On Blanchot and Heidegger," *Research in Phenomenology* 37, no. 1 (2007): 43.

42. Plato, *Symposium,* trans. Alexander Nehamas and Paul Woodruff (Indianapolis: Hackett, 2004), 210A.

43. Ibid., 211A–211D.

44. Georges Bataille, *Inner Experience,* trans. Stuart Kendall (Albany: State University of New York Press, 2014), 198. First ellipsis original.

45. Massie, "The Secret and the Neuter," 36.

46. Georges Bataille, *L'Abbé C,* trans. Philip A. Facey (London: Marion Boyars, 2001), 136.

47. Halberstam, *The Queer Art of Failure,* location 522. I have used "she" as the book was written under the name Judith; Halberstam currently identifies as "he," with the name Jack.

48. Simons, "Power, Resistance," 303. Citing Michel Foucault, *The History of Sexuality, vol. 1: An Introduction,* trans. Robert Hurley (New York: Pantheon Books, 1978), 98.

49. Jordan, *Convulsing Bodies,* 185.

50. Karmen MacKendrick, *counterpleasures* (Albany: State University of New York Press, 1999).

51. Stephen S. Bush, "Sovereignty and Cruelty: Self-Affirmation, Self-Dissolution, and the Bataillean Subject," in *Negative Ecstasies: Georges Bataille and the Study of Religion,* ed. Jeremy Biles and Kent Brintnall (New York: Fordham University Press, 2015), 40. I should note that this is not Bush's own position; he simply does a clear and concise job of summarizing both the promise in and the objections to a Bataillean ethics.

52. Sally Munt articulates this concern particularly well: "It is my contention . . . that shame, working at different levels, performs culturally to mark out certain groups. The political effects of shame can be observed on a national and global stage. . . . Shame operates more visibly within nation states to single out particular groups and stigmatise them; many of these groups are common targets whose vicitimsation remains historically long-lasting, typically: the underclass and the urban poor, rural labourers and peasants, 'gypsies' or Travellers, homosexuals, sex-workers, and racial enmities . . ." What holds for the group extends to those within it: "groups that are shamed contain individuals who internalize the stigma of shame into the tapestry of their lives, each reproduce discrete, shamed subjectivies, all with their specific pathologies." Sally Munt, *Queer Attachments: The Cultural Politics of Shame* (Aldershot, UK: Ashgate, 2007), 2–3. Kent Brintnall, public presentations and personal communication.

53. Burrus, *Saving Shame,* xi–xii.

54. Kent Brintnall, "Erotic Ruination: Embracing the 'Savage Spirituality' of Barebacking," in Biles and Brintnall, *Negative Ecstasies,* 54. Citing Leo Bersani, "Is the Rectum a Grave?" in *Is the Rectum a Grave? And Other Essays* (Chicago: University of Chicago Press, 2010), 25.

55. Ellis Hanson, "Teaching Shame," in Halperin and Traub, *Gay Shame*, 133.

56. Huffer, *Mad for Foucault*, 54.

57. Ibid., 1. Citing Michel Foucault, *History of Madness*, trans. Jonathan Murphy and Jean Khalfa (London, Routledge, 2006), xxxii.

58. Huffer, *Mad for Foucault*, 57.

59. Ibid., 55.

60. Jacob Rogozinski, *The Ego and the Flesh: An Introduction to Ego Analysis*, trans. Robert Vallier (Stanford: Stanford University Press, 2010), 173.

61. Julia Kristeva, *Powers of Horror: An Essay on Abjection*, trans. Leon S. Roudiez (New York: Columbia University Press, 1982), 85.

62. All discussion of abjection is indebted to the anthropologist Mary Douglas, who laid forth the structure of the abject in *Purity and Danger: An Analysis of Concepts of Pollution and Taboo* (New York: Routledge, 1966).

63. Halberstam, *The Queer Art of Failure*, locations 1664–66. Citing Heather Love, *Feeling Backwards: Loss and the Politics of Queer History* (Cambridge, MA: Harvard University Press, 2009), and José E. Muñoz, *Cruising Utopia: The There and Then of Queer Utopia* (New York: New York University Press, 2009).

64. Halberstam, *The Queer Art of Failure*, location 1843: "[I]n true camp fashion, the queer artist works with rather than against failure and inhabits the darkness. Indeed the darkness becomes a crucial part of a queer aesthetic."

65. Ibid., location 2232.

66. Maurice Blanchot, *The Step/Not Beyond*, trans. Lycette Nelson (Albany: State University of New York Press, 1992), 50, 137.

67. Plato, *Symposium*, 211A-C.

68. See, for example, Pseudo-Dionysius, *Celestial Hierarchy*, in *The Works of Dionysius the Areopagite*, Part II, trans. Rev. John Parker (London and Oxford: James Parker and Co., 1899), 2.2: "For any one might say that the cause why forms are naturally attributed to the formless, and shapes to the shapeless, is not alone our capacity which is unable immediately to elevate itself to the intelligible contemplations, and that it needs appropriate and cognate instructions which present images, suitable to us, of the formless and supernatural objects of contemplation; but further, that it is most agreeable to the revealing Oracles to conceal, through mystical and sacred enigmas, and to keep the holy and secret truth respecting the supermundane minds inaccessible to the multitude."

69. Meister Eckhart, Sermon 83, "Renovamini spiritu," in *The Essential Sermons, Commentaries, Treatises, and Defense*, trans. Edmund Colledge and Bernard McGinn (Mahwah, NJ: Paulist Press, 1981), 207.

70. See the helpful discussion in Charles Stang, *Apophasis and Pseudonymity in Dionysius the Areopagite: "No Longer I"* (Oxford: Oxford University Press, 2012).

71. See Enrica Ruaro, "God and the Worm: The Twofold Otherness in Pseudo-Dionysius's Theory of Dissimilar Images," *American Catholic Philosophical Quarterly* 82, no. 4 (2008): 589.

72. Pseudo-Dionysius, *Celestial Hierarchy*, II, 5 (145A–B). Thus cited in Ruaro, "God and the Worm," 587.

73. Maurice Blanchot, *L'Attente, l'Oubli* (Paris: Gallimard, 2008), 35. In English as *Awaiting Oblivion*, trans. John Gregg (Lincoln: University of Nebraska Press, 1999), 16.

74. Ann Smock, "Translator's Introduction," in Maurice Blanchot, *The Space of Literature*, ed. and trans. Ann Smock (Lincoln: University of Nebraska Press, 1989), 13.

75. Samuel Beckett, *Worstward Ho*, in *Nohow On: Company, Ill Seen Ill Said, and Worstward Ho* (New York: Grove Press, 1990), 89.

76. Leo Bersani and Ulysse Dutoit, *Arts of Impoverishment: Beckett, Rothko, Resnais* (Cambridge, MA: Harvard University Press, 1993), 77.

77. Ibid., 11, 51. Bersani and Dutoit also point out Beckett's efforts to drive language to the failure of expression (17), to create in dramatic storytelling the dual failure to begin (27–38) and to end (38–49), and to generate failures of relation and connection (throughout).

78. Beckett, *Worstward Ho*, 95.

79. Ibid., 90.

80. Alfred, Lord Douglas, "Two Loves," at https://www.poets.org/poetsorg/poem/two-loves.

81. Alfred, Lord Douglas, "In Praise of Shame," at https://www.poets.org/poetsorg/poem/praise-shame.

82. Laurie Anderson, "Language Is a Virus (From Outer Space)," on *Home of the Brave*, Warner Bros., 1986, Vinyl. William S. Burroughs, *The Ticket that Exploded* (New York: Grove Press, 1962), 49–50.

83. Jordan, *Convulsing Bodies*, 198. Citing Michel Foucault, *Le beau danger: Entretiens avec Claude Bonnefoy*, ed. Philipe Artières (Paris: Éditions EHESS, 2011), 40, 57–58. Jordan's translation.

84. Jordan, *Convulsing Bodies*, 185.

85. Jacques Derrida, *The Animal that Therefore I Am*, trans. David Wills, ed. Marie-Louise Mallet (New York: Fordham University Press, 2008), 1.

86. Michel de Certeau, *The Mystic Fable, vol. 1: The Sixteenth and Seventeenth Centuries*, trans. Michael B. Smith (Chicago: University of Chicago Press, 1992), 175. Delightfully, the section in which these remarks occur is entitled "The Lie, or the Function of Saying."

87. "In the face of contradiction this intense, precursor of things sacred if not uncanny, there surfaces the problem its demands make on language, as if there is a firm link between the logical possibilities for expression, even with a poetic language, and the exceeding of such possibilities by defacement." Taussig, *Defacement*, 50.

88. Jacques Derrida, "Composing 'Cirumfession,'" in *Augustine and Postmodernism: Confession and Circumfession*, ed. John D. Caputo and Michael J. Scanlon (Indianapolis: Indiana University Press, 2005), 24. Cited in Burrus, *Saving Shame*, 115.

89. Blanchot, *The Writing of the Disaster*, trans. Ann Smock (Lincoln: University of Nebraska Press, 1995), 11.

90. Sweedler, *The Dismembered Community*, 108.

91. Ibid. The text reads "bear," but I have assumed that this is a typographical error.

92. Leiris's multivolume autobiography (if one may call the curious collection by that name) includes numerous considerations both of shame and of the rich layers of association that that words always bore for him. The series comprises *Manhood: A Journey from Childhood into the Fierce Order of Virility*, trans. Richard Howard (Chicago, University of Chicago Press, 1992); *Rules of the Game: Scraps*, trans. Lydia Davis (Baltimore: Johns Hopkins University Press, 1997), and *Rules of the Game: Scratches*, trans. Lydia Davis (Baltimore: Johns Hopkins University Press, 1997).

93. Bataille, *L'Abbé C*, 129. Robert's shameful secret is that, under torture for his work in the Resistance, he kept silent the names of his comrades, but gave away those of people he loved.

94. Certeau, *The Mystic Fable*, 78.

95. Jordan, *Convulsing Bodies*, 191.

96. Ibid., 199.

97. Cf. ibid., 191: "Truth telling will always demand that someone cry out—and that someone register the cry."

CHAPTER TWO. UNWILLING

1. Quran 2:35–37: And We said, "O Adam, dwell, you and your wife, in Paradise and eat therefrom in [ease and] abundance from wherever you will. But do not approach this tree, lest you be among the wrongdoers." But Satan caused them to slip out of it and removed them from that [condition] in which they had been. And We said, "Go down, [all of you], as enemies to one another, and you will have upon the earth a place of settlement and provision for a time." Then Adam received from his Lord [some] words, and He accepted his repentance. Indeed, it is He who is the Accepting of repentance, the Merciful. All citations from the Quran are from *The Noble Qur'an*, Quran.com, 2016. http://quran.com/.

2. The punishments are detailed in Genesis 3:14–19. The issue of mortality is somewhat tricky. God's specific worry is that now that the humans share divine knowledge, they might also eat from the tree of life and become immortal (3:22–24). This suggests that mortality is less imposed upon them than continued for them, and so the primary punishment would be exile. However, the Christian version of this myth links this Fall directly to redemption by the sacrifice of Christ, and that redemption is held to be from lasting death. All Biblical references from *The Catholic Study Bible*, New American Bible translation, ed. Donald Senior, John J. Collins, and Mary Ann Getty (Oxford: Oxford University Press, 2010).

3. Particularly Romans 5:12–21 and 1 Corinthians 15: 7–22.

4. The Quran suggests something similar. See, e.g., 2:10: "In their hearts is disease, so Allah has increased their disease." *Qur'an*, http://quran.com/2.

5. In fact, the unfamiliar stirring of this disobedient flesh is one of the first signs of post-lapsarian separation. See Augustine, *City of God*, trans. Henry Bettenson (New York: Penguin, 2003), 4.14. See also 14.26.

6. This, too, is based upon the text of Romans.

7. Augustine, *City of God*, 22.17.

8. Ibid., 22.30.

9. Ibid., 4.14.

10. "The mind commands itself and meets resistance. . . . The mind orders the mind to will. The recipient of the order is itself, yet it does not perform it. What causes this . . . ? . . . For it is the will that commands the will to exist, and it commands not another will but itself." Augustine, *Confessions*, trans. Henry Chadwick (Oxford: Oxford University Press, 1991), 7.8.20–7.9.21.

11. Kant also wrote a much longer work on ethics, the *Critique of Practical Reason*, trans. Werner S. Pluhar (Indianapolis: Hackett, 2002). Though his ideas are developed more

thoroughly there, that text is considerably less accessible and less attended-to than the more concise *Groundwork*. Immanuel Kant, *Grounding for the Metaphysics of Morals,* with *On a Supposed Right to Lie Because of Philanthropic Concerns*, trans. James W. Ellington (Indianapolis: Hackett, 1993).

12. Kant, *Grounding*, 4:Ak 431; my italics.

13. Kant, *Grounding*, 4:Ak 439; italics original.

14. Kant does not extend moral dignity to animals. Some philosophers have criticized him for this. See, e.g., Christina Hoff, "Kant's Invidious Humanism," *Environmental Ethics* 5 (Spring 1983): 63–70, or James Rachels's *Created from Animals: The Moral Implications of Darwinism* (Oxford: Oxford University Press, 1990). Others have extended to animals our obligations within a Kantian system. Christine Korsgaard regards other animals as nonrational (though intelligent), but argues that Kantian ethics *does* extend our obligations to cover other animals, on the grounds that cruelty to them is nearly analogous to cruelty to other humans, and has a morally detrimental effect upon the doer. See *Fellow Creatures: Kantian Ethics and Our Duties to Animals, Tanner Lectures on Human Values* (Ann Arbor: University of Michigan Press, 2004). I am unaware of suggestions that Kant himself would argue that we have moral duties to other animals for their own sake, but my knowledge of the field is far from complete.

15. This is the formula of the kingdom of ends (*Groundwork* Ak 4:437f), and the basis for Robert Paul Wolff's *In Defense of Anarchism* (Berkeley: University of California Press, 1998).

16. Kant, *Grounding*, Ak 4. 440.

17. Jeremy Waldron, "Cruel, Inhuman and Degrading Treatment: The Words Themselves," 2008, New York University School of Law, Public Law and Legal Theory Research Paper Series, Working Paper 08-36, at http://ssrn.com/abstract=1278604, 41.

18. Martha Nussbaum, "The Capabilities of People with Cognitive Disabilities," *Metaphilosophy* 40, nos. 3–4 (2009): 335. See also Martha Nussbaum, *Frontiers of Justice: Disability, Nationality, Species Membership* (Cambridge, MA: Belknap Press, 2007), ch. 5.

19. See particularly ibid.

20. For a useful summary and consideration of the capabilities approach and the extent of its reach, see Mary Leukam, "Dignified Animals: How 'Non-Kantian' is Nussbaum's Conception of Dignity?" Thesis, Georgia State University, 2011. Accessed February 23, 2017, at http://scholarworks.gsu.edu/philosophy_theses/89.

21. See "dignity" and "decent" in the Online Etymology Dictionary, http://etymonline.com/. As Michael Rosen points out in his history of dignity, "Terms to express similar conceptions exist in most languages, including ancient ones." Michael Rosen, *Dignity: Its History and Meaning* (Cambridge, MA: Harvard University Press, 2012), 11.

22. Ibid.

23. Patrick Geary, "The Humiliation of Saints," in *Saints and their Cults: Studies in Religious Sociology, Folklore, and History*, ed. Stephen Wilson (Cambridge: Cambridge University Press, 1983), 136.

24. Clément, in Clément and Kristeva, *The Feminine and the Sacred,* 90.

25. Giovanni Pico della Mirandola, *Oration on the Dignity of Man*, trans. A. Robert Caponegri (Washington, DC: Gateway Editions, 1996). See also Rosen, *Dignity*, 14–15. Even after Pico, some resistance lingers—aristocracies, Alexis de Tocqueville declares, "raise greatly the general pitch of society. In aristocratic ages vast ideas are commonly entertained of the dignity, the power, and the greatness of man." No such elevation pulls up the democratic populace,

which too easily drags us all to the lowest level. Alexis de Tocqueville, *Democracy in America* (1831), trans. Henry Reeve (1839), Book 1, chapter 10. Via Project Gutenberg at http://xroads.virginia.edu/~hyper/DETOC/ch1_10.htm. In fact, Waldron argues, "the modern notion of human dignity does not cut loose from the idea of rank" even in an attempt at equality; "instead it involves an upwards equalization of rank, so that we now try to accord to every human being something of the dignity, rank, and expectation of respect that was formerly accorded to nobility." Jeremy Waldron, *Dignity, Rank, and Rights* (Cambridge, MA: Harvard University Press, 2012), 229. See also 210.

26. Waldron, *Dignity, Rank, and Rights;* Ronald Dworkin, *Justice for Hedgehogs* (Cambridge, MA: Belknap Press, 2011); Rosen, *Dignity.* Dworkin writes firmly, "[Justice] is drawn from dignity and aims at dignity," 423.

27. See Rosen, *Dignity*, 53–62.

28. For Dworkin, the principles of dignity are self-respect and authenticity, "personal responsibility for identifying what counts as success in his own life; . . . a personal responsibility to create that life through a coherent narrative or style that he endorses." Dworkin, *Justice for Hedgehogs*, 203–204. Rosen writes, "To respect someone's dignity requires that one treats them 'with dignity'—that is, they must not be treated in ways that degrade, insult, or express contempt." Rosen, *Dignity*, 129.

29. If we are moving toward a culture of victimization, as various corners of the internet insist, this distinction may be involved in interesting changes. Victimization implies both a greater demand for respect and a greater alienability of dignity than we are accustomed to considering. Bradley Campbell and Jason Manning argue that we may be seeing "large-scale moral change such as the emergence of a victimhood culture that is distinct from the honor cultures and dignity cultures of the past." Bradley Campbell and Jason Manning, "Microaggressions and Moral Culture," *Comparative Sociology* 13, no. 6 (2014): 692.

30. Basil of Caesarea, *The Asketicon of Basil the Great*, ed. and trans. Anna Silvas (Oxford: Oxford University Press, 2005), 255, 434. Also see 193, 215, 219, 220, 231–32, 336, 359, 366, 381.

31. Benedict of Nursia, *Saint Benedict's Rule for Monasteries*, trans. Leonard J. Doyle OblSB, (Collegeville, MN: Order of St. Benedict, 2001), ch. 7.

32. All, ibid.

33. Sara Maitland, "Saints for Today," *The Way* 36, no. 4 (October 1996): 275–76. See also Chloë Taylor, *The Culture of Confession from Augustine to Foucault: A Genealogy of the "Confessing Animal"* (New York: Routledge, 2009), 17: "At the same time, the discipline involved would augment and aim toward obedience rather than autonomy, an anxiety-ridden obedience to a doctrine within a hierarchy ever less clearly and less calmly chosen."

34. Augustine, *Confessions,* 9.1.1. The text cites Matt. 11:30.

35. "This is our freedom, when we are subject to the truth; and the truth is God himself, who frees us from death, that is, from the state of sin. For that truth, speaking as a human being to those who believe in him, says, 'If you abide in my word, you are truly my disciples. And you shall know the truth, and the truth shall make you free' (John 8:31–32)." Augustine, *On the Free Choice of the Will*, trans. Thomas Williams (Indianapolis: Hackett, 1993), 57. A similar point is made by, among others, Nicholas of Cusa, who declares, "Since the intellectual spirit is not constrained by the influence of the heavens, but is absolutely free, it cometh not to perfection unless it submit itself through faith unto the word of God, like a free disciple, under no control, who is not perfected unless by faith he submit himself unto the word of a master: he needs must have confidence in the master and listen unto him. The intellect is

perfected by the Word of God, and groweth, and becometh continually more receptive and apt, and liker unto the Word." Nicolas of Cusa, *The Vision of God,* trans. Emma Gurley Salter (New York: Frederick Ungar, 1928), 123.

36. On which point Meister Eckhart is succinct: "There are some people who want to have their own will in everything; that is bad, and there is much harm in it. Those are a little better who do want what God wants, and want nothing contrary to his will; if they were sick, what they would wish would be for God's will to be for them to be well. So these people want God to want according to their will, not for themselves to want according to his will." German Sermon 6, "Justi vivent in aeternum," in *The Essential Sermons, Commentaries, Treatises, and Defense,* 186.

37. Joseph Delany, "Obedience," in *The Catholic Encyclopedia,* Vol. 11 (New York: Robert Appleton Company, 1911), 182.

38. Thomas Aquinas, *Summa Theologiae,* trans. The Fathers of the English Dominican Province (Cincinnati: Benziger Brothers, 1947), 2.2, Question 104, Article 2.

39. J. Giles Milhaven, "Asceticism and the Moral Good: A Tale of Two Pleasures," in *Asceticism,* ed. Vincent Wimbush and Richard Valentasis (Oxford: Oxford University Press, 1998), 389.

40. Basil of Caesarea, *The Asketicon,* 185.

41. See Peter Brown, *The Body and Society: Men, Women, and Sexual Renunciation in Early Christianity* (New York: Columbia University Press, 1988), 425: "The fatal flaw of concupiscence would not have seemed so tragic to Augustine, if he had not become ever more deeply convinced that human beings had been created to embrace the material world. The body was a problem to him precisely because it was to be loved and cherished."

42. Ibid., 417; see also 421.

43. Ibid., 422, citing Augustine, *Confessions* 10.30.42, and *de Genesi ad litteram* 12.15.31. Available in English as *The Literal Meaning of Genesis,* trans. John Hammond Taylor (Mahwah, NJ: Paulist Press, 1982).

44. Ibid., 423: "Meanwhile, the monk was encouraged to scan his dreams for welcome signals of the approach of peace of heart. Businesslike as ever, Apa Moses declared that three emissions a year, without sexual fantasies, would be what the good monk might expect."

45. John Cassian, *John Cassian: The Conferences,* trans. Boniface Ramsey (Mahwah, NJ: Paulist Press, 1997), Conference 19, ch. 1.

46. Léon Wurmser, *The Mask of Shame* (Baltimore: Johns Hopkins University Press, 1981), 61–62.

47. Ibid., 63.

48. R. F. Newbold, "Personality Structure and Response to Adversity in Early Christian Hagiography," *Numen* 31, no. 2 (1984): 200. By contrast, however, consider Tobin Siebers, "Sex, Shame, and Disability Identity: With Reference to Mark O'Brien," in Halperin and Traub, *Gay Shame,* 204: "Having nothing to be ashamed of . . . is not a sign of either moral integrity or moral failure. It is a sign of social worthlessness. Any human being will display shame if only his or her social value is sufficient to merit being asked a prying question." As shall soon be clear, my sympathies are more with Siebers than with Prudentius.

49. Thomas Aquinas, *Summa Theologiae,* 2.2, Question 104, Article 2.

50. Ibid., Article 3: "Therefore, properly speaking, the virtue of obedience, whereby we contemn our own will for God's sake, is more praiseworthy than the other moral virtues, which contemn other goods for the sake of God."

51. Ibid., 2.2, Question 105, Article 2.

52. This is particularly apparent in the first three books of his *Confessions*.

53. Burrus, *Saving Shame*, 108.

54. Jacob Rogozinski, *The Ego and the Flesh: An Introduction to Egoanalysis*, trans. Robert Vallier (Stanford: Stanford University Press, 2010), 301.

55. There are exceptions to this reading, of course. Most significantly, death of God theology (particularly for Thomas J. J. Altizer) holds that divinity itself dies with the crucifixion. (See especially *The New Gospel of Christian Atheism* [Aurora, CO: The Davies Group, 2003]). A more conventional and broadly held opinion is that this emptying would undo dual-natured Christology or hypostatic union (the idea that Christ is fully human and fully divine), so that Christ must only have acted as if he did not possess these divine privileges; that is, he continued to possess them, but refused to exercise them.

56. Matt 26:39, Mark 14:36, Luke 22:42.

57. John 4:34, 5:30, 6:38.

58. Rogozinski, *The Ego and the Flesh*, 301.

59. Kristeva, *Powers of Horror*, 5.

60. "Any secretion or discharge, anything that leaks out of the feminine or masculine body defiles. After a reference to sacrifice ... we have again a designation of the impurity of blood." Kristeva, *Powers of Horror*, 102.

61. Ibid., 107.

62. John Chrysostom, "Homily Against the Marcionists and the Manicheans," trans. W. R. W. Stephens, in *Nicene and Post-Nicene Fathers*, First Series, vol.9, ed. Philip Schaff (Buffalo: Christian Literature, 1889), sec. 4.

63. John Cassian, Conference 19, ch. 6.

64. Benedict, *Rule*, ch. 5, citing John 6:38.

65. Hans Urs von Balthasar, *Mysterium Paschale*, trans. Aidan Nichols, OP (Grand Rapids: William B. Eerdmans, 1990), 105.

66. Ibid., i, 111.

67. Bataille, *Inner Experience*, 69.

68. Georges Bataille, *On Nietzsche*, trans. Stuart Kendall (Albany: State University of New York Press, 2015), 44.

69. Kristeva, *Powers of Horror*, 120.

70. Ibid., 123.

71. Ibid.

72. Carson, *Eros the Bittersweet*, 17: "Eros is a verb."

73. Burrus, *Saving Shame*, 46.

74. Kristeva, *Powers of Horror*, 124–25.

75. Taylor, *The Culture of Confession*, 21. Citing Michel Foucault, "Christianity and Confession," in *About the Beginning of a Hermeneutics of the Self: Lectures at Dartmouth College, 1980*, trans. Graham Burchell (Chicago: University of Chicago Press, 2016), 214.

76. Bataille attended the lectures of the Hegel scholar Alexandre Kojève, and his view of the necessary conflict between two autonomous beings, or even between one autonomous being and a recalcitrant world, is influenced by Hegel's discussion of the development of the

146

NOTES TO CHAPTER TWO

human subject in *The Phenomenology of Spirit*. Alexandre Kojève, *Introduction to the Reading of Hegel: Lectures on the Phenomenology of Spirit*, trans. James H. Nichols Jr. (Ithaca: Cornell University Press, 1980), esp. "In Place of an Introduction," 3–30.

77. Bataille, *Inner Experience*, 91.

78. Ibid.

79. Sean Connolly, "Laure's War: Selfhood and Sacrifice in Colette Peignot," *French Forum* 35, no. 1 (Winter 2010): 20.

80. Halberstam, *The Queer Art of Failure*, location 2633. Citing Elizabeth Freeman, *Time Binds: Queer Temporalities* (Durham: Duke University Press, 2010).

81. Ibid., location 2643.

82. Kristeva, in Clément and Kristeva, *The Feminine and the Sacred*, 118.

83. Foucault, "On the Government of the Living," 157.

84. Bataille, *Inner Experience*, 65. We have need, even, for another: "But I do not attain the extremity on my own and really I cannot believe the extremity has been attained, since I never remain there." Ibid., 48.

85. Ibid., 99.

86. Simone Weil, *Gravity and Grace*, trans. Emma Crawford and Mario van der Ruhr (New York: Routledge, 2007), 3.

87. Friedrich Nietzsche, *On the Genealogy of Morality*, trans. Maudemarie Clark and Alan J. Swensen (Indianapolis: Hackett, 1998), 78.

88. Burrus, *Saving Shame*, 81.

89. Weil, *Gravity and Grace*, 59.

90. Ibid., 49.

91. Benedict, *Rule*, ch. 7, degrees 5–7.

92. William Ian Miller, *Humiliation: And Other Essays on Honor, Social Discomfort, and Violence* (Ithaca: Cornell University Press, 1999), 147.

93. Nietzsche, "What Do Ascetic Ideals Mean?" in *On the Genealogy of Morality*, 67–118.

94. Augustine, *The Rule of St. Augustine*, in *Augustine's Rule: A Commentary*, Adolar Zumkeller OSA, trans. Matthew J. O'Connell, ed. John E. Rotelle OSA (Villanova, PA: Augustinian Press, 1987), 7.46–47.

95. Georges Bataille, *The Unfinished System of Nonknowledge*, ed. Stuart Kendall, trans. Michelle Kendall and Stuart Kendall (Minneapolis: University of Minnesota Press, 2001), 269.

96. Rudolph Bell, *Holy Anorexia* (Chicago: University of Chicago Press, 1985), of Catherine of Siena, 42.

97. Ibid., 160.

98. Teresa of Avila, *The Life of Saint Teresa of Avila, by Herself*, trans. J. M. Cohen (New York: Penguin, 1988), 207–208.

99. Kenneth Baxter Wolf has translated the testimony from Elizabeth's canonization and supplemented it with exegeses, in Kenneth Baxter Wolf, *The Life and Afterlife of Elizabeth of Hungary: Testimony from her Canonization Hearings* (Oxford: Oxford University Press, 2010).

100. Dossie Easton and Janet W. Hardy, *The New Bottoming Book* (Emeryville, CA: Greenery Press, 2001), 28. See also Dossie Easton and Janet W. Hardy, *The New Topping Book* (Emeryville,

CA: Greenery Press, 2003). The original editions of each book, by the same authors, were published by Greenery Press in 1998 and 1995.

101. Jeanette Winterson, *Oranges Are not the Only Fruit* (New York: Grove Press, 1985), 170.

102. This invocation occurs several times in Augustine, *Confessions*, Book 10.

103. See Nietzsche, *Genealogy of Morality*.

104. Wallace Stevens, "Notes Toward a Supreme Fiction," in *The Collected Poems: Corrected Edition* (New York: Vintage, 2015), 401–34.

105. Neil Bartlett, "Plunge into Your Shame," in Halperin and Traub, *Gay Shame,* 354–55. Final ellipsis original.

CHAPTER THREE. UNMAKING

1. "There is a correlation between disclosure of the self . . . and the renunciation of the self." Michel Foucault, *Ethics, Subjectivity, and Truth: The Essential Works of Michel Foucault*, ed. Paul Rabinow (New York: The New Press, 1997), 274; "Technologies of the Self" in *Technologies of the Self: A Seminar with Michel Foucault*, ed. Luther H. Martin et al., (Amherst: University of Massachusetts Press, 1988), 48.

2. David Brakke, "Making Public the Monastic Life: Reading the Self in Evagrius Ponticus' *Talking Back,*" in *Religion and the Self in Antiquity*, ed. David Brakke, Michael L. Satlow, and Steven Weitzman (Bloomington: Indiana University Press, 2005), 222. Citing Charles Taylor, *Sources of the Self: The Making of the Modern Identity* (Cambridge: Harvard University Press, 1989), 127–42.

3. Michel Foucault, "About the Beginning of the Hermeneutics of the Self," in Carrette, *Religion and Culture*, 174, 177–79.

4. Johanna Oksala, "From Biopower to Governmentality," in Falzon, O'Leary, and Sawacki, *A Companion to Foucault*, 328. In the modern state, Oksala writes, "subjectivity must be shaped in a specific form through forms of individualizing knowledge and continuous techniques of normalizing power. The state must subject its population to continuous care, control, and guidance in the name of its wellbeing." Jon Simons also draws out the pastoral element of modern state power: "Combining pastoralism and reason of state, modern government is interested in population and welfare in so far as they contribute to state power. The care of the individual becomes a duty for the state, because each individual can contribute to the strength of the state." Jon Simons, "Power, Resistance," 147.

5. Simons, "Power, Resistance," 313. Citing *Power: Essential Works of Foucault 1954–1984*, 332–34, and *The Foucault Reader*, 47–48.

6. Simons, "Power, Resistance," 313, citing Foucault, *Power: Essential Works*, 334–35.

7. See Taylor, *The Culture of Confession*, 14.

8. Kristeva, *Powers of Horror*, 130.

9. Ibid. Nor is Anthony alone in this, as Kristeva notes: "Pachomius (290–346) took up the same point: 'It is greatly wrong not to let the state of one's soul immediately be known to a man practised in spiritual discernment.'"

10. In William Robert, *Exposures: Of Angela of Foligno*, in manuscript, 56: "In 1215, the Fourth Lateran Council mandated that Christians confess at least once a year." Taylor, *The*

Culture of Confession, 46, provides several references: Jacques Le Goff, The Birth of Purgatory (Chicago: University of Chicago Press, 1984); Robb Meens, "Frequency and Nature of Early Medieval Penance," in Handling Sin: Confession in the Middle Ages, ed. Peter Briller and A. J. Minnie (York, UK: York Medieval Press, 1998), 35–55, and R. C. Mortimer, The Origins of Private Penance in the Western Church (Oxford: Clarendon Press, 1939).

11. Taylor notes some slightly amusing modes of resistance—for instance, all members of a church would go at the same time of year, "guaranteeing congestion, noise, and speed." Taylor, The Culture of Confession, 54.

12. Ibid., 49.

13. Kristeva, Powers of Horror, 131.

14. Ibid., 132.

15. Ibid., 130.

16. Taylor, The Culture of Confession, 48.

17. Ibid., 63–64. Citing W. David Meyers, "Poor Sinning Folk": Confession and Conscience in Counter-Reformation Germany (Ithaca: Cornell University Press, 1996), 65.

18. Jordan, Convulsing Bodies, 139.

19. For confession as construction, see especially Michel Foucault, About the Beginning of the Hermeneutics of the Self.

20. Jordan, Convulsing Bodies, 135.

21. Ibid., 159. At 124, Jordan cites Foucault: "Why do we will, we others, and why have we willed, we European others, for millennia, to know the truth of our sex rather than to achieve intensity of pleasure?" Michel Foucault, "Sexualité et pouvoir," in Dits et écrits, vol. 3, ed. Jacques Lagrange under the direction of Daniel Defert and François Ewald (Paris: Gallimard, 1994), 556–57. Jordan's translation.

22. Foucault, The History of Sexuality, vol. 1: An Introduction, 60. Taylor notes that, in the converse of lay resistance, the desire to confess also became problematically intense after confession was imposed as an obligation upon the laity: "For some, confession had become an internalized desire to the extent that, despite the prohibitive fact that confessants had to pay alms in order to confess, confession manuals soon reflect the problem of repeated and excessively detailed confessions, of fabricated confessions manufactured by overly-anxious minds, and of priests overworked, exhausted, and exasperated by too many confessions. 'Scrupulousness,' or excessive self-examination and confession, became a new sin, a sin that one might (scrupulously) need to confess to, since such meticulous penitents were accused of not having enough faith in the mercy of God, or enough humility to submit to Him without these constant confessional interventions." Taylor, The Culture of Confession, 60. Citing Thomas N. Tentler, Sin and Confession on the Eve of the Reformation (Princeton: Princeton University Press, 1977), 114.

23. Jordan notes a humorous variant of this talk of flesh: flesh that talks. "Setting most of its delightful detail aside, Foucault takes just the conceit of talking genitals—with one significant change. In Diderot's novel, the genie's magic ring works only on women. If various pseudo-anatomical speculations are presented to account for this sexual specificity, the novel's answer is much simpler: men do not need to be compelled by a ring to boast of their sexual exploits. They do so regularly and sometimes even candidly. It is Foucault who tacitly generalizes the magical conceit to include both sexes. He writes as if all bodies were female and subject to the whimsically sadistic curiosity of a monarchical and decidedly male Power.

Foucault says that the point of the studies he is about to undertake is nothing other than 'to transcribe into history [en histoire] the fable of the Indiscreet Jewels.'" Jordan, *Convulsing Bodies*, 97. Citing Denis Diderot, *Les bijoux indiscrets*, in *Oeuvres complètes*, vol. 3, ed. Jean Macary, Aram Vartanian, and Jean-Louis Leutrat (Paris: Hermann, 1978), 1–290, and Michel Foucault, *Histoire de la sexualité, vol. 1: La volonté de savoir* (Paris: Gallimard, 1976), 101.

24. Jordan, *Convulsing Bodies*, 104.

25. Taylor, *The Culture of Confession*, 57.

26. Ibid., 59.

27. Jordan, *Convulsing Bodies*, 104.

28. Taylor, *The Culture of Confession*, 15–16.

29. Burrus, *Saving Shame*, 3.

30. Brown, *The Body and Society*, 231.

31. See ibid., 433: "The transparency that John Cassian associated with the gift of 'purity of heart' was shown in the body by the ebbing of the sexual drive. . . . If Augustine disagreed with Cassian, it was not because he believed that the body's instincts were any stronger or more corrupt: rather he held that the most humble details of the body's experience of sexuality . . . mirrored a failure of the will more drastic and irrevocable than Cassian had been prepared to admit."

32. Burrus, *Saving Shame*, 9.

33. Taylor, *The Culture of Confession,* 22: "Importantly, another person is required to help the monastic subject reveal the hidden truth of his thoughts. While Seneca, and even Chrysostom, thought one could lie in bed and contemplate one's day silently and alone, for Cassian it is clear that the examination of thoughts needed to be made to one's spiritual director, and that . . . this examination . . . needed to be put into words."

34. Ibid., 23: "Only when speaking a thought in the presence of another does one experience the difficulty of admitting to shameful thoughts and thus realize the extent of their shamefulness and untruth."

35. David Brakke, "The Problematization of Nocturnal Emissions in Early Christian Syria, Egypt, and Gaul," *Journal of Early Christian Studies* 3, no. 4 (1995): 449. Cited in Burrus, *Saving Shame*, 41. See also Burrus, *Saving Shame*, 141, where she notes that both Cassian and Augustine presume "a split between the will and movements of both thought and flesh that evade the will's control, as well as between what can be seen or known and what remains stubbornly secret . . . a split between the self who confesses and the self who is confessed." Also see Jordan, *Convulsing Bodies*, 137: "Foucault claims a Christian origin for the link between doubling and verbalization."

36. Cf. Burrus's description in *Saving Shame*, 9: "Not an eradication of shame but a continuous turning within shame—a sustained state of contrition, repentance, conversion. Not a catharsis but an ongoing responsiveness—a painfully unrelieved openness."

37. Lazy Domme, "Humiliation in Private," July 29, 2011. http://lazydomme.blogspot.com/2011/07/humiliation-in-private.html.

38. Taylor, *The Culture of Confession*, 87.

39. Bruno Latour, *Rejoicing: Or the Torments of Religious Speech*, trans. Julie Rose (Cambridge: Polity Press, 2013), 20–21. See also 14: "It's very simple: those texts, those words do not provide access to anything whatever; they do not form the first link in a chain of reference

that would, in the end, if all the links hold firm, allow us to find ourselves on familiar turf, to have seen in advance what we were dealing with."

40. Ibid., 102.

41. Ibid., 67–68.

42. Ibid., 120–21.

43. Ibid., 150: "Can I now forget about the comminatory question: 'Is it real or is it made?' and, here too, substitute the question:'How do you tell the difference between what is well and what is badly made?'"

44. Jordan, *Convulsing Bodies*, 17.

45. Bataille, *Inner Experience*, 128–29. See also Judith Butler, *Giving an Account of Oneself* (New York: Fordham University Press, 2005), 37, where Butler writes that it is "only in dispossession that I can and do give any account of myself."

46. Amalia Ziv clarifies the connection in "Shameful Fantasies: Cross-Gender Queer Sex in Lesbian Erotic Fiction," in Halperin and Traub, *Gay Shame*, 170: "For Bataille, eroticism always entails violation of individual boundaries and loss of self-possession. Humiliation, like other forms of violence, violates—if only temporarily—our sense of self. Hence, by dissolving our boundaries and divesting us of our discontinuous self, humiliation can inaugurate us into the erotic."

47. Georges Bataille, *My Mother*, in *My Mother, Madame Edwarda,* and *The Dead Man*, trans. Austryn Wainhouse (London: Marion Boyars, 2000), 68.

48. This is particularly but not exclusively true of sexual sensation; see John Cassian's *Institutes*, trans. Boniface Ramsey (Westminster, MD: Newman Press, 2000), *passim,* and likewise his *Conferences,* trans. Boniface Ramsey, (Mahwah, NJ: Paulist Press, 1985). See also Brown, *The Body and Society*, esp. 421.

49. And, of course, we do indeed do our best to show and to tell. Jordan, *Convulsing Bodies*, 86: "We talk about it no longer in the confessional but in the clinic. Whatever the site, sexuality as such has always been articulated. 'In a general way, I would say this: sexuality, in the West, is not what one silences; it is not what one is obliged to keep silent but what one is obliged to confess.' To confess—once ritually and sacramentally, now medically and legally." Citing Michel Foucault, *Les anormaux: Cours au Collège de France, 1974–1975*, ed. Valerio Marchetti and Antoinetta Salomoni under the direction of François Ewald and Alesandro Fontana (Paris: Gallimard/ Seuil, 1999), 157. Jordan's translation.

50. Huffer, *Mad for Foucault*, 65. Citing Joan Scott, "The Evidence of Experience," *Lesbian and Gay Studies Reader*, ed. Henry Abelove, Michèle Aina Barale, and David M. Halperin (New York: Routledge, 1993), 412.

51. Bataille, *The Unfinished System of Nonknowledge*, 98.

52. Jordan, *Convulsing Bodies*, 136. Citing Michel Foucault, *Du gouvernement des vivants: Cours au Collège de France, 1979–1980*, ed. Michel Senellart under the direction of François Ewald and Alessandro Fontana (Paris: EHESS, Gallimard, and Seuil, 2012), 175, 222. Jordan's translation.

53. Tobin Siebers, "Sex, Shame, and Disability Identity: With Reference to Mark O'Brien," in Halperin and Traub, *Gay Shame,* 205.

54. Ana-Karina Schneider sums up liminality succinctly: "Liminality is conventionally defined as the in-between condition traversed as part of rites of passage (see van Gennep), a 'liminal phase between rites of separation and reincorporation' (Aguirre et al. 7), or 'a state or

process which is betwixt-and-between the normal, day-to-day cultural and social states and processes of getting and spending, preserving law and order, and registering structural status' (Turner, 'Frame, Flow and Reflection' 465)." Ana-Karina Schneider, "Skin as a Trope of Liminality in Anne Enright's *The Gathering*," in *Contemporary Women's Writing* 8, no. 2 (2014): 208. Citing Manuel Aguirre, Roberta Quance, and Philip Sutton, *Margins and Thresholds: An Enquiry into the Concept of Liminality in Text Studies: Studies in Liminality and Literature 1* (Madrid: The Gateway Press, 2000); Victor Turner, "Frame, Flow and Reflection: Ritual and Drama as Public Liminality," *Japanese Journal of Religious Studies* 6, no. 4 (December 1979): 465–99; with reference to Arnold van Gennep, *The Rites of Passage*, trans. Monika B. Vizedom and Gabrielle L. Caffee (New York: Routledge Library Editions, 1960).

55. Schneider, "Skin as Trope," 208. Citing Victor Turner, "Liminality and Communitas," in Victor Turner, ed., *The Ritual Process: Structure and Anti-Structure* (Ithaca: Cornell University Press, 1977), 106–107.

56. Schneider, "Skin as Trope," 209. Citing Victor Turner, "Betwixt and Between: The Liminal Period in Rites de Passage," in Victor Turner, *The Forest of Symbols: Aspects of Ndembu Ritual* (Ithaca: Cornell University Press, 1970), 97–98.

57. Schneider, "Skin as Trope," 209.

58. Colette Peignot, *Laure: The Collected Writings*, trans. Jeannine Herman (San Francisco: City Lights, 2001), 151.

59. Certeau, *The Mystic Fable*, 232.

60. Ibid., 187.

61. Taylor notes the potential for complication here: The confessant's desire to speak "has not been separable from a discussion of the confessor's desire—or lack of desire—to hear the confession, whether the confessor is a lover, a priest, a psychoanalyst, or a police officer. A rebounding form of discipline has been observed, as for instance when priests themselves grew scrupulous, or when the analyst's desire became implicated in his confessant's story. The one who listens, as in the case of the scrupulous priest or the counter-confessing analyst, may become the one who speaks, internalizing the desire to confess which he claims to inculcate in the other." Taylor, *The Culture of Confession*, 166.

62. Sean Connolly, "Laure's War: Selfhood and Sacrifice in Colette Peignot," *French Forum* 35, no. 1 (Winter 2010): 28.

63. David M. Halperin and Valerie Traub, "Beyond Gay Pride," in Halperin and Traub, *Gay Shame*, 38.

64. Latour, *Rejoicing*, 123.

65. Ibid., 103: "The creationists and other literalists can no longer even remember that there was a time when people spoke to designate something other than access to the distant." And, 35: "Why has it become so hard to mark the difference between what allows access to the distant—reference—and what allows us to transform someone distant into someone close—conversion?"

66. Ibid., 131.

67. Bataille, *L'Abbé C*, 57.

68. Jordan, *Convulsing Bodies*, 136. Citing Foucault, *Du gouvernement des vivants*, 207. Jordan's translation.

69. Huffer, *Mad for Foucault*, 32. Citing Michel Foucault, *History of Madness*, trans. Jonathan Murphy and Jean Khalfa (London: Routledge, 2006), 7.

70. Sarah Hamilton, "Doing Penance," in *Medieval Christianity in Practice*, ed. Miri Rubin (Princeton: Princeton University Press, 2009), 141.

71. Both of these passages are cited by Sarah Hamilton, "Doing Penance," 138. Her source is *Die Bussbücher und das kanonische Bussverfahren nachhandschriftlichen Quellen*, ed. Hermann J. Schmitz (Schwann: Düsseldorf, 1898), 402–407. Corrected against manuscript Vaticana ms. Vat. Lat. 4772, fols. 190v–194v (Vatican City: Biblioteca Apostolica).

72. Jordan, *Convulsing Bodies*, 89. Citing Foucault, *Les anormaux*, 198. Jordan's translation.

73. Teresa of Avila, *The Life*, 174.

74. Virginia Burrus, "A Saint of One's Own: Emmanuel Levinas, Eliezer ben Hyrcanus, and Eulalia of Mérida," *L'Esprit Créateur* 50, no. 1 (Spring 2010): 8. Citing Derek Krueger, *Writing and Holiness: The Practice of Authorship in the Early Christian East* (Philadelphia: University of Pennsylvania Press, 2004), 94–109.

75. Jeanine Herman, introduction, *Laure*, ix.

76. Peignot, *Laure*, 177.

77. Miller, *Humiliation*, 137.

78. Ibid., 170.

79. Georges Bataille, *Blue of Noon*, trans. Harry Matthews (New York: Urizen Books, 1978), 34.

80. Taylor summarizes: "Shame and guilt require confession, while confession produces more shame and guilt and pleasure in this shame and guilt, and hence the need and the desire for more confession. . . . [O]ne can confess even to the pleasures one took in one's confessions, to taking pleasure in shame, and to inventing confessions in order to produce this pleasurable shame." Taylor, *The Culture of Confession*, 105, citing Paul de Man, "Excuses (*Confessions*)," in *Allegories of Reading: Figural Language in Rousseau, Nietzsche, Rilke, and Proust* (New Haven: Yale University Press, 1998), 84–90.

81. Jean-Luc Nancy, "The Confronted Community," trans. Jason Kemp Winfree, in *The Obsessions of Georges Bataille: Community and Communication*, ed. Andrew J. Mitchell and Jason Kemp Winfree (Albany: State University of New York Press, 2009), 26.

82. Bataille, *On Nietzsche*, 34.

83. Kristeva, *Powers of Horror*, 129–30.

84. Bataille, *On Nietzsche*, 33.

85. Ibid.

86. Simone Weil, *Ouevres completes* (Paris: Gallimard, 1988), 6.2.482, cited and translated by William Robert, "A Mystic Impulse: From Apophatics to Decreation in Pseudo-Dionysius, Meister Eckhart, and Simone Weil," *Medieval Mystical Theology* 21 (2012): 115.

87. Ibid., 126, citing and translating Weil, *Ouevres completes*, 6.2.368.

88. William Robert, *Exposures: Of Angela of Foligno*, in manuscript, 57. Citing *Decrees of the Ecumenical Councils*, ed. Norman P. Tanner (Washington, DC: Georgetown University Press, 1990), 245, regarding the Fourth Lateran council. Compare Hamilton, *Doing Penance*, in Rubin, *Medieval Christianity*, 139: "[W]e plead to you, humbly, that you confer your forgiveness on this your servant, who has converted to the right life, and wipe him clean so that the wounds of all his faults which he incurred after baptism may be obliterated and healed through pure and true confession so that no sign remains in him."

89. Julie B. Miller, "Eroticized Violence In Medieval Women's Mystical Literature: A Call for a Feminist Critique," *Journal of Feminist Studies in Religion* 15, no. 2 (1999): 32–33. Citing

Beatrice of Nazareth, *The Seven Manners of Holy Love*, trans. Roger de Ganck (Kalamazoo: Cistercian Publications, 1991), 311; *Angela of Foligno: Complete Works*, trans. Paul Lachance (New York: Paulist Press, 1993), 226, 227; *The Letters of Catherine of Siena*, trans. Suzanne Noffke (Binghamton, NY: Medieval and Renaissance Texts and Studies, 1988), 1:38–39; Catherine of Genoa, *Purgation and Purgatory and The Spiritual Dialogue*, trans. Serge Hughes (New York: Paulist Press, 1979), 109.

90. Frank Graziano, *Wounds of Love: The Mystical Marriage of Saint Rose of Lima* (Oxford: Oxford University Press, 2004), 213. Citing Juan Meléndez, *Tesoros verdaderos de las Indias: Historia de la provincial de San Juan Baptista del Peru de la orden de Predicadores*, 3 vols (Rome, 1681–82), 2:279. Also citing Jacinto de la Parra, *Rosa Laureada entre los santos* (Madrid: Domingo Garcia Morras, 1670), 27, and Teresa of Avila, *The Life*, ch. 29. For a devout review of several similar instances, see Michael Freze, *They Bore the Wounds of Christ: The Mystery of the Sacred Stigmata* (Huntington, IN: Our Sunday Visitor, 1989), esp. 168–96.

91. Anonymous, *The Cloud of Unknowing* (London: Aeterna Press, 2015), ch. 12.

92. Bataille, in *Laure*, 87. Cited in Sweedler, *The Dismembered Community*, 70.

93. L. Bernd Mattheus, *Georges Bataille: eine Thanatographie* (Munich: Matthes und Seitz, 1984), 1:428. Cited in Sweedler, *The Dismembered Community*, 70.

94. Sweedler, *The Dismembered Community*, 70, 84.

95. Jordan, *Convulsing Bodies*, 10.

96. This is primarily true for European and African Christianities; Latin American crucifixes continue for some time to be more vividly physical.

97. Jordan, *Convulsing Bodies*, 159. "Again, since the object of passion is most of all truth, desire rather than fulfillment is the stuff of true love. Most interestingly, philosophy pushes stylization of free erotic relations toward the strictest austerity, an indefinite abstention. In true love, you stylize bodily erotics by not acting out, by intensifying desire through its endless restraint." Citing Foucault, *Histoire de sexualite, vol. 2: L'usage des plaisirs* (Paris: Gallimard, 1984), 266–268.

98. Kristeva, in Clément and Kristeva, *The Feminine and the Sacred*, 15.

99. Georges Bataille, *Guilty*, trans. Stuart Kendall (Albany: State University of New York Press, 2011), 22.

100. A particularly direct discussion of this risk occurs in Raymond of Capua's *The Life of St. Catherine of Siena*, trans. George Lamb (London: Harvill Press, 1960), Part 2, chapter 4.

101. Shannon Winnubst, "The Missing Link: *Homo Economicus* (Reading Bataille and Foucault Together)," in Falzon, O'Leary, and Sawicki, *A Companion to Foucault*, 456. Citing Georges Bataille, *The Accursed Share, vol. 1: An Essay on General Economy*, trans. Robert Hurley (New York: Zone Books, 1991), 21.

102. Georges Bataille, *The Unfinished System of Non-knowledge*, 33.

103. Derrida, "Composing 'Circumfession,'" in *Augustine and Postmodernism: Confession and Circumfession*, ed. John D. Caputo and Michael J. Scanlon (Indianapolis: Indiana University Press, 2005), 25; cited in Burrus, *Saving Shame*, 10.

104. Bataille, *Guilty*, 99.

105. Blanchot, *The Writing of the Disaster*, 137. Cited in Massie, "The Secret and the Neuter," 40.

106. Massie, "The Secret and the Neuter," 49: "Yet, to talk of the neuter rather than the sacred is, for Blanchot, a matter of taking his distance from a religious/mystical understanding of

the secret. The term 'neuter' hints to 'the renunciation of mystery, the ultimate insignificance of lightness.' Before the neuter no transfiguration is to be expected, no meaning is to be revealed. The neuter so defined (if it can be defined) indicates the namelessness of the name that exceeds the name; for the neuter is never just a name. It precedes the oppositions of sensible and intelligible, visible and invisible, presence and absence. The neuter names an erasure that is neither simply present nor simply absent, but is postponement of presence." Citing Maurice Blanchot, *The One Who Would Not Accompany Me*, trans. Lydia Davis (Barrytown, NY: Station Hill Press, 1993), 43.

107. Bataille, *L'Abbé C*, 88. There are in this text other references to failed desires or efforts to speak; see, e.g., 86, 89.

108. Certeau, *The Mystic Fable*, 97.

109. Foucault, *The History of Sexuality, vol. 1*, 62.

110. Taussig, *Defacement*, 2. Citing Walter Benjamin, *The Origin of German Tragic Drama*, trans. John Osborne (London: Verso, 1998), 25.

111. Latour, *Rejoicing*. 131: "These are sacramental words that oblige those who utter them to do what they say—or to lie." And 170: "Thomas Aquinas defines a sacrament as a sign that 'effects what it signifies.'" From Thomas Aquinas, *Summa Theologiae*, 3, Question 62, Article 1.

112. For more on the mystery of the sacramental, see my *Divine Enticement* (New York: Fordham University Press, 2013), esp. 71–100.

113. Latour, *Rejoicing*, 121: "This regime of utterance, we now realize, is not complicated: it is simply fragile."

114. Ibid., 132.

115. Sweedler, *The Dismembered Community*, 135.

116. Colette Peignot was ill with tuberculosis from the age of thirteen, and died at thirty-five, at Bataille's home.

117. Certeau, *The Mystic Fable*, 175.

118. Huffer, *Mad for Foucault*, 80.

119. Bataille, *L'Abbé C*, 120.

120. A similar instance occurs in *My Mother*, in a note that is part of the novel: "At this point the text becomes difficult to follow. . . . Georges Bataille seems to hesitate throughout between the crudest, the most direct descriptive vocabulary and the circumlocutions he has been employing since the opening pages of the manuscript. For some additions, appearing as notes, a definite place has not been assigned, and several passages, bracketed but not deleted, are uncertain." Bataille, *My Mother, Madame Edwarda, and The Dead Man*, 127.

121. Certeau, *The Mystic Fable*, 297.

CHAPTER FOUR. UNCOVERING

1. Augustine, *Confessions*, 10.35.

2. Ibid., 10.35.

3. Aristotle, *Poetics*, trans. S. H. Butcher (New York: Hill and Wang, 1961), 55.

4. Augustine, *Confessions*, 10.35. Augustine uses the example of a wounded corpse, but also the examples of a dog chasing rabbits and spiders or lizards catching flies.

5. Michel Foucault, "Christianity and Confession," in *The Politics of Truth* (Los Angeles: Semiotext(e), 1997), 207. Cited in Taylor, *The Culture of Confession*, 19.

6. Eusebius, *Historia Ecclesiastica*, trans. Arthur Cushman McGiffert, in *Nicene and Post-Nicene Fathers, Second Series, vol. 1*, ed. Philip Schaff and Henry Wace (Buffalo: Christian Literature Publishing, 1890), 5:28. Cited in Taylor, *The Culture of Confession*, 19.

7. From William Robert, *Exposures: Of Angela of Foligno* (in manuscript), 29. Citing Thomas Lentes, "'As Far as the Eye Can See . . .': Rituals of Gazing in the Late Middle Ages," in *The Mind's Eye: Art and Theological Argument in the Middle Ages*, ed. Jeffrey F. Hamburger and Anne-Marie Bouché (Princeton: Princeton University Press, 2005), 371.

8. Robert, *Exposures*, 45. Citing Sara Lipton, "Images and Their Uses," in *The Cambridge History of Christianity: Christianity in Western Europe c. 1000–c.1500*, ed. Miri Rubin and Walter Simons (Cambridge: Cambridge University Press, 2009), 270.

9. Jean-Luc Nancy, *The Birth to Presence,* trans. Brian Holmes et al. (Stanford: Stanford University Press, 1993), 44.

10. Bataille, *My Mother, Madame Edwarda, and the Dead Man*, 150.

11. Derrida, *The Animal that Therefore I Am*, 4: "Ashamed of what and before whom? Ashamed of being as naked as a beast."

12. Ibid., 3–4.

13. See Miller, *Humiliation*, 160–61: "[I]n embarrassment we are intensely aware of our faces. The face, after all, is often the culprit, as when one speaks amiss or when spinach is stuck between the teeth . . . the face also indicates embarrassment with blushing and linguistic glitches that indicate fluster. And it falls to the face to do the work of amelioration, again by blushing or by apologizing, that is, by deflecting attention from other bodily areas that might have been the source of embarrassment. . . . With humiliation, the feeling may also lead to blushing and rising temperature, but the center of feeling is the gut. The stomach goes queasy, the bowel contracts. . . . If embarrassment lingers on the surface of the body, humiliation is located at its deepest center. We may even pale in humiliation rather than blush."

14. J. David Velleman, "The Genesis of Shame," *Philosophy and Public Affairs* 30, no. 1 (2001): 35. Velleman refers to Georg Simmel, "The Secret and the Secret Society," Part IV of *The Sociology of Georg Simmel*, trans. Kurt H. Wolff (Glencoe, IL: The Free Press, 1950), 311–12: "All we communicate to another individual by means of words or perhaps in another fashion—even the most subjective, impulsive, intimate matters—is a selection from that psychological-real whole whose absolutely exact report (absolutely exact in terms of content and sequence) would drive everybody into the insane asylum—if a paradoxical expression is permissible. In a quantitative sense, it is not only fragments of our inner life which we alone reveal, even to our closest fellowmen. What is more, these fragments are not a representative selection, but one made from the standpoint of reason, value, and relation to the listener and his understanding. . . . We simply cannot imagine any interaction or social relation or society which are not based on this teleologically determined non-knowledge of one another."

15. Ibid., 37: "You thus have a fundamental interest in being recognized as a self-presenting creature, an interest that is more fundamental, in fact, than your interest in presenting any particular public image. Not to be seen as honest or intelligent or attractive would be socially disadvantageous, but not to be seen as a self-presenting creature would be socially disqualifying: it would place you beyond the reach of social intercourse altogether. Threats to your

standing as a self-presenting creature are thus a source of deep anxiety, and anxiety about the threatened loss of that standing is, in my view, what constitutes the emotion of shame."

16. Ibid., 50–51. Though it is not directly relevant to the present work, I cannot resist passing along a fascinating conclusion from Velleman's essay, p. 50: "My account of shame has a present-day moral. We often hear that our culture has lost its sense of shame—an observation that I think is largely true. Some moralists take this observation as grounds for trying to rescandalize various conditions that used to be considered shameful, such as out-of-wedlock birth or homosexuality. These moralists reason that nothing is shameful to us because nothing is an object of social disapproval, and hence that reviving disapproval is the only way to reawaken shame. In my view, however, nothing is shameful to us because nothing is private: our culture has become too confessional and exhibitionistic. The way to reawaken shame is to revive our sense of privacy, which needn't require disapproval at all. . . .What's responsible for the exhibitionism of our culture, I think, is a mistake . . . about the dishonesty of self-presentation. People now think that not to express inclinations or impulses is in effect to claim that one doesn't have them, and that honesty therefore requires one to express whatever inclinations or impulses one has. What they forget is that the overt personas we compose are not interpreted as accurate representations of our inner lives. . . . No one believes that our public faces perfectly reflect our private selves, and so we shouldn't be tempted to pretend that they do, or to accuse ourselves of dishonesty when they don't."

17. Emmanuel Levinas, *On Escape*, trans. Bettina Bergo (Stanford: Stanford University Press, 2003), 65.

18. Ibid., 63: "Yet shame's whole intensity, everything it contains that stings us, consists precisely in our inability not to identify with this being who is already foreign to us and whose motives for acting we can no longer comprehend."

19. Benedicta Ward, trans. *The Life of Mary of Egypt*, in Ward, ed., *Harlots of the Desert: A Study of Repentance in Early Monastic Sources* (Kalamazoo: Cistercian Publications, 1987), 26–56.

20. Palladius, *The Lausiac History of Palladius*, trans. W. K. Lowther Clarke (London and New York: The Macmillan Company, 1918), 37.13–16. Available at http://www.tertullian.org/fathers/palladius_lausiac_02_text.htm#C37. Burrus recounts this story in *Saving Shame*, 92.

21. Angela of Foligno, *Angela of Foligno's Memorial,* trans. John Cirignano, with introduction, notes and interpretive essay by Cristina Mazzoni (Rochester: Boydell and Brewer, 1999), step 8, 26.

22. Michel Foucault, "Sexuality and Power," trans. Richard A. Lynch, in *Religion and Culture,* selected and ed. Jeremy R. Carrette (New York: Routledge, 1999), 115–30. Also, "About the Beginning of the Hermeneutics of the Self," 1980, transcript Thomas Keenan and Mark Blasius, in idem., 158–81, and "The Battle for Chastity," trans. Anthony Forester, in idem., 188–97.

23. Angela of Foligno, *St. Angela of Foligno: Complete Works*, trans. Paul Lachance and Romana Guarnieri (Mahwah, NJ: Paulist Press, 1993), 219.

24. Robert, *Exposures,* 232. Citing *De vitis partum, Verba seniorum*, book 5, ch. 6, sec. 16, in *Patrologia latina*, vol. 73, ed. J.-P. Migne (Paris, 1879), col. 891.

25. *The Little Flowers of St. Francis of Assisi*, Part II.

26. Certeau, *The Mystic Fable*, 88.

27. Bataille, *The Unfinished System of Nonknowledge*, 98.

28. Peignot, *Laure*, 64 (ellipsis original).

29. Ibid.

30. Virginia Burrus, *The Sex Lives of Saints: An Erotics of Ancient Hagiography* (Philadelphia: University of Pennsylvania Press, 2003), 141.

31. *Life of Pelagia*, ch. 5, trans. Sebastian P. Brock and Susan Ashbrook Harvey, in *Holy Women of the Syrian Orient*, ed. Brock and Harvey (Berkeley: University of California Press), 40–62. Cited in Burrus, *Sex Lives*, 138.

32. *Life of Pelagia*, ch. 7. Cited in Burrus, *Sex Lives*, 139.

33. Rudolph Bell, *Holy Anorexia* (Chicago: University of Chicago Press, 1985), 67.

34. Ibid., 99.

35. Catherine had exterior motivation in this act as well: the Sisters of Penance had told her mother that Catherine would be allowed to join them only if she was not too pretty. As by that time Catherine had had disfiguring pox, we might think that she was not at great risk of this. When she finally persuaded a priest of the sincerity of her religious vows, he said that she could show her seriousness by cutting off all of her hair, which she immediately did. Bell, 41, 45.

36. Geronima Vaccari and Cecilia de Ansalono, *La leggenda della beata Eustochia da Messina. Testo volgare del sec. XV restituito all' originaria lezione*, 2nd edition, ed. Michele Catalono (Messina: Libreria d'Anna, 1975), 74–76. Thus cited in Bell, *Holy Anorexia*, 143.

37. "St. Rose of Lima," Accessed at http://www.catholic.org/saints/saint.php?saint_id=446.

38. Burrus, *Sex Lives*, 144.

39. Ibid., 146. Citing Patricia Cox Miller, "Is There a Harlot in This Text? Asceticism and the Grotesque," *Journal of Early Christian Studies* 33, no. 3 (2003).

40. Carolyn Korsmeyer, *Savoring Disgust: The Foul and the Fair in Aesthetics* (Oxford: Oxford University Press, 2011), 71.

41. Velleman, "The Genesis of Shame," 29. Velleman notes, "This example is discussed by Gabrielle Taylor, *Pride, Shame, and Guilt: Emotions of Self-Assessment* (Oxford: Oxford University Press, 1985), 60–61; and by Richard Wollheim, *On the Emotions*, (New Haven: Yale University Press, 1999), 159–63. Wollheim traces it to Max Scheler, "Ober Scham und Schmagefühle," in *Schriften aus dem Nachlass* (Bern: Francke Verlag, 1957), Vol. 1.

42. Donald L. Nathanson, *Shame and Pride: Affect, Sex, and the Birth of the Self* (New York: W. W. Norton, 1992), 295.

43. Korsmeyer, *Savoring Disgust*, 103.

44. Nathanson, *Shame and Pride*, 160.

45. Ibid., 163.

46. Burrus, *The Sex Lives of Saints*, 31.

47. There are also important connections between shame and gender-ambiguous, gender fluid, or intergendered bodies. To explore these across a broad historical range would require a separate volume, but it is important to acknowledge, even as my focus here is on the influential gender binary. Burrus notes the ambivalent humility of femaleness in *Saving Shame*, 92.

48. Burrus, *Saving Shame*, 92.

49. Examples are too numerous to annotate, but can be found especially throughout Teresa's *The Life*, and in Hildegard's letters, in *The Personal Correspondence of Hildegard of Bingen*, ed. Joseph L. Baird, trans. Joseph L. Baird and Radd K. Ehrman (Oxford: Oxford University Press, 2006).

50. Wurmser, *The Mask of Shame*, 174–75.

51. Bartlett, "Plunge Into Your Shame," 344.

52. Derrida, *The Animal*, 13.

53. Ibid.

54. Jean-Christophe Bailly, *The Animal Side*, trans. Catherine Porter (New York: Fordham, 2011), 91–92.

55. Bataille, *The Unfinished System*, 29.

56. Bataille, *On Nietzsche*, 40.

57. Ibid., 39.

58. Virginia Burrus, "Wyschogrod's Hand: Saints, Animality, and the Labor of Love," *Philosophy Today* 55, no. 4 (Winter 2011): 419.

59. Page duBois, *Torture and Truth* (New York: Routledge, 1991), 6.

60. Ibid., 130. Citing Martin Heidegger, "Plato's Doctrine of Truth," trans. John Barlow, in *Philosophy in the Twentieth Century*, vol. 3, ed. William Barrett and Henry D. Aiken (Random House: New York, 1962), 260. The German verbs *entrissen* and *geraubt* support the sense of aggression and even theft. Martin Heidegger, *Platons Lehre von der Wahrheit* (Bern: A. Francke, 1947), 32: "Das Unverborgene muß einer Verborgenheit entrissen, dieser im gewissen Sinne geraubt warden."

61. duBois, *Torture and Truth*, 132. Citing Martin Heidegger, *Being and Time*, trans. John Macquarrie and Edward Robinson (New York: Harper and Row, 1962), 265. Here the verb *abgerungen* implies extraction by force, even to the extent of bending or twisting. Martin Heidegger, *Sein und Zeit* (Halle: Max Niemeyer Verlag, 1941), 222: "Die Wahrheit (Entdecktheit) muß dem Seienden immer erst abgerungen werden. Das Seiende wird der Verborgenheit entriffen."

62. Diane L. Prosser MacDonald, *Transgressive Corporeality: The Body, Poststructuralism, and the Theological Imagination* (Albany: State University of New York Press, 1995), 120–21.

63. duBois, *Torture and Truth*, 85–86.

64. Taussig, *Defacement*, 3–4.

65. duBois, *Torture and Truth*, 87.

66. Taylor, *The Culture of Confession*, 75.

67. Burrus, *Saving Shame*, 87.

68. Sarah Lucas, "Chicken Knickers," 1997, photograph, 17 x 17 inches. Tate Collection, London. Accessed at http://www.tate.org.uk/art/artworks/lucas-chicken-knickers-p78210.

69. cf. Bataille: "Paradoxically, intimacy is violence . . ." Georges Bataille, *Theory of Religion*, trans. Robert Hurley (New York: Zone Books, 1992), 51.

70. Jonathan Sawday, *The Body Emblazoned: Dissection and the Human Body in Renaissance Culture* (London: Routledge, 1995), 8.

71. By my count, tears appear at 31, 33, 49, 67, 82, 101, 131, 141, 149, and 150; sweat at 47, 92, 94, and 100; blood as blush at 16, 70, and 124, and as bleeding at 17, 51, 139, and 148; urine at 17 (with feces), 62 (with vomit); and vomit again at 4, 65, and 95 (with spittle). Bataille, *Blue of Noon*.

72. Elizabeth Grosz, *Volatile Bodies: Toward a Corporeal Feminism* (Indianapolis: Indiana University Press, 1994), 203.

73. Clément, in Clement and Kristeva, *The Feminine and the Sacred*, 15.

74. Benedicta Ward, trans., *The Life of St. Thaïs the Harlot*, in Ward, *Harlots of the Desert*, 83.

75. "Anastasia the Roman," accessed at http://orthodoxwiki.org/Anastasia_the_Roman.

76. Zeynep Direk, "Bataille and Kristeva on Religion," in Biles and Brintnall, *Negative Ecstasies*, 190–91.

77. I suspect that the ever-fascinating zombie plays upon this particular monstrosity: what if the body in its purest materiality, the corpse itself, without ceasing to hold just barely together, nonetheless lived, like us, reminding us of how much we too are like it? Might it eat our brains as another attempt to acquire our secret knowledge?

78. Maurice Blanchot, *The Step / Not Beyond*, trans. Lycette Nelson (Albany: State University of New York Press, 1992), 107. Cited in Massie, "The Secret and the Neuter," 34.

79. Raymond of Capua, *The Life of St. Catherine of Siena*, 191. Thus in Bell, *Holy Anorexia*, 30.

80. Bataille, *Blue of Noon*, 51.

81. Daniel Kelly, *Yuck! The Nature and Moral Significance of Disgust* (Cambridge: MIT Press, 2011), 28. Citing Palut Rozin, J. Haidt, and C. R. McCauly, "Disgust," in *Handbook of Emotions,* 3rd edition, ed. M. Lewis, J. M. Haviland-Jones, and L. F. Barret (New York: Guilford Press, 2010), 757–76; A. Angyal, "Disgust and Related Aversions," *Journal of Abnormal and Social Psychology* 36 (1941): 393–412; J. Haidt, C. McCauly, and P. Rozin, "Individual Differences in Sensitivity to Disgust: A Scale Sampling Seven Domains of Disgust Elicitors," *Personality and Individual Differences* 16 (1994): 701–13; P. Rozin, C. Nemeroff, M. Horowitz, B. Gordon, and W. Voet, "The Borders of the Self: Contamination Sensitivity and Potence of the Mouth, Other Apertures, and Body Parts," *Journal of Research in Personality* 29 (1995): 318–40; and William Miller, *The Anatomy of Disgust* (Cambridge, MA: Harvard University Press, 1997).

82. Burrus, *Sex Lives*, 142.

83. Bailly, *The Animal Side*, 17. Citing Walter Benjamin, *The Work of Art in the Age of Its Technological Reproduction*, trans. Edmund Jephcott, in *The Work of Art in the Age of Its Technological Reproduction, and Other Writings on Media*, ed. Michael W. Jennings, Brigid Doherty, and Thomas Y. Levin (Cambridge: Harvard University Press, 2008), 285.

84. Bruno Latour, *Rejoicing: Or The Torments of Religious Speech* (Cambridge: Polity Press, 1992), 131.

85. Burrus, *Saving Shame*, 2.

86. Aurel Kolnai, *On Disgust*, ed. Barry Smith and Carolyn Korsmeyer (Chicago: Open Court Press, 2004), 79.

87. Peignot, *Laure*, 8.

88. Ibid., 11. "A child's curiosity about her belly precisely when she knows that God sees all and follows her into the attic. Curiosity and then terror. Life soon managed to oscillate between these two poles: one sacred, venerated, which must be exhibited...; the other dirty, shameful, which must not be named. Both more mysterious, more appealing, more intense than a bleak and unchanging life."

89. Ibid., 152.

90. Ibid., 3–4.

91. Ibid., 188.

92. Georges Bataille, "Abjection and Miserable Forms," trans. Yvonne Shafir, in *More & Less*, ed. Sylvere Lotringer (Brooklyn: Semiotexte/ Autonomedia, 1999), 11.

93. Ibid., 10.

94. Ibid., 11.

95. Cary Howie and William Burgwinkle, *Sanctity and Pornography in Medieval Culture: On the Verge* (Manchester, UK: Manchester University Press, 2010), 15.

96. Sweedler, *The Dismembered Community*, 42.

97. Ibid., 43-44. Citing Luce Irigaray, *Speculum of the Other Woman*, trans. Gillian C. Gill, (Ithaca: Cornell University Press, 1985), 199. Translation modified by Sweedler.

98. Howie and Burgwinkle, *Sanctity and Pornography*, 39.

99. Ibid., 20.

100. Meister Eckhart, German sermon on Ecclesiasticus 24:30. In *Meister Eckhart: Selected Writings*, ed. and trans. Oliver Davies (New York: Penguin Books, 1994), 179.

101. Thomas F. Glick, Steven John Livesey, and Faith Wallis, *Medieval Science, Technology And Medicine: An Encyclopedia* (New York: Routledge, 2005), 373-74.

102. Howie and Burgwinkle, *Sanctity and Pornography*, 38.

103. Jacques Lacan, *Four Fundamental Concepts of Psychoanalysis*, trans. Alan Sheridan (New York: W. W. Norton, 1978), esp. 181-83.

104. Georges Bataille, *The Story of the Eye*, trans. Joachim Neugroschel (San Francisco: City Lights Books, 1977), 83-84.

105. Eve Kosofsky Sedgwick, *Touching Feeling: Affect, Pedagogy, Performativity* (Durham: Duke University Press, 2003), 50.

106. The description of the infant's world as "one great blooming, buzzing confusion" comes from William James, *Principles of Psychology*, vol. 1 (Mineola, NY: Dover, 1950), 488.

107. Here, too, the self is made as it is known; for Lacan, who makes famous the idea of the "mirror stage" of self-development, the whole self perceived in the mirror is necessarily a constructed fiction. See Jacques Lacan, *Écrits*, trans. Bruce Fink with Héloïse Fink and Russell Grigg (New York: W. W. Norton, 2002), 75-81.

108. Lacan, *Four Fundamental Concepts*, 72.

109. Ibid., 75.

110. Wurmser, *The Mask of Shame*, 54. "Even a small child hides his face if he is shamed—retreats into a corner or another room or at least hides his face. The 'aim' of anxiety in general is flight, and hiding is a form of flight."

111. J. Brooks Bouson, *Embodied Shame: Uncovering Female Shame in Contemporary Women's Writings* (Albany: State University of New York Press, 2009), 166. Citing Lucy Grealy, *Autobiography of a Face* (New York: Houghton Mifflin, 1994), 62.

112. Bouson, *Embodied Shame*, 119. Citing Judith Moore, *Fat Girl: A True Story* (New York: Plume, 2005).

113. I except here exhibitionism to which the viewer has not consented and would not consent given the opportunity—the classic display of the "flasher"—in which the viewer's embarrassment or disgust appears to be central. This is an interesting class of pleasures, but presents both experiential and ethical issues very different from those of humiliation begun in mutual desire.

114. Bouson, *Embodied Shame*, 61. Citing Toni Morrison, *The Bluest Eye* (New York: Knopf, 1993), 48.

115. Bouson, *Embodied Shame*, 62, citing Wurmser, *The Mask of Shame*, 81.

116. Paul de Man, "Shame is primarily exhibitionistic." "Excuses (Confessions)," 285. Cited thus in Burrus, *Saving Shame*, 112.

117. Clement of Alexandria, *Exhortation to the Greeks*, trans. G. W. Butterworth, in *Clement of Alexandria*, Loeb Classical Library 92 (Cambridge, MA: Harvard University Press, 1919), 29. A similar discussion appears in the first two books of Clement's *Exhortation to the Heathen*, trans. William Wilson, in *Ante-Nicene Fathers*, vol. 2, ed. Alexander Roberts, James Donaldson, and A. Cleveland Cox (Buffalo: Christian Literature Publishing, 1885).

118. Clement, *Exhortation to the Greeks*, 33.

119. Ibid. Demeter provides particularly vivid examples, as her mysteries commemorate her "amorous embraces" with her son Zeus, "on account of which she is said to have received the name Brimo (the Terrible One); also the supplications of Zeus, the drink of bile, the tearing out the heart of the victims, and unspeakable obscenities." If not appalling, these rituals are laughable: "If I go on further to quote the symbols of initiation into this mystery they will, I know, move you to laughter." While Demeter mourns the loss of her daughter, a woman called "Baubo, having received Demeter as a guest, offers her a draught of wine and meal. She declines to take it . . . on account of her mourning. Baubo is deeply hurt, thinking she has been slighted, and thereupon uncovers her secret parts and exhibits them to the goddess." Note here an intriguing reversibility—display can shame, but it can insult as well, or move to laughter. "Demeter is pleased at the sight, and now at last receives the draught,—delighted by the spectacle! These are the secret mysteries of the Athenians!"

120. Ibid., 45.

121. Irenaeus, *Against Heresies*, trans. Alexander Roberts and W. H. Rambaut (Edinburgh: T&T Clark, 1869), 1.6.3.5.

122. Ibid.

123. Raynaldus, "Annales," in S. R. Maitland, trans., *History of the Albigenses and Waldenses*, (London: C. J. G. and F. Rivington, 1832), 392–94.

124. Tertullian, "Tertulliani Adversus Valentinianos," trans. Mark T. Riley, 1971. Tertullian Project. Accessed at http://gnosis.org/library/ter_val_riley.htm.

125. Richard D. E. Burton, *Holy Tears, Holy Blood: Women, Catholicism, and the Culture of Suffering in France, 1840–1970* (Ithaca: Cornell University Press, 2004), 152.

126. Jacques Derrida, *The Gift of Death*, trans. David Wills (Chicago: University of Chicago Press, 1995), 92.

127. Jean Baudrillard, "The Ecstasy of Communication," in *The Anti-Aesthetic: Essays in Postmodern Culture*, ed. Hal Foster (New York: The New Press, 2002), 150–51.

128. Robert Mills, "'Whatever You Do Is a Delight to Me!' Masculinity, Masochism, and Queer Play in Representations of Male Martyrdom," *Exemplaria* 13, no. 1 (2001): 3. Citing Simon Gaunt, "Straight Minds/'Queer' Wishes in Old French Hagiography: La vie de sainte Euphrosine," *GLQ: A Journal of Lesbian and Gay Studies* 1, no. 4 (1995): 441, 453.

CHAPTER FIVE. UNDIGNIFIED

1. Debra Bergoffen, *Contesting the Politics of Genocidal Rape: Affirming the Dignity of the Vulnerable Body* (Routledge, 2012), 74–75. Cited in Ellen Feder, *Making Sense of Intersex: Changing Ethical Perspectives in Biomedicine* (Bloomington: Indiana University Press, 2014), 179.

2. Ibid., 2. Cited in Feder, *Making Sense of Intersex*, 177.

3. Ibid., 31. Cited in Feder, *Making Sense of Intersex,* 180.

4. Ibid.

5. Feder, *Making Sense of Intersex,* 173–74: "If the 'protection' that parents seek to extend to their child with atypical sex is an effort to 'clear an easier path for the child,' it must also be understood as an effort to diminish the vulnerability of the child to what parents and doctors see as the inevitable consequences of a stigmatized anatomical difference."

6. Ibid., esp. 181–83.

7. Ibid., esp.186–92.

8. Laura Kipnis, "Sexual Paranoia Strikes Academe," *Chronicle of Higher Education,* February 27, 2015. Accessed at http://chronicle.com/article/Sexual-Paranoia-Strikes/190351/. Student petition, March 2015. Accessed at https://docs.google.com/forms/d/12sbmVqpNGQPY-QEYG5N7-VIUsXigVg3l9itcX4yTDcA/viewform. Both, cited in Emily Bazelon, "The Return of the Sex Wars," *New York Times,* September 10, 2015. Accessed at http://www.nytimes.com/2015/09/13/magazine/the-return-of-the-sex-wars.html?_r=0.

9. Burrus, *Saving Shame,* 23.

10. Ibid., 99.

11. John Keats, *The Complete Poetical Works and Letters of John Keats,* ed. Horace Elisha Scudder (Boston and New York: Houghton, Mifflin, 1899, reprint 2010), 277.

12. Ibid.

13. Roberto Mangabiera Unger, *False Necessity: Anti-Necessitarian Social Theory in the Service of Radical Democracy* (New York: Verso, 2004), 279.

14. This is supported particularly by Unger's insistence on labor's dignity; see his introduction to *False Necessity,* esp. 26–35.

15. Hélène Cixous and Mireille Calle-Gruber, *Rootprints: Memory and Life Writing,* trans. Eric Prenowitz (London: Routledge, 1997), 35.

16. Ibid., 16.

17. Kolnai, *On Disgust,* 42.

18. Ibid., 76.

19. Ibid., 76–77.

20. Ibid., 62.

21. Ibid., 65: "Although there is a change of affect from recoil to savor [his example here is the delight that some people take in eating stinky cheeses], the shadow of the former lingers; indeed, it is in that shadow that the sophisticated depth of flavor resides. On the other hand, though the sensation has shifted only a little, the affective response has radically altered, having switched from recoil to appetite. Disgust has been replaced by savoring." (Kolnai cites Palut Rozin and April Fallon, "A Perspective on Disgust," *Psychological Review* 94, no. 1 [1987]: 24 n. 1.) In literature and drama, tragedy and sublimity similarly transform the recoil of fear.

22. Ibid., 67; emphasis mine.

23. Sweedler, *The Dismembered Community,* 77.

24. Ziv, "Shameful Fantasies," 168. Compare Wurmser, *The Mask of Shame,* 92: "The most radical shame is to offer oneself and be rejected as unlovable."

25. Nathanson, *Shame and Pride,* 17.

26. Ibid., 16.

27. Bartlett, "Plunge into Your Shame," 345.

28. Nathanson, *Shame and Pride*, 332.

29. Ibid., 254.

30. Wurmser, *The Mask of Shame*, 41.

31. Ellis Hanson, "Teaching Shame," 132.

32. Gerber also notes that director John Waters and his drag queen star Divine celebrate the connections among fat, excess, and waste in their films together—in, for example, a famous scene in *Pink Flamingos* in which Divine eats dog excrement from the street. Lynne Gerber, "Movements of Luxurious Exuberance: Georges Bataille and Fat Politics," in Biles and Brintnall, *Negative Ecstasies*, 30.

33. Ibid., 28.

34. Sedgwick, *Touching Feeling*, 63–64.

35. Easton and Hardy, *The New Bottoming Book*, 148.

36. Mollena Williams, "Digging in the Dirt: The Lure of Taboo Role Play," in *The Ultimate Guide to Kink: BDSM, Role Play and the Erotic Edge*, ed. Tristan Taormino (Berkeley: Cleis Press, 2012), 373.

37. Ibid. Similarly, Easton and Hardy remark, "We know lots more people of color who are interested in playing slave than we do white folks who are comfortable being Simon Legree." Easton and Hardy, *The New Bottoming Book*, 148.

38. In addition to Williams (esp. 383–84), other rich sources include the film *Fetishes*, directed by Nick Broomfield (New York: HBO, 1996), and Gloria G. Brame, William D. Brame, and Jon Jacobs, *Different Loving: The World of Sexual Dominance and Submission* (New York: Villard, 1993).

39. Halperin and Traub, "Beyond Gay Pride," 9. Hanson, "Teaching Shame," 132.

40. Burrus, *Saving Shame*, 14.

41. See ibid., 152.

42. Williams, "Digging in the Dirt," 383.

43. Ibid.

44. Ibid., 382.

45. Susan Bordo, *Unbearable Weight: Feminism, Western Culture, and the Body,* (Berkeley: University of California Press, 1994), 3, 8. Cited in Bouson, *Embodied Shame*, 3f. Léon Wurmser likewise notes that a woman may be contemptuously regarded as "a debased, dirty thing—a derided and low animal." Wurmser, *The Mask of Shame*, 81. Cited and glossed in Bouson, *Embodied Shame*, 152.

46. Williams, "Digging in the Dirt," 384, 386.

47. Ibid., 384–85.

48. Ibid., 384.

49. Ibid., 383.

50. Burrus, *Saving Shame,* 87–88.

51. Miller, *Humiliation*, 10–11.

52. Waldron, "Cruel, Inhuman," 37.

53. *Different Loving* notes footstools or ottomans, tables, hat stands, ashtrays, and sofa cushions. Brame et al., *Different Loving*, 157.

54. Waldron, "Cruel, Inhuman," 38.

55. For some particularly creative artistic images, see http://www.bernadinism.com/forniphilia-human-furniture/.

56. See Waldron, "Cruel, Inhuman," 39: "How important is it that the degradation be experienced subjectively as humiliating? Some European Convention on Human Rights commentators suggest that the connection is definitional, but this is not so, at least not in my dictionary. However it is very common in the case law to emphasize the subjective element almost to the exclusion of everything else. Treatment is degrading, we are told, if it arouses in its victim 'feelings of fear, anguish and inferiority capable of humiliating'." Citing D. J. Harris, M. O'Boyle, C. Warbrick, *Law of the European Convention on Human Rights* (Oxford: Oxford University Press, 1995), 80. Waldron disagrees because his interest is legal more than phenomenological, erotic, or theological; from those perspectives, I think, the "conflation" is more properly permissible. Unexpectedly to me, Waldron associates the desecration of corpses with bestialization, believing that only humans tend to their dead.

57. Aristotle, *Politics*, from *Aristotle in 23 Volumes*, Vol. 21, trans. H. Rackham (Cambridge, MA: Harvard University Press and London: William Heinemann, 1944), 1253b.

58. Charles Taylor, "Self-Interpreting Animals," in *Human Agency and Language: Philosophical Papers* (Cambridge: Cambridge University Press, 1985), 53. Cited in Alice M. Ramos, *Dynamic Transcendentals: Truth, Goodness, and Beauty from a Thomistic Perspective* (Washington, DC: Catholic University of America Press, 2012), 109–10.

59. Gloria Steinem's classic 1993 essay, "Erotica vs. Pornography," refers to pornography in which women dominate men as "role-reversal pornography," in which men only pretend to victimhood. In this essay Steinem does not consider it possible that women might enjoy this genre; it is entirely a matter of male pretense without danger, though it is not clear why men would thus pretend. The essay appears in *Transforming a Rape Culture,* ed. E. Buchwald, P. R. Fletcher, M. Roth (Minneapolis: Milkweed Editions, 1993), 31–46. It may be relevant that Steinem there identifies all power play as pornographic: "As for class bias, it's simply not accurate to say that pornography is erotica with less education. . . . Pornography is about dominance. Erotica is about mutuality. Any man able to empathize with women can easily tell the difference by looking at a photograph or film and putting himself in the woman's skin." Steinem, "Erotica," 41–42.

60. Halberstam, *The Queer Art of Failure*, location 160.

61. Unsurprisingly, there are many sites providing long lists of such stories, albeit at varying levels of literacy. Sites including Literotica (literotica.com) and the Femdom Library (femdomlibrary.com) include sections on forced feminization, and there are more specialized sites such as *I Enjoy Forced Feminization* (http://www.experienceproject.com/groups/Enjoy-Forced-Feminization-Stories/) as well. While there are still print sources for pornographic stories, internet access has increasingly shifted the medium to online forums.

62. Uncondemned does not mean uncomplicated. See, e.g., Burrus, *Saving Shame*, 35: "Like Perpetua's transgendering, Thecla's transvestitism marks her as both woman and man: shamed like a woman (shamed *as* a woman) through her bodily exposure and vulnerability to sexual assault, she is now able to display shamelessly the perverse virility of a woman 'who is no bride.'"

63. Leslie Feinberg, *Stone Butch Blues* (Ann Arbor, MI: Firebrand Books, 1993), 8–9.

64. Burrus, *Saving Shame*, 34.

65. The phrase "boasting of beatings" is Jennifer Glancy's, from her excellent article "Boasting of Beatings (Corinthians 11:23–25)," *Journal of Biblical Literature* 123, no. 1 (Spring 2004): 99–135.

66. Mills, "'Whatever You Do Is a Delight to Me!'" 12.

67. Robert Mills, "Violence, Community, and the Materialisation of Belief," in *A Companion to Middle English Hagiography*, ed. Sarah Salih (Cambridge: Boydell and Brewer, 2006), 94. Mills cites Sarah Kay, *Courtly Contradictions: The Emergence of the Literary Object in the Twelfth Century* (Stanford: Stanford University Press, 2002), 226; Mills, "Whatever You Do Is a Delight to Me," 7, 13–14; and Samantha Riches, "St. George: as a Male Virgin Martyr," in *Gender and Holiness: Men, Women, and Saints in Late Medieval Europe*, ed. Samantha J. E. Riches and Sarah Salih (London: Routledge, 2002), 72.

68. Maureen Moran, "The Art of Looking Dangerously: Victorian Images of Martyrdom," *Victorian Literature and Culture* 32, no. 2 (2004): 480.

69. Clément, in Clément and Kristeva, *The Feminine and the Sacred*, 30.

70. Ibid.

71. Ibid., 31.

72. Kristeva, in Clément and Kristeva, *The Feminine and the Sacred*, 50.

73. Ibid. 37.

74. Max Riley Sissy, "Forced Feminization Story (True Series), Part 1." Last edited May 22, 2015. Accessed at http://maxrileysissy.deviantart.com/journal/Forced-Feminization-Story-True-Series-Part-1-534584924.

75. I find it intriguing that in the 1996 documentary *Fetishes*, the segment on infantilism begins with a man's description of the pleasure that he has long taken in dressing in women's clothing, with some minutes passing before there is any mention of age play.

76. Brame et al., *Different Loving*, 122–26.

77. Waldron, "Cruel, Inhuman," 38.

78. Tristan Taormino, "Still in Diapers," *Village Voice*, August 13, 2002. Accessed at http://www.villagevoice.com/news/still-in-diapers-6396960.

79. Ibid.

80. Ignacio Rivera, aka Papí Coxxx, "Age Role Play," in Taormino, *The Ultimate Guide to Kink*, 353.

81. Nathanson, *Shame and Pride*, 163: "[H]eight [is] a source of pride, and lack of it a source of shame" "Bigness is associated with power—the ability to accomplish tasks—and therefore efficacy."

82. Tracy Clark-Fory, "I'm Hung Like a Toddler: Meet a Man with a Micropenis," *Salon*, February 23, 2015. Accessed at http://www.salon.com/2015/02/24/i%E2%80%99m_hung_like_a_toddler_meet_a_man_with_a_micropenis/.

83. Natalie Corner, "Are These the Bravest Men in the Country?" *The Mirror*, January 20, 2016. Accessed at http://www.mirror.co.uk/tv/tv-news/bravest-men-country-three-men-7268368.

84. Halberstam, *The Queer Art of Failure*, location 564.

85. Kristeva, *The Feminine and the Sacred*, 37.

86. Korsmeyer, *Savoring Disgust*, 104.

87. Waldron, "Cruel, Inhuman," 38.

88. Lee Harrington, "A Romp on the Wild Side: Erotic Human Animal Role Playing," in Taormino, *The Ultimate Guide to Kink*, 267–68.

89. Chris Brooke, "'I'm a Human Pet': The Goth Teenager Whose Fiancé Walks Her around on a Dog Lead," *Daily Mail*, 23 January 2008. Accessed at http://www.dailymail.co.uk/news/article-509713/Im-human-pet-The-Goth-teenager-fiance-walks-dog-lead.html#ixzz46nHQ9ex9.

90. Harrington, "A Romp on the Wild Side," in Taormino, *The Ultimate Guide to Kink*, 269.

91. Brame et al., *Different Loving*, 152.

92. Peignot, *Laure*, 168.

93. Bataille, Appendix, in Peignot, *Laure*, 237. Ellipsis in original. "Wartberg" is the name Bataille gives to Eduard Trautner.

94. Miller, *Humiliation*, 206. Citing Richard Rorty, *Contingency, Irony, and Solidarity* (Cambridge: Cambridge University Press, 1989).

95. Clément, in Clément and Kristeva, *The Feminine and the Sacred*, 32. Gustave Flaubert's *The Temptation of St. Anthony* is available in a translation by Lafacadio Hearn (Rockville, MD: Wildside Press, 2008).

96. A. Voöbus, *History of Asceticism in the Syrian Orient. A Contribution to the History of Culture in the Near East, II, Early Monasticism in Mesopotamia and Syria* (Leuven: Corpus Scriptorum Christianorum Orientalium, 1960), 25.

97. Ibid., 26.

98. Ephrem the Syrian, cited in Kenelm Henry Digby, *Compitum: Or the Meeting of the Ways at the Catholic Church* (London: C. Dolman, 1854), 58–59.

99. Andrew Jotischky, "Eats Roots and Leaves," *History Today* 61, no. 4 (April 2011): 19.

100. Violet McDermot, *The Cult of the Seer in the Ancient Middle East: A Contribution to Current Research on Hallucinations Drawn from Coptic and Other Texts* (Berkeley: University of California Press, 1971), 278. Cited in Patrick Olivelle, "The Beast and the Ascetic: The Wild in the Indian Religious Imagination," in *Collected Essays*, Volume 2 (Florence: Firenze University Press, 2008), 91–92. Olivelle points out, "In some Hindu traditions ascetics deliberately reject the trapping of civilization, and a translation of the *Majjhima Nikaya* declares that the Indian ascetics who acted like bovines 'anticipated by a thousand years those Christian anchorites who "derived their name from their humble practice of grazing in the fields of Mesopotamia with the common herd."'" Olivelle cites *Majjhima Nikaya*, trans. Lord Robert Chalmers (Oxford: Oxford University Press, 1948), l.xvi. Chalmers in turn is quoting Edward Gibbon, *The History of the Decline and Fall of the Roman Empire* (Boston: Philips, Samson, 1852), 538, though Olivelle's text does not seem to note this.

101. Jotischky, "Eats Roots and Leaves," 21.

102. Reforming monks in eleventh and twelfth-century Europe, such as Robert of Arbrissel and Stephen of Obazine, are often described as spending periods of rejection and angst in the wild, digging up roots and forest plants and even stripping the bark off trees to eat. Ibid., 20.

103. See for example Plato, *Republic*, trans. C. D. C. Reeve (Indianapolis: Hackett, 2004), 571c, in which the "wild beast" within us seeks to satisfy desire without "shame or sense." At 589, the tyrant is described as having the beast of desire so overgrown in his soul that both the

"good" animal of spirit (metaphorized as a lion) and wholly human reason are enslaved by it.

104. Anthony Steinbock, *Moral Emotions: Reclaiming the Evidence of the Heart* (Evanston: Northwestern University Press, 2014), 68. Citing G. W. F. Hegel, *Enzyklopädie der philosophischen Wissenschaften im Grundrisse (1830), Erster Teil*, in *Werke*, vol. 8 (Frankfurt am Main: Suhrkamp, 1970), 89–90. Steinbock does not himself stop at Hegel's position.

105. See, e.g., Giorgio Agamben, *The Open: Man and Animal*, trans. Kevin Attell (Stanford: Stanford University Press, 2004), 30.

106. Ibid., 12.

107. Edith Wyschogrod, *Saints and Postmodernism: Revisioning Moral Philosophy* (Chicago: University of Chicago Press, 1990), 82. Cited in Virginia Burrus, "Wyschogrod's Hand: Saints, Animality, and the Labor of Love," *Philosophy Today* 55, no. 4 (Winter 2011): 415.

108. Ibid., 83. Cited in Burrus, "Wyschogrod's Hand," 416.

109. Enkidu, who is part "beast" and part human, is civilized and made wholly human by the priestess Shamhat, who has sexual intercourse with him and gives him bread and beer. Sex, eating, and drinking are all pleasures shared across most animals, but Shamhat knows the arts that make them uniquely human practices. I recommend Stephen Mitchell, trans., *Gilgamesh: A New English Version* (New York: Free Press, 2004).

110. Waldron, "Cruel, Inhuman," 39.

111. Zeynep Direk, "Bataille and Kristeva on Religion," 186.

112. Jeffrey Kosky, "Georges Bataille's Religion without Religion: A Review of the Possibilities Opened by the Publication of *The Unfinished System of Nonknowledge*," *Journal of Religion* 84, no. 1 (2004): 83.

113. Georges Bataille, *The Accursed Share vols. 2 and 3: The History of Eroticism and Sovereignty*, trans. Robert Hurley (New York: Zone Books, 1993), 92–93.

114. Halberstam, *The Queer Art of Failure*, locations 582–86. Peter Lord and Nick Park, directors, *Chicken Run*, Aardman Animations, 2000.

115. Ibid., locations 2226–32.

116. Peignot, *Laure*, 39.

117. Ibid., 39n.

118. Hanson, "Teaching Shame," 134.

119. Burrus, *Saving Shame*, 8.

120. Virginia Burrus, "A Saint of One's Own: Emmanuel Levinas, Eliezer ben Hyrcanus, and Eulalia of Mérida," *L'Esprit Créateur* 50, no. 1 (2010): 17.

121. Hanson, "Teaching Shame," 151.

CHAPTER SIX. UNFINISHED

1. Plato, *Symposium*, 210D–212A.

2. See Huffer, *Mad for Foucault*, 259–60: "This modern relation between subjectivity and truth, where access to truth does not require self-transformation, is what Foucault calls, in *Hermeneutics*, philosophy. In contrast to philosophy, Foucault names the other mode of access to truth spirituality, that mode of relation between subjectivity and truth we have already seen, both in *Madness* and *Hermeneutics*, in the mad dreamers of the nineteenth century."

3. Ibid., 273.

4. Teresa of Avila, *The Life*, 49.

5. Halberstam, *The Queer Art of Failure*, locations 301–302.

6. Edmond Jabès, *The Book of Questions, Volume II,* trans. Rosmarie Waldrop (Hanover, NH: Wesleyan University Press, 1991), 193.

7. Kristeva, in Clément and Kristeva, *The Feminine and the Sacred*, 24.

8. Cixous and Calle-Gruber, *Rootprints*, 55.

9. Ibid., 54.

10. George Bataille, *Erotism: Death and Sensuality*, trans. Mary Dalwood (San Francisco: City Lights, 1986), 12–13.

11. Cixous, *Rootprints*, 54.

12. Bataille, *Erotism*, 11.

13. See Online Etymology Dictionary, entries for *perverse, perversion, perversity, pervert, and perverted*. Accessed at Etymonline.com.

14. See Sigmund Freud, "The Sexual Aberrations," in *Three Essays on the Theory of Sexuality*, trans. James Strachey (New York: Basic Books, 2000), 1–38.

15. Jacques Lacan, "The Subversion of the Subject and the Dialectic of Desire in Freudian Psychoanalysis," in Fink et al., *Écrits*, 699.

16. Jacques Lacan, *The Seminar, Book XI. The Four Fundamental Concerns of Psychoanalysis, 1964*, trans. Alan Sheridan (New York: W. W. Norton, 1978), 182–85.

17. Ibid.

18. So he said, "Go forth and stand on the mountain before the Lord." And behold, the Lord was passing by! And a great strong wind was rending the mountains and breaking in pieces the rocks before the Lord, but the Lord was not in the wind. And after the wind an earthquake, but the Lord was not in the earthquake. After the earthquake a fire, but the Lord was not in the fire, and after the fire a sound of a gentle blowing. When Elijah heard it, he wrapped his face in his mantle and went out and stood in the entrance of the cave. And behold, a voice came to him and said, "What are you doing here, Elijah?"

19. Adrian Price, "The Invocatory Drive: From a Small Still Voice to the Scream of Nature," conference presentation, Dublin, The Irish Circle of Lacanian Orientation—New Lacanian School seminar, December 2014. Accessed at www.iclo-nls.org/wp-content/uploads/Pdf/Price.Invocatory.pdf.

20. Ibid.

21. Jean Charmoille, "The Invocatory Drive," conference presentation, "The Purpose Behind Mis-hearing." Paris 2003. Accessed at http://www.sonecrit.com/texte/PDF/anglais/Pulsion-Invocante.pdf.

22. Robert Harari, *Lacan's Four Fundamental Concepts of Psychoanalysis: An Introduction*, trans. Judith Filk (New York: Other Press, 2004), 110–12.

23. This is Roland Barthes's description as he discusses the grain of the voice: "It granulates, it crackles, it caresses, it grates, it cuts, it comes: that is bliss." Roland Barthes, *The Pleasure of the Text*, trans. Richard Miller (New York: Hill and Wang, 1975), 67.

24. Blanchot, *The Writing of the Disaster*, 131.

25. Bataille, *L'Abbé C*, 146.

26. Blanchot, *The Writing of the Disaster*, 137. Translation modified by Massie, "The Secret and the Neuter," 48. Note that "enigma" here is differentiated from "secret." However, Massie also writes of "the illusion of a restraint that could be removed in favor of a revelation. To talk of illusion is to confuse the enigma with a secret awaiting to be revealed; it is to confuse the absence of any 'beyond' with a further reserve of meaning." Massie, 40.

27. Sedgwick, "Shame, Theatricality, and Queer Performativity: Henry James's The Art of the Novel," in *Touching Feeling*, 51.

28. Michael Warner says of the queer imperative to pride that it is "too safe to be sexy and too dishonest to be safe." Michael Warner, "The Pleasures and Dangers of Shame," in Halperin and Traub, *Gay Shame*, 287.

29. Peignot, *Laure*, 101.

30. Ibid., 81.

31. Ibid., 181.

32. Ibid., 150.

33. Ibid., 182.

34. Clément, in Clément and Kristeva, *The Feminine and the Sacred*, 29.

35. Rogozinski, *The Ego and the Flesh*, 301.

36. See, for example, Richard D. E. Burton, who asserts that Peignot "is clearly sexually and psychologically disturbed, speaking of her 'shame of her nether regions' (basses régions), and of her desire to 'soil' or 'dirty' herself." *Holy Tears, Holy Blood*, 164. Citing Jérôme Peignot and Anne Roche, eds., *Laure: Une Rupture (1934)—Correspondances croisée de Laure avec Boris Souvarine, sa famille, Georges Bataille, Pierre et Jenny Pascal, Simone Weil* (Paris: Editions des Cendres, 1999), 96, 34.

37. Georges Bataille, Appendix, in Peignot, *Laure*, 238.

38. George Chauncey, "The Trouble with Shame," in Halperin and Traub, *Gay Shame*, 281.

39. Jacques Derrida and Maurizio Ferraris, *A Taste for the Secret*, trans. Giacomo Donis (Cambridge: Polity Press, 2001), 59. Thus cited in Catherine Keller and Stephen Moore, "Derridapocalypse," in *Derrida and Religion: Other Testaments*, ed. Yvonne Sherwood and Kevin Hart (New York: Routledge, 2005), 200.

40. Jacques Lacan, *The Seminar of Jacques Lacan: Crucial Problems for Psychoanalysis 1964–1965*, Seminar from March 17, 1965, trans. Cormac Gallagher, 14. Accessed at http://users.clas.ufl.edu/burt/Lacan%20Seminars%20pdfs/12-Crucial-problems-for-psychoanalysis.pdf.

41. Ibid., 16.

Works Cited

Agamben, Giorgio. *The Open: Man and Animal.* Translated by Kevin Attell. Stanford: Stanford University Press, 2003.

Aguirre, Manuel, Roberta Quance, and Philip Sutton. *Margins and Thresholds: An Enquiry into the Concept of Liminality in Text Studies: Studies in Liminality and Literature 1.* Madrid: The Gateway Press, 2000.

Altizer, Thomas J. J. *The New Gospel of Christian Atheism.* Aurora, CO: The Davies Group, 2003.

Anderson, Laurie. "Language is a Virus (From Outer Space)." *Home of the Brave.* Warner Bros., 1986. Vinyl.

Angela of Foligno. *St. Angela of Foligno: Complete Works.* Translated by Paul Lachance. New York: Paulist Press, 1993.

———. *Angela of Foligno's Memorial.* Translated by John Cirignano. Introduction, Notes, and Interpretive Essay by Cristina Mazzoni. Rochester: Boydell and Brewer, 1999.

Angyal, A. "Disgust and Related Aversions." *Journal of Abnormal and Social Psychology* 36 (1941): 393–412.

Anonymous. "Anastasia the Roman." Last modified October 22, 2012. orthodoxwiki.org/Anastasia_the_Roman.

———. *The Cloud of Unknowing.* London: Aeterna Press, 2015.

———. The Femdom Library. Accessed March 25, 2017, at femdomlibrary.com.

———. "Forniphilia (Human Furniture)." Accessed February 23, 2017, at www.bernadinism.com/forniphilia-human-furniture/.

———. "Humiliation in Private." Accessed February 23, 2017, at lazydomme.blogspot.com/2011/07/humiliation-in-private.html.

———. "I Enjoy Forced Feminization." Accessed February 23, 2017, at www.experienceproject.com/groups/Enjoy-Forced-Feminization-Stories/141432.

———. Literotica. Accessed March 25, 2017, at literotica.com.

————."Petition for Administrative Response to Prof. Kipnis." Accessed March 10, 2017, at docs. google.com/forms/d/12sbmVqpNGGQPY-QEYG5N7-VIUsXigVg3l9itcX4yTDcA/ viewform.

————. "Rose of Lima." Accessed February 23, 2017, at www.catholic.org/saints/saint. php?saint_id=446.

Antoci, Peter M. "Scandal and Marginality in the Vitae of Holy Fools." *Christianity and Literature* 44, no. 3–4 (Spring-Summer 1995): 275–88.

Aristotle. *Metaphysics*. Translated by Hugh Tredennick. In *Aristotle in 23 Volumes*, edited by Hugh Tredennick. Cambridge, MA: Harvard University Press; London: William Heinemann, 1933, 1989. Vols. 17, 18.

————. *Poetics*. Translated by S. H. Butcher. New York: Hill and Wang, 1961.

————. *Politics*. Translated by H. Rackham. In *Aristotle in 23 Volumes*, edited by Hugh Tredennick. Cambridge, MA: Harvard University Press; London: William Heinemann, 1944. Vol. 21.

Augustine. *City of God*. Translated by Henry Bettenson. New York: Penguin, 2003.

————. *Confessions*. Translated by Henry Chadwick. Oxford: Oxford University Press, 1991.

————. *The Literal Meaning of Genesis*. Translated by John Hammond Taylor. Mahwah, NJ: Paulist Press, 1982.

————. *On the Free Choice of the Will*. Translated by Thomas Williams. Indianapolis: Hackett, 1993.

————. *The Rule of St. Augustine*. In *Augustine's Rule: A Commentary*. Adolar Zumkeller OSA, translated by Matthew J. O'Connell, edited by John E. Rotelle OSA. Villanova, PA: Augustinian Press, 1987.

Bailly, Jean-Christophe. *The Animal Side*. Translated by Catherine Porter. New York: Fordham University Press, 2011.

von Balthasar, Hans Urs. *Mysterium Paschale*. Translated by Aidan Nichols, OP. Grand Rapids, MI: William B. Eerdmans, 1990.

Barthes, Roland. *The Pleasure of the Text*. Translated by Richard Miller. New York: Hill and Wang, 1975.

Bartlett, Neil. "Plunge into Your Shame." In *Gay Shame*, edited by David M. Halperin and Valerie Traub, 339–56. Chicago: University of Chicago Press, 2009.

Basil of Caesarea. *The Asketicon of Basil the Great*. Edited and translated by Anna Silvas. Oxford: Oxford University Press, 2005.

Bataille, Georges. *L'Abbé C.* Translated by Philip A. Facey. London: Marion Boyars, 2001.

————. "Abjection and Miserable Forms." Translated by Yvonne Shafir. In *More & Less*, edited by Sylvere Lotringer, 8–13. Brooklyn, NY: Semiotexte/ Autonomedia, 1999.

————. *The Accursed Share vol. 1: An Essay on General Economy*. Translated by Robert Hurley. New York: Zone Books, 1991.

————. *The Accursed Share vols. 2 and 3: The History of Eroticism and Sovereignty*. Translated by Robert Hurley. New York: Zone Books, 1993.

————. *Blue of Noon*. Translated by Harry Matthews. New York: Urizen Books, 1978.

————. *Erotism: Death and Sensuality*. Translated by Mary Dalwood. San Francisco: City Lights Books, 1986.

————. *Guilty*. Translated by Stuart Kendall. Albany: State University of New York Press, 2011.

————. *Inner Experience.* Translated by Stuart Kendall. Albany: State University of New York Press, 2014.

————. *My Mother, Madame Edwarda, and The Dead Man.* Translated by Austryn Wainhouse. London: Marion Boyars, 2000.

————. *On Nietzsche.* Translated by Stuart Kendall. Albany: State University of New York Press, 2015.

————. *The Story of the Eye.* Translated by Joachim Neugroschel. San Francisco: City Lights Books, 1977.

————. *Theory of Religion.* Translated by Robert Hurley. New York: Zone Books, 1992.

————. *The Unfinished System of Nonknowledge.* Edited by Stuart Kendall. Translated by Michelle Kendall and Stuart Kendall. Minneapolis: University of Minnesota Press, 2001.

Baudrillard, Jean. "The Ecstasy of Communication." In *The Anti-Aesthetic: Essays in Postmodern Culture*, edited by Hal Foster, 145–54. New York: The New Press, 2002.

Bazelon, Emily. "The Return of the Sex Wars." *New York Times*, September 10, 2015. Accessed March 10, 2017, at www.nytimes.com/2015/09/13/magazine/the-return-of-the-sex-wars.html?_r=0.

Beatrice of Nazareth. *The Seven Manners of Holy Love.* Translated by Roger de Ganck. Kalamazoo: Cistercian Publications, 1991.

Beckett, Samuel. *Worstward Ho.* In *Nohow On: Company, Ill Seen Ill Said, and Worstward Ho*, 87–116. New York: Grove Press, 1990.

Bell, Rudolph. *Holy Anorexia.* Chicago: University of Chicago Press, 1985.

Benedict of Nursia. *Saint Benedict's Rule for Monasteries.* Translated by Leonard J. Doyle OblSB. Collegeville, MN: Order of Saint Benedict, 2001.

Benjamin, Walter. *The Origin of German Tragic Drama.* Translated by John Osborne. London: Verso, 1998.

————. *The Work of Art in the Age of its Technological Reproduction, and Other Writings on Media.* Translated by Edmund Jephcott, edited by Michael W. Jennings, Brigid Doherty, and Thomas Y. Levin. Cambridge, MA: Harvard University Press, 2008.

Bergoffen, Debra. *Contesting the Politics of Genocidal Rape: Affirming the Dignity of the Vulnerable Body.* London: Routledge, 2012.

Bernauer, James. "Secular Self-Sacrifice: On Michel Foucault's Courses at the Collège de France." In *Foucault's Legacy*, edited by C. G. Prado, 146–60. London: Continuum, 2009.

Bersani, Leo. "Is the Rectum a Grave?" In *Is the Rectum a Grave? And Other Essays*, 3–31. Chicago: University of Chicago Press, 2010.

————, and Ulysse Dutoit. *Arts of Impoverishment: Beckett, Rothko, Resnais.* Cambridge, MA: Harvard University Press, 1993.

Blanchot, Maurice. "De l'angoisse au langage." In *Faux pas*, 10–23. Paris: Gallimard, 1943. In English as "From Dread to Language." In *The Station Hill Blanchot Reader: Fiction and Literary Essays*, edited by George Quasha; translated by Lydia Davis and Paul Auster, 343–99. Barrytown, NY: Station Hill, 1999.

————. *L'Attente, L'Oubli.* Paris: Gallimard, 2008. In English as *Awaiting Oblivion.* Translated by John Gregg. Lincoln: University of Nebraska Press, 1999.

————. *The Book to Come.* Translated by Charlotte Mandell. Stanford: Stanford University Press, 2002.

————. *The One Who Would Not Accompany Me.* Translated by Lydia Davis. Barrytown, NY: Station Hill Press, 1993.

————. *The Step/Not Beyond.* Translated by Lycette Nelson. Albany: State University of New York Press, 1992.

————. *The Writing of the Disaster.* Translated by Ann Smock. Lincoln: University of Nebraska Press, 1995.

Bordo, Susan. *Unbearable Weight: Feminism, Western Culture, and the Body.* Berkeley: University of California Press, 1994.

Bouson, J. Brooks. *Embodied Shame: Uncovering Female Shame in Contemporary Women's Writings.* Albany: State University of New York Press, 2009.

Brakke, David. "Making Public the Monastic Life: Reading the Self in Evagrius Ponticus' *Talking Back.*" In *Religion and the Self in Antiquity*, edited by David Brakke, Michael L. Satlow, and Steven Weitzman, 222–33. Bloomington: Indiana University Press, 2005.

————. "The Problematization of Nocturnal Emissions in Early Christian Syria, Egypt, and Gaul." *Journal of Early Christian Studies* 3, no. 4 (1995): 419–60.

Brame, Gloria G., William D. Brame, and Jon Jacobs. *Different Loving: The World of Sexual Dominance and Submission.* New York: Villard, 1993.

Brintnall, Kent. *Ecce Homo: The Male-Body-in-Pain as Redemptive Figure.* Chicago: University of Chicago Press, 2012.

————. "Erotic Ruination: Embracing the 'Savage Spirituality' of Barebacking." In *Negative Ecstasies: Georges Bataille and the Study of Religion*, edited by Jeremy Biles and Kent Brintnall, 51–67. New York: Fordham University Press, 2015.

Brock, Sebastian P., and Susan Ashbrook Harvey, trans. "Pelagia." In *Holy Women of the Syrian Orient*, edited and translated by Sebastian P. Brock and Susan Ashbrook Harvey, 40–62. Berkeley: University of California Press, 1987.

Brooke, Chris. "'I'm a Human Pet': The Goth Teenager Whose Fiance Walks Her around on a Dog Lead." *Daily Mail*, January 23, 2008. Accessed March 10, 2017, at www.dailymail.co.uk/news/article-509713/Im-human-pet-The-Goth-teenager-fiance-walks-dog-lead.html#ixzz46nHQ9ex9.

Broomfield, Nick. *Fetishes*. Directed by Nick Broomfield. New York: HBO, 1996.

Brown, Peter. *The Body and Society: Men, Women, and Sexual Renunciation in Early Christianity.* New York: Columbia University Press, 1988.

Burroughs, William S. *The Ticket that Exploded.* New York: Grove Press, 1962.

Burrus, Virginia. "A Saint of One's Own: Emmanuel Levinas, Eliezer ben Hyrcanus, and Eulalia of Mérida." *L'Esprit Créateur* 50, no. 1 (2010): 6–30.

————. *Saving Shame: Martyrs, Saints, and Other Abject Subjects.* Philadelphia: University of Pennsylvania Press, 2008.

————. *The Sex Lives of Saints: An Erotics of Ancient Hagiography.* Philadelphia: University of Pennsylvania Press, 2003.

————. "Wyschogrod's Hand: Saints, Animality, and the Labor of Love." *Philosophy Today* 55, no. 4 (November 2011): 412–21.

Burton, Richard D. E. *Holy Tears, Holy Blood: Women, Catholicism, and the Culture of Suffering in France, 1840–1970.* Ithaca: Cornell University Press, 2004.

Bush, Stephen S. "Sovereignty and Cruelty: Self-Affirmation, Self-Dissolution, and the

Bataillean Subject." In *Negative Ecstasies: Georges Bataille and the Study of Religion*, edited by Jeremy Biles and Kent Brintnall, 38–50. New York: Fordham University Press, 2015.

Butler, Judith. *Giving an Account of Oneself.* New York: Fordham University Press, 2005.

Campbell, Bradley, and Jason Manning. "Microaggressions and Moral Culture." *Comparative Sociology* 13, no. 6 (2014): 692–726.

Carson, Anne. *Eros the Bittersweet*. McLean, IL: Dalkey Archive Press, 1998.

Catherine of Genoa. *Purgation and Purgatory* and *The Spiritual Dialogue*. Translated by Serge Hughes. New York: Paulist Press, 1979.

Catherine of Siena. *The Letters of Catherine of Siena*. Translated by Suzanne Noffke. Binghamton, NY: Medieval and Renaissance Texts and Studies, 1988.

de Certeau, Michel. *The Mystic Fable, vol. 1: The Sixteenth and Seventeenth Centuries*. Translated by Michael B. Smith. Chicago: University of Chicago Press, 1992.

Chalmers, Lord Robert, trans. *Majjhima Nikaya*. Oxford: Oxford University Press, 1948.

Charmoille, Jean. "The Invocatory Drive." Paper presented at "The Purpose Behind Mis-hearing," Paris, 2003. Accessed March 10, 2017, at http://www.sonecrit.com/texte/PDF/anglais/Pulsion-Invocante.pdf.

Chauncey, George. "The Trouble with Shame." In *Gay Shame*, edited by David M. Halperin and Valerie Traub, 277–82. Chicago: University of Chicago Press, 2009.

Cixous, Hélène, and Mireille Calle-Gruber. *Rootprints: Memory and Life Writing*. Translated by Eric Prenowitz. London: Routledge, 1997.

Clark-Fory, Tracy. "I'm Hung Like a Toddler: Meet a Man with a Micropenis." *Salon*, February 23, 2015. Accessed March 17, 2017, at www.salon.com/2015/02/24/i%E2%80%99m_hung_like_a_toddler_meet_a_man_with_a_micropenis/.

Clement of Alexandria. *Exhortation to the Greeks*. Translated by G. W. Butterworth. In *Clement of Alexandria*. Loeb Classical Library 92, 3–263. Cambridge, MA: Harvard University Press, 1919.

———. *Exhortation to the Heathen*. In *Ante-Nicene Fathers*, Vol. 2, edited by Alexander Roberts, James Donaldson, and A. Cleveland Coxe, translated by William Wilson, 171–206. Buffalo, NY: Christian Literature Publishing, 1885.

Clément, Catherine, and Julia Kristeva. *The Feminine and the Sacred*. Translated by Jane Marie Todd. New York: Columbia University Press, 2001.

Connolly, Sean. "Laure's War: Selfhood and Sacrifice in Colette Peignot." *French Forum* 35, no. 1 (Winter 2010): 17–37.

Corner, Natalie. "Are These The Bravest Men in the Country?" *The Mirror*, January 30, 2016. Accessed March 10, 2017, at www.mirror.co.uk/tv/tv-news/bravest-men-country-three-men-7268368.

Deigh, John. "The Politics of Disgust and Shame." *Journal of Ethics* 10, no. 4 (December 2006): 383–418.

Derrida, Jacques. *The Animal that Therefore I Am*. Edited by Marie-Louise Mallet and translated by David Wills. New York: Fordham University Press, 2008.

———. "Composing 'Cirumfession.'" In *Augustine and Postmodernism: Confession and Circumfession*, edited by John D. Caputo and Michael J. Scanlon, 19–27. Indianapolis: Indiana University Press, 2005.

———. *The Gift of Death*. Translated by David Wills. Chicago: University of Chicago Press, 1995.

————. "How to Avoid Speaking: Denials." In *Languages of the Unsayable: The Play of Negativity in Literature and Literary Theory,* edited by Sanford Budick and Wolfgang Iser, 3–70. Stanford: Stanford University Press, 1987.

————, and Maurizio Ferraris. *A Taste for the Secret.* Translated by Giacomo Donis. Cambridge: Polity Press, 2001.

Diderot, Denis. *Les bijoux indiscrets.* In *Oeuvres completes,* vol.3, edited by Jean Macary, Aram Vartanian, and Jean-Louis Leutrat, 1–290. Paris: Hermann, 1978.

Digby, Kenelm Henry. *Compitum: Or the Meeting of the Ways at the Catholic Church.* London: C. Dolman, 1854.

Diogenes Laërtius. "The Life of Diogenes." In *Lives and Opinions of Eminent Philosophers: Including the Biographies of the Cynics and the Life of Epicurus,* Vol. 2, Book VI, §§20–81. New York: Gottfried and Fritz, 2015. Kindle edition.

Pseudo-Dionysius the Areopagite. *The Celestial Hierarchy.* In *The Works of Dionysius the Areopagite,* Part II, translated by Rev. John Parker, 1–66. London and Oxford: James Parker, 1899.

Direk, Zeynep. "Bataille and Kristeva on Religion." In *Negative Ecstasies: Georges Bataille and Religion,* edited by Jeremy Biles and Kent Brintnall, 185–201. New York: Fordham University Press, 2015.

Alfred, Lord Douglas. "In Praise of Shame." Accessed February 23, 2017, at www.poets.org/poetsorg/poem/praise-shame.

————. "Two Loves." Accessed February 23, 2017, at www.poets.org/poetsorg/poem/two-loves.

Douglas, Mary. *Purity and Danger: An Analysis of Concepts of Pollution and Taboo.* New York: Routledge, 1966.

duBois, Page. *Torture and Truth.* New York: Routledge, 1991.

Dworkin, Ronald. *Justice for Hedgehogs.* Cambridge, MA: Belknap Press, 2011.

Easton, Dossie, and Janet W. Hardy. *The New Bottoming Book.* Emeryville, CA: Greenery Press, 2001.

Meister Eckhart. "Justi vivent in aeternum." In *Meister Eckhart: The Essential Sermons, Commentaries, Treatises, and Defense,* edited and translated by Edmund Colledge and Bernard McGinn, 185–89. Mahwah, NJ: Paulist Press, 1981.

————. "Qui audit me non confundetur." In *Meister Eckhart: Selected Writings,* edited and translated by Oliver Davies, 175–180. New York: Penguin, 1994.

————. "Renovamini Spiritu." In *The Essential Sermons, Commentaries, Treatises, and Defense,* translated by Edmund Colledge and Bernard McGinn, 207–208. Mahwah, NJ: Paulist Press, 1981.

Eusebius. *Historia Ecclesiastica.* In *Nicene and post-Nicene Fathers, Second Series,* Vol. 1, edited by Phillip Schaff and Henry Wace, translated by Arthur Cushman McGiffert, 73–387. Buffalo, NY: Christian Literature Publishing, 1890.

Eustochius. *Vita Sanctae Pelagiae, Meretricis.* Patrologia Latina vol. 73, columns 663–672. Paris: Migne, 1849. In English as *The Life of Saint Pelagia the Harlot.* In *Harlots of the Desert: A Study of Repentance in Early Monastic Sources,* edited and translated by Benedicta Ward, 57–75. Kalamazoo: Cistercian Publications, 1986.

Feder, Ellen. *Making Sense of Intersex: Changing Ethical Perspectives in Biomedicine.* Bloomington: Indiana University Press, 2014.

Fedotov, George P. "The Holy Fools." *St. Vladimir's Quarterly* 3, no. 3 (Fall 1959): 2–17.

Feinberg, Leslie. *Stone Butch Blues*. Ann Arbor: Firebrand Books, 1993.

Flaubert, Gustave. *The Temptation of St. Anthony*. Translated by Lafcadio Hearn. Rockville, MD: Wildside Press, 2008.

Foucault, Michel. "About the Beginning of the Hermeneutics of the Self." Transcript by Thomas Keenan and Mark Blasius. In *Religion and Culture*, edited by Jeremy Carrette, 158–81. London: Routledge, 1999.

———. *About the Beginning of the Hermeneutics of the Self*. Translated by Graham Burchell. Chicago: University of Chicago Press, 2016.

———. *Les anormaux: Cours au Collège de France, 1974–1975*. Edited by Valerio Marchetti and Antoinetta Salomoni under the direction of François Ewald and Alessandro Fontana. Paris: Gallimard/Seuil, 1999.

———. "The Battle for Chastity." Translated by Anthony Forester. In *Religion and Culture*, edited by Jeremy Carrette, 188–97. London: Routledge, 1999.

———. *Le beau danger: Entretiens avec Claude Bonnefoy*. Edited by Philipe Artières. Paris: Éditions EHESS, 2011.

———. *Le courage de la vérité: Le gouvernement de soi et des autres II: Cours au Collège de France, 1983–1984*. Edited by Frédéric Gros under the direction of François Ewald and Alessandro Fontana. Paris: Gallimard/Seuil, 2009.

———. *Ethics, Subjectivity, and Truth: The Essential Works of Michel Foucault*. Edited by Paul Rabinow. New York: The New Press, 1997.

———. *The Foucault Reader*. Edited by Paul Rabinow. New York: Pantheon Books, 1984.

———. "On the Genealogy of Ethics: An Overview of Work in Progress." In Michel Foucault, *Ethics, Subjectivity, and Truth: The Essential Works of Michel Foucault*, vol. 1, edited by Paul Rabinow, 253–80. New York: The New York Press, 1998.

———. *Du gouvernement des vivants: Cours au Collège de France, 1979–1980*. Edited by Michel Senellart under the direction of François Ewald and Alessandro Fontana. Paris: EHESS, Gallimard, and Seuil, 2012. In English as "On the Government of the Living." In *Religion and Culture*, edited by Jeremy Carrette, 154–57. London: Routledge, 1999.

———. *Histoire de la sexualité, vol. 1: La volonte de savoir*. Paris: Gallimard, 1976. In English as *The History of Sexuality, vol. 1: An Introduction*. Translated by Robert Hurley. New York: Pantheon Books, 1978.

———. *Histoire de sexualite, vol. 2: L'usage des plaisirs*. Paris: Gallimard, 1984. In English as *The History of Sexuality, vol. 2: The Use of Pleasure*. Translated by Robert Hurley. New York: Vintage, 1990.

———. *Power: Essential Works of Foucault 1954–1984*. Edited by James D. Faubion. New York: The New Press, 1998.

———. "Sexualité et pouvoir." In *Dits et écrits*, vol. 3, edited by Jacques Lagrange under the direction of Daniel Defert and François Ewald, 552–70. Paris: Gallimard, 1994. In English as "Sexuality and Power." Translated by Richard A. Lynch. In *Religion and Culture*, edited by Jeremy Carrette, 115–30. London: Routledge, 1999.

———. *Technologies of the Self: A Seminar with Michel Foucault*. Edited by Luther H. Martin, Huck Gutman, and Patrick H. Hutton. Amherst: University of Massachusetts Press, 1988.

Frankfurter, David. "Martyrology and the Prurient Gaze." *Journal of Early Christian Studies* 17, no. 2 (2009): 215–45.

Fraser, Nancy. "Rethinking the Public Sphere." In *Habermas and the Public Sphere*, edited by Craig Calhoun, 109–42. Cambridge, MA: MIT Press, 1992.

Freeman, Elizabeth. *Time Binds: Queer Temporalities*. Durham: Duke University Press, 2010.

Freud, Sigmund. "The Sexual Aberrations." In *Three Essays on the Theory of Sexuality*, translated by James Strachey, 1–38. New York: Basic Books, 2000.

Freze, Michael. *They Bore the Wounds of Christ: The Mystery of the Sacred Stigmata*. Huntington, IN: Our Sunday Visitor, 1989.

Gaunt, Simon. "Straight Minds/'Queer' Wishes in Old French Hagiography: La vie de sainte Euphrosine." *GLQ: A Journal of Lesbian and Gay Studies* 1, no. 4 (1995): 439–57.

Geary, Patrick. "The Humiliation of Saints." In *Saints and their Cults: Studies in Religious Sociology, Folklore, and History*, edited by Stephen Wilson, 123–40. Cambridge: Cambridge University Press, 1983.

van Gennep, Arnold. *The Rites of Passage*. Translated by Monika B. Vizedom and Gabrielle L. Caffee. New York: Routledge Library Editions, 1960.

Gerber, Lynne. "Movements of Luxurious Exuberance: Georges Bataille and Fat Politics." In *Negative Ecstasies: Georges Bataille and the Study of Religion*, edited by Jeremy Biles and Kent Brintnall, 19–37. New York: Fordham University Press, 2015.

Gibbon, Edward. *The History of the Decline and Fall of the Roman Empire*. Boston: Philips, Samson, 1852.

Glancy, Jennifer. "Boasting of Beatings (Corinthians 11:23–25)." *Journal of Biblical Literature* 123, no. 1 (Spring 2004): 99–135.

Glick, Thomas F., Steven John Livesey, and Faith Wallis. *Medieval Science, Technology and Medicine: An Encyclopedia*. New York: Routledge, 2005.

le Goff, Jacques. *The Birth of Purgatory*. Chicago: University of Chicago Press, 1984.

Graziano, Frank. *Wounds of Love: The Mystical Marriage of Saint Rose of Lima*. Oxford: Oxford University Press, 2004.

Grealy, Lucy. *Autobiography of a Face*. New York: Houghton Mifflin, 1994.

Grosz, Elizabeth. *Volatile Bodies: Toward a Corporeal Feminism*. Indianapolis: Indiana University Press, 1994.

Haidt, J., C. McCauly, and P. Rozin. "Individual Differences in Sensitivity to Disgust: A Scale Sampling Seven Domains of Disgust Elicitors." *Personality and Individual Differences* 16 (1994): 701–13.

Halberstam, Judith. *The Queer Art of Failure*. Durham: Duke University Press, 2011. Kindle edition.

Halperin, David M., and Valerie Traub. "Beyond Gay Pride." In *Gay Shame*, edited by David M. Halperin and Valerie Traub, 3–40. Chicago: University of Chicago Press, 2009.

Hamilton, Sarah. "Doing Penance." In *Medieval Christianity in Practice*, edited by Miri Rubin, 135–43. Princeton: Princeton University Press, 2009.

Hanson, Ellis. "Teaching Shame." In *Gay Shame*, edited by David M. Halperin and Valerie Traub, 132–64. Chicago: University of Chicago Press, 2009.

Harari, Robert. *Lacan's Four Fundamental Concepts of Psychoanalysis: An Introduction*. Translated by Judith Filk. New York: Other Press, 2004.

Harrington, Lee. "A Romp on the Wild Side: Erotic Human Animal Role Playing." In *The Ultimate Guide to Kink*, edited by Tristan Taormino, 264–78. Berkeley: Cleis Press, 2012.

Harris, D. J., M. O'Boyle, and C. Warbrick. *Law of the European Convention on Human Rights*. Oxford: Oxford University Press, 1995.

Hegel, G. W. F. *Enzyklopädie der philosophischen Wissenschaften im Grundrisse (1830), Erster Teil*. In *Werke*, vol. 8. Frankfurt am Main: Suhrkamp, 1970.

Heidegger, Martin. *Platons Lehre von der Wahrheit*. Bern: A. Francke Verlag, 1947. In English as "Plato's Doctrine of Truth." Translated by John Barlow. In *Philosophy in the Twentieth Century*, edited by William Barrett and Henry D. Aiken, 251–70. New York: Random House, 1962.

———. *Sein und Zeit*. Halle: Max Niemeyer Verlag, 1941. In English as *Being and Time*. Translated by John Macquarrie and Edward Robinson. New York: Harper and Row, 1962.

Hildegard of Bingen. *The Personal Correspondence of Hildegard of Bingen*. Edited by Joseph L. Baird, translated by Joseph L. Baird and Radd K. Ehrman. Oxford: Oxford University Press, 2006.

Hoff, Christina. "Kant's Invidious Humanism." *Environmental Ethics* 5 (Spring 1983): 63–70.

Howie, Cary, and William Burgwinkle. *Sanctity and Pornography in Medieval Culture: On the Verge*. Manchester, UK: Manchester University Press, 2010.

Huffer, Lynn. "Foucault's Eros: For an Ethics of Living in Biopower." In *A Companion to Foucault*, edited by Christopher Falzon, Timothy O'Leary, and Jana Sawicki, 436–53. West Sussex, UK: Wiley-Blackwell, 2013.

———. *Mad for Foucault: Rethinking the Foundations of Queer Theory*. New York: Columbia, 2009.

Irenaeus. *Against Heresies*. In *The Writings of Irenaeus*. Translated by Alexander Roberts and W. H. Rambaut. Edinburgh: T&T Clark, 1869.

Irigaray, Luce. *Speculum of the Other Woman*. Translated by Gillian C. Gill. Ithaca: Cornell University Press, 1985.

Jabès, Edmond. *The Book of Questions, Volume II*. Translated by Rosmarie Waldrop. Hanover, NH: Wesleyan University Press, 1991.

James, William. *The Principles of Psychology*. Mineola, NY: Dover Books, 1950.

John Cassian. *John Cassian: The Conferences*. Translated by Boniface Ramsey. Mahwah, NJ: Paulist Press, 1947.

———. *John Cassian's Institutes*. Translated by Boniface Ramsey. Westminster, MD: Newman Press, 2000.

John Chrysostom. "Homily against the Marcionists and the Manicheans." In *Nicene and Post-Nicene Fathers*, First Series, volume 9, edited by Philip Schaff, translated by W. R. W. Stephens, 201–207. Buffalo, NY: Christian Literature Publishing, 1889.

Jordan, Mark. *Convulsing Bodies: Religion and Resistance in Foucault*. Stanford: Stanford University Press, 2015.

Jotischky, Andrew. "Eats Roots and Leaves." *History Today* 61, no. 4 (April 2011): 19–24.

Kant, Immanuel. *Critique of Practical Reason*. Translated by Werner S. Pluhar. Indianapolis: Hackett, 2002.

———. *Grounding for the Metaphysics of Morals*, with *On a Supposed Right to Lie Because of Philanthropic Concerns*. Translated by James W. Ellington. Indianapolis: Hackett, 1993.

Kay, Sarah. *Courtly Contradictions: The Emergence of the Literary Object in the Twelfth Century*. Stanford: Stanford University Press, 2002.

Keats, John. *The Complete Poetical Works and Letters of John Keats*. Edited by Horace Elisha Scudder. Boston and New York: Houghton, Mifflin, 1899. Reprint, 2010.

Keller, Catherine, and Stephen Moore. "Derridapocalypse." In *Derrida and Religion: Other Testaments*, edited by Yvonne Sherwood and Kevin Hart, 189–208. New York: Routledge, 2005.

Kelly, Daniel. *Yuck! The Nature and Moral Significance of Disgust*. Cambridge, MA: MIT Press, 2011.

Kipnis, Laura. "Sexual Paranoia Strikes Academe." *Chronicle of Higher Education*, February 27, 2015. chronicle.com/article/Sexual-Paranoia-Strikes/190351/.

Kojève, Alexandre. *Introduction to the Reading of Hegel: Lectures on the Phenomenology of Spirit*. Translated by James H. Nichols. New York: Basic Books, 1969.

Kolnai, Aurel. *On Disgust*. Edited by Barry Smith and Carolyn Korsmeyer. Chicago: Open Court Press, 2004.

Korsgaard, Christine. *Fellow Creatures: Kantian Ethics and Our Duties to Animals: Tanner Lectures on Human Values*. Anne Arbor: University of Michigan Press, 2004.

Korsmeyer, Carolyn. *Savoring Disgust: The Foul and the Fair in Aesthetics*. Oxford: Oxford University Press, 2011.

Kosky, Jeffrey. "Georges Bataille's Religion without Religion: A Review of the Possibilities Opened by the Publication of *The Unfinished System of Nonknowledge*." *Journal of Religion* 84, no.1 (2004): 78–87.

Kristeva, Julia. *Powers of Horror: An Essay on Abjection*. Translated by Leon S. Roudiez. New York: Columbia University Press, 1982.

Kruger, Derek. *Writing and Holiness: The Practice of Authorship in the Early Christian East*. Philadelphia: University of Pennsylvania Press, 2004.

Lacan, Jacques. *Four Fundamental Concepts of Psychoanalysis*. Translated by Alan Sheridan. New York: W. W. Norton, 1978.

———. *Écrits*. Translated by Bruce Fink with Héloïse Fink and Russell Grigg. New York: W. W. Norton, 2002.

———. *The Seminar of Jacques Lacan, Book XII: Crucial Problems for Psychoanalysis 1964–1965*, Seminar from March 17, 1965. Translated by Cormac Gallagher. Accessed March 10, 2017, at http://users.clas.ufl.edu/burt/Lacan%20Seminars%20pdfs/12-Crucial-problems-for-psychoanalysis.pdf.

Latour, Bruno. *Rejoicing: Or the Torments of Religious Speech*. Translated by Julie Rose. Cambridge: Polity Press, 2013.

Leiris, Michel. *Manhood: A Journey from Childhood into the Fierce Order of Virility*. Translated by Richard Howard. Chicago: University of Chicago Press, 1992.

———. *Rules of the Game: Scraps*. Translated by Lydia Davis. Baltimore: Johns Hopkins University Press, 1997.

———. *Rules of the Game: Scratches*. Translated by Lydia Davis. Baltimore: Johns Hopkins University Press, 1997.

Lentes, Thomas. "'As Far as the Eye Can See . . .': Rituals of Gazing in the Late Middle Ages." In *The Mind's Eye: Art and Theological Argument in the Middle Ages*, edited by Jeffrey F. Hamburger and Anne-Marie Bouché, 360–73. Princeton: Princeton University Press, 2005.

Leukam, Mary. "Dignified Animals: How 'Non-Kantian' is Nussbaum's Conception of Dignity?" Thesis, Georgia State University, 2011. Accessed February 23, 2017, at scholarworks. gsu.edu/philosophy_theses/89.

Levinas, Emmanuel. *On Escape*. Translated by Bettina Bergo. Stanford: Stanford University Press, 2003.

Lipton, Sara. "Images and their Uses." In *The Cambridge History of Christianity: Christianity in Western Europe c. 1000–c.1500*, edited by Miri Rubin and Walter Simons, 254–83. Cambridge: Cambridge University Press, 2009.

Lord, Peter, and Nick Park, dir. *Chicken Run*. Bristol, UK: Aardman Animations, 2000.

Love, Heather. *Feeling Backwards: Loss and the Politics of Queer History*. Cambridge, MA: Harvard University Press, 2009.

Lucas, Sarah. "Chicken Knickers." 1997. Photograph, 17 x 17 in. Tate Collection, London. Accessed March 11, 2017, at http://www.tate.org.uk/art/artworks/ lucas-chicken-knickers-p78210.

MacDonald, Diane L. Prosser. *Transgressive Corporeality: The Body, Poststructuralism, and the Theological Imagination*. Albany: State University of New York Press, 1995.

MacKendrick, Karmen. *counterpleasures*. Albany: State University of New York Press, 1999.

———. *Divine Enticement*. New York: Fordham University Press, 2013.

Maitland, Sara. "Saints for Today." *The Way* 36, no. 4 (October 1996): 275–84.

Maitland, S. R., trans. *History of the Albigenses and Waldenses*. London: C. J. G. and F. Rivington, 1832.

de Man, Paul. "Excuses (*Confessions*)." In *Allegories of Reading: Figural Language in Rousseau, Nietzsche, Rilke, and Proust*, 278–302. New Haven: Yale University Press, 1998.

Manning, H. E., ed. and trans. *The Little Flowers of St. Francis of Assisi*. London: Burns and Lambert, 1884.

Massie, Pascal. "The Secret and the Neuter: On Heidegger and Blanchot." *Research in Phenomenology* 37, no. 1 (2007): 32–55.

Mattheus, L. Bernd. *Georges Bataille: eine Thanatographie*. Munich: Matthes und Seitz, 1984.

McDermot, Violet. *The Cult of the Seer in the Ancient Middle East: A Contribution to Current Research on Hallucinations Drawn from Coptic and Other Texts*. Berkeley: University of California Press, 1971.

Meens, Rob. "Frequency and Nature of Early Medieval Penance." In *Handling Sin: Confession in the Middle Ages*, edited by Peter Briller and A. J. Minnie, 35–55. York, UK: York Medieval Press, 1998.

Meléndez, Juan. *Tesoros verdaderos de las Indias: Historia de la provincial de San Juan Baptista del Peru de la orden de Predicadores*, 3 vols. Rome, 1681–82.

Meyers, W. David. *"Poor Sinning Folk": Confession and Conscience in Counter-Reformation Germany*. Ithaca: Cornell University Press, 1996.

Migne, Jacques Paul, ed. *De vitis patrum, Verba seniorum*. In *Patrologia latina* Series 1, Vol. 73. Imprimerie Catholique: Paris, 1879.

Milhaven, J. Giles. "Asceticism and the Moral Good: A Tale of Two Pleasures." In *Asceticism*, edited by Vincent Wimbush and Richard Valentasis, 375–94. Oxford: Oxford University Press, 1998.

Miller, Julie B. "Eroticized Violence in Medieval Women's Mystical Literature: A Call for a Feminist Critique." *Journal of Feminist Studies in Religion* 15, no. 2 (1999): 25–49.

Miller, Patricia Cox. "Is There a Harlot in This Text? Asceticism and the Grotesque." *Journal of Early Christian Studies* 33, no. 3 (2003): 419–35.

Miller, William Ian. *The Anatomy of Disgust.* Cambridge, MA: Harvard University Press, 1997.

———. *Humiliation: And Other Essays on Honor, Social Discomfort, and Violence.* Ithaca: Cornell University Press, 1993.

Mills, Robert. "Violence, Community, and the Materialisation of Belief." In *A Companion to Middle English Hagiography,* edited by Sarah Salih, 87–103. Cambridge: Boydell and Brewer, 2006.

———. "'Whatever You Do Is a Delight to Me!' Masculinity, Masochism, and Queer Play in Representations of Male Martyrdom." *Exemplaria* 13, no. 1 (2001): 1–37.

Mitchell, Stephen, trans. *Gilgamesh: A New English Version.* New York: Free Press, 2004.

Moon, Jennifer. "Gay Shame and the Politics of Identity." In *Gay Shame,* edited by David M. Halperin and Valerie Traub, 357–68. Chicago: University of Chicago Press, 2009.

Moore, Judith. *Fat Girl: A True Story.* New York: Plume, 2005.

Moran, Maureen. "The Art of Looking Dangerously: Victorian Images of Martyrdom." *Victorian Literature and Culture* 3, no. 2 (2004): 475–93.

Morrison, Toni. *The Bluest Eye.* New York: Knopf, 1993.

Mortimer, R. C. *The Origins of Private Penance in the Western Church.* Oxford: Clarendon Press, 1939.

Muñoz, José E. *Cruising Utopia: The There and Then of Queer Utopia.* New York: New York University Press, 2009.

Munt, Sally. *Queer Attachments: The Cultural Politics of Shame.* Aldershot, UK: Ashgate, 2007.

Nancy, Jean-Luc. "The Confronted Community." Translated by Jason Kemp Winfree. In *The Obsessions of Georges Bataille: Community and Communication,* edited by Andrew J. Mitchell and Jason Kemp Winfree, 19–30. Albany: State University of New York Press, 2009.

———. *The Birth to Presence.* Translated by Brian Holmes et al. Stanford: Stanford University Press, 1993.

Nathanson, Donald L. *Shame and Pride: Affect, Sex, and the Birth of the Self.* New York: W. W. Norton, 1992.

Nicolas of Cusa, *The Vision of God.* Translated by Emma Gurley Salter. New York: Frederick Ungar, 1928.

Newbold, R. F. "Personality Structure and Response to Adversity in Early Christian Hagiography." *Numen* 31, no. 2 (1984): 199–215.

Nietzsche, Friedrich. *The Gay Science.* Translated by Walter Kaufmann. New York: Vintage, 1974.

———. *On the Genealogy of Morality.* Translated by Maudemarie Clark and Alan J. Swensen. Indianapolis: Hackett, 1998.

Nussbaum, Martha. "The Capabilities of People with Cognitive Disabilities." *Metaphilosophy* 40, no. 3–4 (2009): 331–51.

———. *Frontiers of Justice: Disability, Nationality, Species Membership.* Cambridge, MA: Belknap Press, 2007.

————. "Replies." *Journal of Ethics* 10, no. 4 (December 2006): 463–506.

Oksala, Johanna. "From Biopower to Governmentality." In *A Companion to Foucault*, edited by Christopher Falzon, Timothy O'Leary, and Jana Sawicki, 320–36. West Sussex, UK: Wiley-Blackwell, 2013.

Olivelle, Patrick. "The Beast and the Ascetic: The Wild in the Indian Religious Imagination." In *Collected Essays, Volume 2*, 91–100. Florence: Firenze University Press, 2008.

Online Etymology Dictionary. Accessed March 11, 2017, at etymonline.com/.

Palladius. *The Lausiac History of Palladius.* Translated by W. K. Lowther Clarke. London and New York: Macmillan, 1918.

de la Parra, Jacinto. *Rosa Laureada entre los santos.* Madrid: Domingo Garcia Morras, 1670.

Peignot, Collette. *Laure: The Collected Writings.* Translated by Jeanine Herman. San Francisco: City Lights Books, 2001.

Peignot, Jérôme, and Anne Roche, eds. *Laure: Une Rupture (1934)—Correspondances croisée de Laure avec Boris Souvarine, sa famille, Georges Bataille, Pierre et Jenny Pascal, Simone Weil.* Paris: Editions des Cendres, 1999.

Pico della Mirandola, Giovanni. *Oration on the Dignity of Man.* Translated by A. Robert Gaponegri. Washington, DC: Gateway Editions, 1996.

Plato. *Republic.* Translated by C. D. C. Reeve. Indianapolis: Hackett, 2004.

————. *Symposium.* Translated by Alexander Nehamas and Paul Woodruff. Indianapolis: Hackett, 1989.

Poulakou-Rebelakou, E., A. Liarmakopoulos, C. Tsiamis, and D. Ploumpidis. "Holy Fools: A Religious Phenomenon of Extreme Behaviour." *Journal of Religious Health* 53 (2014): 95–104.

Price, Adrian. "The Invocatory Drive: From a Small Still Voice to the Scream of Nature." Paper presented at The Irish Circle of Lacanian Orientation—New Lacanian School seminar. Dublin, December 2014. Accessed February 23, 2017, at www.iclo-nls.org/wp-content/uploads/Pdf/Price.Invocatory.pdf.

Probyn, Elspeth. *Blush: Faces of Shame.* Minneapolis: University of Minnesota Press, 2005.

Rachels, James. *Created from Animals: The Moral Implications of Darwinism.* Oxford: Oxford University Press, 1990.

Ramos, Alice M. *Dynamic Transcendentals: Truth, Goodness, and Beauty from a Thomistic Perspective.* Washington, DC: Catholic University of America Press, 2012.

Raymond of Capua. *Life of Saint Catherine of Siena.* Translated by George Lamb. London: Harvill Press, 1960.

Raynaldus. "Annales." In *History of the Albigenses and Waldenses*, translated by S. R. Maitland, 392–94. London: C. J. G. and F. Rivington, 1832.

Riches, Samantha. "St. George: as a Male Virgin Martyr." In *Gender and Holiness: Men, Women, and Saints in Late Medieval Europe*, edited by Samantha J. E. Riches and Sarah Salih, 65–85. London: Routledge, 2002.

Rivera, Ignacio. "Age Role Play." In *The Ultimate Guide to Kink: BDSM, Role Play, and the Erotic Edge*, edited by Tristan Taormino, 352–65. Berkeley: Cleis Press, 2012.

Robert, William. "Antigone's Nature." *Hypatia* 25, no. 2 (Spring 2010): 412–36.

————. *Exposures: Of Angela of Foligno*, in manuscript.

————. "A Mystic Impulse: From Apophatics to Decreation in Pseudo-Dionysius, Meister Eckhart, and Simone Weil." *Medieval Mystical Theology* 21 (2012): 113–32.

————. "Performing Religiously Between Passion and Resistance." *Journal for Cultural and Religious Theory* 12, no. 2 (Fall 2012): 69–84.

Rogozinski, Jacob. *The Ego and the Flesh: An Introduction to Egoanalysis.* Translated by Robert Vallier. Stanford: Stanford University Press, 2010.

Rorty, Richard. *Contingency, Irony, and Solidarity.* Cambridge: Cambridge University Press, 1989.

Rosen, Michael. *Dignity: Its History and Meaning.* Cambridge, MA: Harvard University Press, 2012.

Rozin, Palut, J. Haidt, and C. R. McCauly. "Disgust." In *Handbook of Emotions,* 3rd edition, edited by M. Lewis, J. M. Haviland-Jones, and L. F. Barret, 757-76. New York: Guilford Press.

————, C. Nemeroff, M. Horowitz, B. Gordon, and W. Voet. "The Borders of the Self: Contamination Sensitivity and Potence of the Mouth, Other Apertures, and Body Parts." *Journal of Research in Personality* 29 (1995): 318–40.

————, and April Fallon. "A Perspective on Disgust." *Psychological Review* 94, no. 1 (1987): 23–41.

Ruaro, Enrica. "God and the Worm: The Twofold Otherness in Pseudo-Dionysius's Theory of Dissimilar Images." *American Catholic Philosophical Quarterly* 82, no. 4 (2008): 581–92.

Rydén, Lennart, ed. *Das Leben des heiligen Narren Symeon von Leontios von Neapolis.* Uppsala: Almquist and Wiksell, 1963.

von Sacher-Masoch, Leopold. *Venus in Furs.* Translated by Fernanda Savage. Digital: Project Gutenberg, 2011. Kindle edition.

de Sade, D. A. F. *Marquis de Sade: 120 Days of Sodom and Other Writings.* Compiled and translated by Austryn Wainhouse and Richard Seaver. New York: Grove Press, 1994.

————. *Juliette, or The Misfortunes of Virtue.* Tranlsated by Austryn Wainhouse. New York: Grove Press, 1968.

————. *Justine.* Translated by John Philips. Oxford: Oxford University Press, 2012.

Sawday, Jonathan. *The Body Emblazoned: Dissection and the Human Body in Renaissance Culture.* London: Routledge, 1995.

Scheler, Max. "Ober Scham und Schmagefühle." In *Schriften aus dem Nachlass: Gesammelte Werke* vol. 10. Bern: A Francke Verlag, 1957.

Schmitz, Hermann, ed. *Die Bussbücher und das kanonische Bussverfahren nachhandschriftlichen Quellen.* Düsseldorf: Schwann, 1898. Corrected against manuscript Vat. Lat. 4772. Vatican City: Biblioteca Apostolica Vaticana.

Schneider, Ana-Karina. "Skin as a Trope of Liminality in Anne Enright's *The Gathering.*" *Contemporary Women's Writing* 8, no. 2 (2014): 206–22.

Scott, Joan. "The Evidence of Experience." In *The Lesbian and Gay Studies Reader,* edited by Henry Abelove, Michèle Aina Borale, and David M. Halperin, 397–415. New York: Routledge, 1993.

Sedgwick, Eve Kosofsky. *Touching Feeling: Affect, Pedagogy, Performativity.* Durham: Duke University Press, 2003.

Siebers, Tobin. "Sex, Shame, and Disability Identity: With Reference to Mark O'Brien." In *Gay Shame,* edited by David M. Halperin and Valerie Traub, 201–18. Chicago: University of Chicago Press, 2009.

Simmel, Georg. "The Secret and the Secret Society." In *The Sociology of Georg Simmel*, translated by Kurt H. Wolff, 330–426. Glencoe, IL: The Free Press, 1950.

Simons, Jon. "Power, Resistance, and Freedom." In *A Companion to Foucault*, edited by Christopher Falzon, Timothy O'Leary, and Jana Sawicki, 301–19. West Sussex, UK: Wiley-Blackwell, 2013.

Sissy, Max Riley. "Forced Feminization Story (True Series), Part I." Last edited May 22, 2015. Accessed March 10, 2017, at maxrileysissy.deviantart.com/journal/Forced-Feminization-Story-True-Series-Part-1-53484924.

Smock, Ann. "Translator's Introduction." In Maurice Blanchot, *The Space of Literature*, translated by Ann Smock, 1–18. Lincoln: University of Nebraska Press, 1989.

Stang, Charles. *Apophasis and Pseudonymity in Dionysius the Areopagite: "No Longer I."* Oxford: Oxford University Press, 2012.

Steinbock, Anthony. *Moral Emotions: Reclaiming the Evidence of the Heart*. Evanston: Northwestern University Press, 2014.

Steinem, Gloria. "Erotica vs. Pornography." In *Transforming a Rape Culture,* edited by E. Buchwald, P. R. Fletcher, and M. Roth, 31–46. Minneapolis: Milkweed Editions, 1993.

Stevens, Wallace. *The Collected Poems: Corrected Edition*. New York: Vintage Books, 2015.

Sweedler, Milo. *The Dismembered Community: Bataille, Blanchot, Leiris, and the Remains of Laure.* Newark, DE: University of Delaware Press, 2009.

Tanner, Norman P., ed. *Decrees of the Ecumenical Councils*. Washington, DC: Georgetown University Press, 1990.

Taormino, Tristan. "Still in Diapers." *Village Voice*. August 13 2002. Accessed March 10, 2017, at www.villagevoice.com/news/still-in-diapers-6396960.

Taussig, Michael. *Defacement: Public Secrecy and the Labor of the Negative*. Stanford: Stanford University Press, 1999.

Taylor, Charles. *Sources of the Self: The Making of the Modern Identity*. Cambridge, MA: Harvard University Press, 1989.

———. "Self-Interpreting Animals." In *Human Agency and Language: Philosophical Papers*, 45–76. Cambridge: Cambridge University Press, 1985.

Taylor, Chloë. *The Culture of Confession from Augustine to Foucault: A Genealogy of the "Confessing Animal."* New York: Routledge, 2009.

Taylor, Gabrielle. *Pride, Shame, and Guilt: Emotions of Self-Assessment*. Oxford: Oxford University Press, 1985.

Tentler, Thomas N. *Sin and Confession on the Eve of the Reformation*. Princeton: Princeton University Press, 1977.

Teresa of Avila. *The Life of Saint Teresa of Avila, by Herself.* Translated by J. M. Cohen. New York: Penguin, 1988.

Tertullian. "Tertulliani Adversus Valentinianos." Text, translation, and commentary by Mark T. Riley. February 1971. Accessed February 23, 2017, at gnosis.org/library/ter_val_riley.htm.

———. *De spectaculis*. In *Tertullian: Apology* and *De spectaculis*, and *Minucius Felix, Octavius*. Translated and edited by T. R. Glover and Gerald H. Rendall. Loeb Classical Library 250. London: Heinemann, 1931.

Thomas Aquinas. *Scriptum super libros Sententiarium (Commentary on the Sentences)*. Edited by R. P. Madonnet, O.P. Paris: P. Lethielleux, 1929.

———. *Summa Theologiae*. Translated by the Fathers of the English Dominican Province. Cincinnati: Benziger Brothers, 1947.

Tomkins, Silvan. *Shame and its Sisters: A Silvan Tomkins Reader*. Edited by Eve Kosofsky Sedgwick and Adam Frank. Durham: Duke University Press, 1995.

de Tocqueville, Alexis. *Democracy in America*. Translated by Henry Reeve. Corrected and revised via Project Gutenberg. Accessed February 23, 2017, at xroads.virginia.edu/~hyper/DETOC/toc_indx.html.

Turner, Victor. "Betwixt and Between: The Liminal Period in Rites de Passage." In *The Forest of Symbols: Aspects of Ndembu Ritual*, edited by Victor Turner, 93–111. Ithaca: Cornell University Press, 1970.

———. "Frame, Flow and Reflection: Ritual and Drama as Public Liminality." *Japanese Journal of Religious Studies* 6, no. 4 (December 1979): 465–99.

———. "Liminality and Communitas." In *The Ritual Process: Structure and Anti-Structure*, edited by Victor Turner, 94–130. Ithaca: Cornell University Press, 1977.

Unger, Roberto Mangabiera. *False Necessity: Anti-Necessitarian Social Theory in the Service of Radical Democracy*. New York: Verso, 2004.

Vaccari, Geronima, and Cecilia de Ansalono. *La leggenda della beata Eustochia da Messina. Testo volgare del sec. XV restituito all' originaria lezione*, 2nd edition. Edited by Michele Catalono. Messina: Libreria d'Anna, 1975.

Velleman, J. David. "The Genesis of Shame." *Philosophy and Public Affairs* 30, no. 1 (2001): 27–52.

Voöbus, A. *History of Asceticism in the Syrian Orient. A Contribution to the History of Culture in the Near East, II. Early Monasticism in Mesopotamia and Syria*. Leuven: Corpus Scriptorum Christianorum Orientalium, 1960.

Waldron, Jeremy. "Cruel, Inhuman and Degrading Treatment: The Words Themselves." New York University School of Law, Public Law and Legal Theory Research Paper Series, Working Paper 08-36, 2008. Accessed February 23, 2017, at ssrn.com/abstract=1278604.

———. *Dignity, Rank, and Rights*. Cambridge, MA: Harvard University Press, 2012.

Ward, Benedicta, trans. *The Life of St. Thaïs*. In *Harlots of the Desert: A Study in Repentance in Early Monastic Sources*, edited by Benedicta Ward, 76–84. Kalamazoo: Cistercian Publications, 1987.

Ward, Benedicta, trans. *Life of Mary of Egypt*. In *Harlots of the Desert: A Study in Repentance in Early Monastic Sources*, edited by Benedicta Ward, 26–56. Kalamazoo: Cistercian Publications, 1987.

Warner, Michael. "The Pleasures and Dangers of Shame." In *Gay Shame*, edited by David M. Halperin and Valerie Traub, 283–96. Chicago: University of Chicago Press, 2009.

Weil, Simone. *Gravity and Grace*. Translated by Emma Crawford and Mario van der Ruhr. New York: Routledge, 2007.

———. "The Needs of the Soul." In *The Need for Roots: Prelude to a Declaration of Duties Towards Mankind*, translated by A. F. Wills, 1–40. New York: G. P. Putnam's Sons, 1953. Reprinted in *Simone Weil: An Anthology*, edited by Siân Miles, 85–120. New York: Grove Press, 1986.

———. *Ouevres completes*. Paris: Gallimard, 1988.

Williams, Mollena. "Digging in the Dirt: The Lure of Taboo Role Play." In *The Ultimate Guide to Kink: BDSM, Role Play, and the Erotic Edge*, edited by Tristan Taormino, 366–87. Berkeley: Cleis Press, 2012.

Winnubst, Shannon. "The Missing Link: *Homo Economicus* (Reading Bataille and Foucault Together)." In *A Companion to Foucault*, edited by Christopher Falzon, Timothy O'Leary, and Jana Sawicki, 454–71. West Sussex, UK: Wiley-Blackwell, 2013.

Winterson, Jeanette. *Oranges Are Not the Only Fruit*. New York: Grove Press, 1985.

Wolf, Kenneth Baxter. *The Life and Afterlife of Elizabeth of Hungary: Testimony from Her Canonization Hearings*. Oxford: Oxford University Press, 2010.

Wolff, Robert Paul. *In Defense of Anarchism*. Berkeley: University of California Press, 1998.

Wollheim, Richard. *On the Emotions*. New Haven: Yale University Press, 1999.

Wurmser, Léon. *The Mask of Shame*. Baltimore: Johns Hopkins University Press, 1981.

Wyschogrod, Edith. *Saints and Postmodernism: Revisioning Moral Philosophy*. Chicago: University of Chicago Press, 1990.

Ziv, Amalia. "Shameful Fantasies: Cross-Gender Queer Sex: Lesbian Erotic Fiction." In *Gay Shame*, edited by David M. Halperin and Valerie Traub, 165–75. Chicago: University of Chicago Press, 2009.

Index

120 Days of Sodom (Sade), 6, 137n28

abasement, 33, 50, 60, 62, 130, 134. *See also* abjection

L'Abbé C (Bataille), 9, 18, 59, 68, 70, 138n46, 141n93, 151n67, 154n107, 154n119, 169n25

abbot, 28, 30, 34, 42, 47–49, 51, 54, 58, 98. *See also* superior

abjection, 33–34, 44, 57, 60, 63, 65, 80, 82, 89–95, 99, 107–110, 113, 115, 117–18, 120, 124, 130, 132–133, 139n62; and remainder, 12, 36, 37, 40, 93, 132; of Christ, 35, 37, 124

"Abjection and Miserable Forms" (Bataille), 159n92

About the Beginning of a Hermeneutics of the Self (Foucault), 145n75, 148n19, 167n2

"About the Beginning of the Hermeneutics of the Self" (Foucault), 147n3, 156n22

Accursed Share, vol. 1, The (Bataille), 153n101

Accursed Share vols. 2 and 3, The (Bataille), 123, 167n113

Acts of the Apostles (Biblical book), 73

Adam (Biblical figure), 23, 141n1

aesthetic, 13, 25, 79, 82, 94, 109, 139n64

affect, 10–11, 30, 57, 80, 96, 108, 112, 125, 136n11, 162n21

Against Heresies (Irenaeus), 161nn121–122

Agamben, Giorgio, 122, 167nn105–106

age, 83, 95–96, 118, 124; and beauty, 77, 81; and gender, 118; role play, 108, 113–114, 118–119, 122–123, 165n75, 165n80

"Age Role Play," 165n80

Aguirre, Manuel, 150–151n54

Altizer, Thomas J. J., 145n55

Anastasia, Saint, 89, 159n75

Anatomy of Disgust, The (W. Miller), 159n81

Anderson, Laurie, 16, 140n82

Angela of Foligno, 56, 64, 78–81, 87, 91–92, 100, 147, 153n89, 155n7, 156n21, 156n23

Angela of Foligno: The Complete Works, 153n89, 155n7, 156n21, 156n2323

Angela of Foligno's Memorial, 156n21

Angyal, A., 159n81

animal, 22, 24, 73, 75, 80, 84–85, 87, 112, 116, 122–124, 129, 142n14, 167n103, 158, 167n109; and divinity, 121–123, 129; role play as, 113–14, 120–123, 129; and woman, 116, 119–120, 122–124, 163n45